THE
Bridal
BIBLE

THE
Bridal
BIBLE

Inspiration for Planning Your Perfect Wedding

SHARON NAYLOR, BLAIR DELAUBENFELS,
CHRISTY WEBER, AND KIM BAMBERG

LYONS PRESS
GUILFORD, CONNECTICUT
AN IMPRINT OF GLOBE PEQUOT PRESS

To buy books in quantity for corporate use
or incentives, call **(800) 962-0973**
or e-mail **premiums@GlobePequot.com.**

Lyons Press is an imprint of Globe Pequot Press.

Editorial Director: Cynthia Hughes Cullen
Editor: Katie Benoit
Project Editor: Tracee Williams
Text Design: Sheryl P. Kober
Layout: Mary Ballachino

The following manufacturers/names appearing in *The Bridal Bible* are trademarks: Band-Aid®, Bumpits™, Converse®, Dove®, Frisbee®, Oscar®, Pantene®, Popsicle®, Rolls Royce®, Suave®, Super 8®

Library of Congress Cataloging-in-Publication Data

Bridal Bible : inspiration for planning your perfect wedding / Sharon Naylor . . . [et al.].
 p. cm.
ISBN 978-0-7627-7251-3
1. Weddings—Planning. I. Naylor, Sharon.
HQ745.B745 2012
395.2'2—dc 23
                          2011026442

Printed in China

10 9 8 7 6 5 4 3 2 1

TABLE of CONTENTS

Photo by Kristen Jensen

Photo by Kristen Jensen

Photo by Kristen Jensen

INTRODUCTION

Lucky you! You're in love and you're getting married! We know without a doubt that your wedding will be unlike any other event you'll ever host again: more romantic, more personal, and much more complicated to plan. You'll soon walk down the aisle, speak your vows for all to witness, seal your promise with a kiss, and celebrate the great love and commitment in your heart, but with all the guests to consider and the details to organize, it may be quite a big undertaking to get from "I will" to "I do." Our goal with this book is to help you make your wedding, as well as your wedding planning, one of the most fun and rewarding projects of your life.

Every bride and groom and every family is totally unique, and what all of our advice comes down to in the end is to be true to yourself. Although others may have invaluable contributions to make, your wedding is a reflection of you and your love. Not your mother's, not your best friend's, and not that of the celebrity you read about in that magazine. Your personalities and how perfectly they complement each other are what your guests will be there to celebrate, so let them shine! The fun and focus of planning your wedding should be on finding all those special little ways to communicate your values, your passions, and your love's uniqueness. Your ceremony, your fashion, your invitation wording, your music—each is a little piece of you. If you can discover your own wedding style that authentically represents you, then you're destined to create an extraordinary celebration. Rest assured that all the logistical advice you need is readily available and we're here to help.

Throughout this book we'll encourage you to first and foremost keep a positive attitude. With the right mix of careful organization, flexibility, proper etiquette, and good humor, you'll sail through all the important decisions you need to make and achieve the goals you're after. We'll help you discover your dreams and expectations, we'll give you tips on how to gracefully respond to the abundant and well-meaning advice of close friends and family members without ruffling feathers, and we'll share loads of useful wedding information on everything from invitation etiquette to how to make and maintain a budget that works for you.

Speaking of budgets, we realize that there is a wide range of them out there. Whether you're looking to throw a grand-scale party in a lavish ballroom that pulls out all the stops or you're planning a more intimate affair in your parents' backyard, we offer plenty of advice and inspiration to satisfy all tastes and needs. We've even included many "do-it-yourself" (DIY) sections for you crafty brides looking to include a unique personal touch or two.

© photo by GH Kim Photography

When it comes to planning your wedding, the choices can sometimes seem endless: Do you want a buffet or sit-down dinner? Red or green for the bridesmaid dresses? Tulips or hyacinths for the flowers? Ponytail or chignon? And so on. We hope this book presents all the choices for you in a stress-free, low-pressure way. We've provided "inspiration galleries" throughout—photo grids that provide all the choices in an easy flip-through presentation—to help you decide what look (style, color, hair, etc.) is best for you. We understand that there's a lot of choice, but always remember: There is no wrong choice, really. It's just a matter of choosing what is best for you both. And we hope this book helps you do that.

After months of planning every detail of your big day, what it all boils down to is this: Your wedding day is about celebrating your union with your significant other, your best friend, the love of your life. Whether you choose to celebrate at a country club, in a grand ballroom, or even in an outdoor venue, the choices you make leading up to that very special day will help make memories to last a lifetime. We hope this book encourages you to have your wedding, your way and helps ensure that, when it's all over, you have fond memories and zero regrets. We wish you all the best in your wedding planning journey. We know your wedding will be a one-of-a-kind celebration that's totally you, and we're thrilled and honored to lend our support.

Inspiration Gallery

© photo by La Vie Photography

© photo by La Vie Photography

© photo by GH Kim Photography

© photo by GH Kim Photography

Chapter 1

CONGRATULATIONS, YOU'RE ENGAGED! NOW WHAT?

Congratulations, you're engaged! You said, "Yes!" You've made a commitment to spend the rest of your lives together. Revel in the reality of how lucky you are before you begin making plans. Say, "I love you" and count the ways. Let your partner know that you're thrilled to be getting married and share all the reasons you think this is the best decision for your life. It will do you both good to hear it.

The next few months might seem like a bit of a whirlwind—after all, you're planning out one of the most important days in your lives. But in the midst of the planning, remember to

sit back, take in some perspective, and, most important, find some time to just breathe. Remember that wedding planning can bring out some crazies, but what's most important here is that you stick to what's true to you, and what's best for each other.

This chapter will help guide you along the first steps of the journey that is wedding planning—how to figure out your wedding style, your budget, and your familial roles. It will provide you with a plethora of options and advice to help make your big day a great one. So please dive right in and have fun planning!

PICKING YOUR WEDDING STYLE

Far and away the hottest trend in wedding planning today is personalization. With a huge array of fabulous choices available to you, both online and where you live, it's never been easier or more fun to make a personal wedding style statement. So don't be shy. Go ahead and join the crowd of happy couples who are personalizing their weddings and making new traditions of their own. Start with what makes you tick. You both know

© photo by GH Kim Photography

1

© photo by La Vie Photography

loved the saxophone since second grade? Then by all means get a jazz band for your reception. Are your best friends all from college? Then ask them all to be part of your wedding party. No matter what decisions you ultimately make, remember that you've already made the most important one: You're getting married. The rest is simply icing on the cake.

Remember to personalize it. These days no two weddings are the same. Each couple's celebration is a unique expression of their sense of style and their ties to family, friends, and faith. Your wedding will offer you a fabulous opportunity for creative expression, so have fun indulging your artistic side and create a wedding that will have everyone saying, "That was just so them!" Nearly any part of your wedding can be personalized. Have fun making it all your own.

what you love, from your favorite music to your favorite dessert, and if you've already made your top-ten priority list, you know what's most important to you both.

Transforming your likes and loves into decisions is a creative process that will help you discover more about who you are as a couple and allow you to create a wedding day like no other. Are you envisioning a classic ceremony or an alternative exchange of vows? Do you want a formal reception or a casual affair? Will your guest list consist of your closest friends and family, or do you want to celebrate with everyone you care about, from your kindergarten teacher to your favorite barista? Once you've answered the basic questions that provide a foundation for your wedding plans, focus on what makes you unique in the world: the people, places, and passions that you hold most dear. Have you

Don't forget to play up your passions. Divide up responsibilities based on passion. If you love flowers and he's crazy about music, then enjoy choosing your bouquets and floral arrangements while he hires the DJ and ceremony musicians. Start with trying to fit as many things from your top-ten list into your wedding plan as possible; then when you run into practical obstacles, see how many things you can let go. Inspiration can come from anywhere; find it in all parts of your lives.

Remember that diversity makes life rich. Look for ways to incorporate your families and your backgrounds into your wedding. Have fun playing up your differences in creative ways rather than viewing them as obstacles. These are the things that make you unique. Help each other keep perspective about the things you really want. Consider which things on your priority list are important to you emotionally and which are items you could do without.

© photo by J. Garre Photography

Enjoy the process. Although it may seem counterintuitive, try not to compromise too much. If you love carrot cake and he loves chocolate, or if you love jazz and he loves rock and roll, there's plenty of room for you both to have what you want. Enjoy the time you get to spend together during your wedding planning process and don't let long to-do lists get in the way of quality time spent side by side.

Your Wedding, Your Way

There are millions of ways to creatively express your love and celebrate your marriage. Finding your own way can be one of the most rewarding things about wedding planning—and one of the most challenging. You want to hang on to the euphoria you felt when you first got engaged without having it turn into worries about planning your wedding. So before you begin to make the many choices that will make your big day unique, stop and spend some special time with your partner, focusing on these simple steps to stress-free wedding planning.

Step one: Share your dreams and expectations of what it means to have a wedding. Talk about the people and traditions you want to honor and the things you're looking forward to.

Step two: Make a top-ten list that emphasizes what each of you considers most important about your wedding day. Then share your lists with each other. Understanding each other's dreams will help you make decisions you'll feel good about when you get married and throughout your years together.

Step three: Once you have your priorities set, decide on a wedding date and whom you

© photo by GH Kim Photography

attended. Focus on the elements that made each of them unique. What parts did you appreciate and find really special, and what parts didn't you personally connect with?

Share your good news. The hustle and bustle of wedding planning is on its way, so be sure to savor the romance of the moment and celebrate this big step together. Agree on a plan for sharing your news before you start. Tell both sets of parents at the same time and before anyone else. Hearing the big news directly from you will be important to them. Share your news with family, close friends, and acquaintances—in that order.

Start living your vows now. Take advantage of opportunities to demonstrate the commitment "for better or worse, for richer or poorer" as you plan your wedding.

Make keeping perspective a family tradition. Give your wedding the weight it deserves without getting weighed down by it. Make a pact to keep your romance alive now and forever, no matter how busy you get. Designate at least one night a week as "date night" and give your partner your undivided attention.

Classic Style

Chic, classic styles honor important traditions while making an elegant statement. Are you inspired by the refined, ladylike looks of Grace Kelly and Audrey Hepburn? Are you perfectly at home sipping champagne in the back of a stretch limousine? Do you adore the idea of kicking up your shiny high heels on a dance

want to tell about your engagement and when to tell them. Consider making your announcement special by hosting an engagement party, sharing it at a family event, or putting it in the paper or on a website.

Step four: Last but not least, have fun finding ways to celebrate your preferences, your backgrounds, and your differences. Use your love and imagination to find new ways to work together. Remember: The partnering skills you'll learn while planning your wedding will be a gift you'll both be grateful for as you share your lives together.

Share your dreams. Really listen and share to find out what's important to you and the one you love. Chances are you'll be delighted, surprised, and occasionally challenged by what you find out, so stay curious and open-minded. Share some stories about weddings you've

© photo by GH Kim Photography

floor full of black ties, tuxes, and tails? Then you probably have a classic sense of style, and a traditional, elegant wedding is what you're looking for. To show off your good taste, choose timeless designs and formal fashions that make a classic style statement, then polish off your planning by weaving together each element to evoke an aura of sophistication. For a wedding full of time-honored tradition, choose your church, synagogue, or mosque for your ceremony, followed up by a swanky reception at a glittering hotel ballroom or sprawling historic mansion. Opt for Old English fonts on your engraved invitations and have silk ribbons woven tightly around your bridal bouquet. Wear your hair in a chignon or an elegant updo. Top off your look with a tiara or full-length veil and make your way down the aisle in a white wedding dress that will leave your guests breathless.

For a wedding that's all about glamour, get married at your place of worship or consider having your ceremony and reception at the same location. Book the penthouse of a private club high above the city lights, or choose a favorite restaurant with a view of the harbor. Wear your hair in finger waves or comb it out

© photo by Yours by John Photography

to impress, indicate the level of attire on your invitation. A white dress worn with a fingertip-length or cathedral-length veil is still the choice of traditional brides. Romantic vintage fashions are a lovely classic alternative. A formal tuxedo or morning suit, with cuff links, a silk tie, and shiny shoes, is still the look for grooms with classic style.

Exceptional service is synonymous with swank soirees. Host a seated dinner, or a delicious buffet, with plenty of staff on hand to attend to your guests' desires. Kick your party off with a first dance that showcases your ballroom skills. Pick a swing band, jazz quartet, or sophisticated DJ who naturally encourages couples to show off their own dancing skills as well. A traditional champagne toast is a must for classic events.

A black-and-white color palette with metallic or bold color accents is always in fashion. Choose calla lilies, orchids, or long-stemmed

perfectly straight and glossy to show off your A-line gown or silky sheath. Keep embellishments refined and to a minimum, and keep your color palette well-defined.

Seize your chance to interpret what "classic" means to you. You'll never have a better excuse to show off your style.

Classic events should begin with a formal invitation printed on linen or cotton stationery and sent in a hand-addressed envelope. A religious ceremony held at your house of worship is the most traditional choice for a wedding. Having your father walk you down the aisle and dance with you after your first dance is a respectful touch that still solicits tears, sighs, and warm hearts from all ages of wedding guests.

Dress is "black-tie" or "very black-tie" for formal events. If you want everyone to dress

© photo by One Thousand Words Photography

red roses and a multitiered white wedding cake to accentuate the romantic tradition. Make your graceful exit in a limousine or vintage Rolls Royce. If you think he's into it, pause when you enter your wedding night bedroom and wait for him to carry you over the threshold.

Casual Style

Lovely, laid-back details create understated elegance and an atmosphere of easy entertaining. Semiformal and informal weddings relax the standards of tradition and take a more carefree approach to both etiquette and style. Casual celebrations give you permission to have fun with the rules, from the way you announce your engagement to where you hold your reception, without sacrificing meaningful traditions or your personal sense of style. Maybe you've been dreaming of walking down the aisle in a fairy-tale wedding dress ever since you were six years old, but the aisle you've dreamed of is a garden path lined with wildflowers. Maybe you've

© photo by John and Joseph Photography

place anywhere you find beautiful or sacred, indoors or outdoors. To create a lovely altar wherever you are, choose a floral arbor, a chuppah, or a decorated fabric pavilion. Walk down the aisle with your father, your best male friend, or all by yourself. A casual ceremony gives you room to interpret tradition.

Choose a comfortably fitting gown that makes you look and feel gorgeous. Wear a tea-length skirt or a dress with peek-a-boo tulle for a fun and feminine look. Wear your hair gently pulled back and put a fresh fragrant flower behind your ear. Suits in colors like dark blue and charcoal gray, or mix-and-match jackets and pants, are perfect for casual weddings. Linen suits and dress shirts without ties look sharp on hot summer days.

Loose bouquets for your ladies and floral headpieces for the little girls add a sweet casual touch. Complementary colors like plum and

envisioned your ring bearer delivering your wedding bands on a favorite pillow from your childhood, but your ring bearer is your beloved black Lab or golden retriever puppy.

Show off your romantic, casual style and embrace what inspires you: a special place, a favorite color scheme, or an overall theme that feels just right. Play up your love for the beach by getting married with your toes in the sand and holding a bouquet of exotic flowers, followed by a sunset reception complete with a steel drum band and seafood buffet. Celebrate your love for the country by tying the knot in an old-fashioned barn lit with antique chandeliers and filled with the sounds of a mandolin and fiddle.

Casual weddings begin with creative invitations, but remember that basic rules of etiquette still apply. Semiformal ceremonies can take

© photo by Positive Light Photography

saffron, chocolate and teal, and pink and lime green contrast beautifully in photographs. Buffets full of yummy comfort foods and fresh seasonal fruits and vegetables are a hit with guests. Cupcakes, chocolate fountains, and candy buffets are easy-to-serve desserts that both adults and kids will love.

Get whisked away in a vintage pickup truck, Mini Cooper, or sporty convertible. Leave the top down during your outdoor wedding and have guests leave their gifts inside. Choose a creative guest book alternative like an instant-photo scrapbook or a bottle of champagne signed by all of your guests to enjoy on your one-year anniversary. If your reception is a dance party that will run late into the night, serve your guests delicious late-night snacks before they head home.

Alternative Style

Out-of-the-box ideas and creative accents combine to produce an unforgettable event. Green weddings, theme weddings, destination weddings, and DIY weddings are popping up everywhere, and they're just a few of the alternative options available to you for your wedding day. Truly, when it comes to planning your wedding, there's only one way to do it—and that's your way. So go for it and have a wedding that's authentically you!

© photo by GH Kim Photography

Are you committed to lessening your carbon footprint? Then reduce, reuse, recycle, and go green! Look for creative ways to cut down on wasted resources, without sacrificing your style.

Pick a theme to liven up your day. Take your guests on a wagon ride for your Wild West ceremony or surprise them with a first-dance fox-trot at your 1920s affair. The choices are limitless when it comes to theme weddings, so let your imagination take flight.

If travel is your thing, choose a desirable destination for your wedding and have your honeymoon before, during, and after your ceremony while you treat your guests to an unforgettable vacation.

DIY weddings are not just for brides on a budget; they allow you to incorporate precious, sentimental accents and the impressive talents of those you love. Ask your kitchen-savvy

© photo by Cheri Pearl Photography

Trust a destination-wedding specialist or your on-site wedding planner to help you organize your wedding details long distance. Be sure to give your guests ample time to plan for travel and a tiered price range of accommodation options.

If you'll be making DIY items for your wedding, be sure they don't have to be assembled the night before. You'll need your energy for your big day. Thank helpful guests publicly at your reception and point out their specific talents.

Choose favors that will live on after your wedding day. Tiny saplings or flower seeds make thoughtful and refreshing gifts. The easiest way to go green is to choose an organic catering company that composts leftovers. Rent, don't buy. Almost anything can be found through party rental companies and specialty companies. What you do buy, buy locally. Choose a local gift registry or ask guests to donate to a favorite charity in lieu of shipping gifts.

mother to bake your cake or your crafts-loving girlfriends to help you make decorations. Use your imagination and have some fun!

If you're dreaming of it, there's a way to incorporate it into your wedding. If you look fabulous in it, then be daring and wear it. Alternative style embraces fashion and gives your inner diva room to shine. Who says he can't wear tennis shoes with his tux? Fashionable grooms make style work for them. The sky's the limit—literally! Enthusiastic couples have had every kind of wedding, even jumping out of planes while saying "I do."

Find ways to express your wedding theme in everything from your apparel to your location to your getaway vehicle. Throw on your red cowboy boots and do the two-step at your country-style wedding. Try on a show-stopping feathered hair accessory for your Hollywood-style affair. Sushi bars, vegetarian meals, and fusion menus grace the tables at alternative weddings. Choose foods that match your theme.

> *Ecofriendly Weddings*
>
> While 100 percent green weddings are still somewhat unusual, weddings that incorporate ecofriendly practices are now commonplace. It's easy to plan a wedding that's friendly to the environment without giving up what's important to you.
>
> ~

Seasonal Style

Seasonal touches inspired by nature bring a special sense of time and place to your celebration. No matter what style suits you best, using seasonal accents in your wedding design will help you create a memorable sense of time and place. In addition, choosing fresh, locally grown foods and flowers will reduce your impact on the environment in uniquely delicious and beautiful ways. Discover what you each love most about the season, and celebrate it.

© photo by GH Kim Photography

© photo by J. Garner Photography

Spring Style: In the spring choose bright yellow daffodils and lipstick pink tulips for your bouquet, and every year when they begin to bloom you'll be reminded that your anniversary is on its way. Have a fresh floral wreath made for your flower girl's hair, use a bird's nest for a ring pillow, or incorporate fashion accessories for your wedding wardrobe in shades of robin's egg blue, soft green, or petal pink.

Paper parasols and antique umbrellas keep spring rain at bay and look sweet and romantic in photos. Lacy loose bouquets of peonies and potted centerpieces of mini daffodils, crocuses, and reticulated irises shout out spring style. Baby carrots, young asparagus, new potatoes, and sugar snap peas evoke the season and taste delicious. Baroque arrangements from composers like Handel and Vivaldi, with an emphasis on trumpets and horns, herald a spring bride down the aisle.

Summer Style: In the heat of the summer, serve up slices of delicious wedding cake filled with fresh berries and other ripe fruit, and accompany them with cold mint juleps, passion fruit punch, or tart lemonade. Have your ceremony programs made up as pretty paper fans to keep your guests cool in the hot summer sun.

Big bright bouquets of sunflowers, dahlias, and delphinium, or fragrant blossoms like roses, stephanotis, and gardenias, show off the season. Decorative metal buckets and watering cans filled with blossoms make smart centerpieces and fun take-home gifts for your family members and bridal party. Don't forget a change of shoes or two to help soothe your hot feet. And carry a powder puff or blotting papers to keep your face and neck pretty and shine free.

Fall Style: For fall play up the harvest season with floral arrangements that include fall leaves and berries. Choose rich oranges, reds, and russets for your color palette. Treat your guests to a hearty buffet of seasonal fresh vegetables, savory entrees, and warm crusty breads, and

© photo by Barbie Hull Photography

serve hot apple cider or mulled spiced wine to keep everyone cozy.

Wineries, orchards, and historic barns are fabulous locations for fall weddings. Homemade preserves, maple syrup, and caramel apples make fun additions to the menu and thoughtful take-home favors. Walkways with luminarias or jack-o'-lanterns with welcoming faces look lovely on an autumn night. Serve pie instead of wedding cake or as an additional dessert. Who doesn't love pumpkin and pecan pie or a warm apple tart with a dollop of vanilla bean ice cream?

Winter Style: Go glam in winter with a black-and-white wedding with splashes of ruby red or emerald green. Find a gorgeous faux-fur wrap to cover your shoulders, or have one designed to match your wedding dress. Hold a candlelight ceremony and decorate your reception with thousands of twinkling lights. Give personalized mugs complete with packets of rich cocoa, chocolate spoons, and mini marshmallows as take-home favors for your guests to enjoy.

Ski lodges, mansions, and intimate venues with fireplaces and dark wood accents feel warm and snug on cold winter days. Use crystals, shiny sugar, and gold and silver decorations in your decor. Give silver dinner bells away as favors. Keep winter travel to a minimum by having your reception near your ceremony or at the same place. Don't forget the mistletoe! Hang it in every doorway to put guests in an affectionate mood.

© photo by GH Kim Photography

GETTING ORGANIZED

You're about to plan one of the most elaborate and momentous events of your life. You'll need lots of support, solid advice, and a flexible attitude to make the most of it. To get off on the right foot, begin by creating your guest list. Make a "must have" list of all the people you simply have to have with you, and a "wish" list of those it would be fun to invite. Soon, when many of your budget decisions come down to "per head" estimates, you can easily compare the two lists and weigh your options.

Create a spreadsheet to help keep your guest list organized. Include contact information and add columns to record your RSVPs, the gifts you give and receive, when you send out your thank-you notes, and miscellaneous information like your bridal party's measurements or which guests need a vegetarian meal.

Buy, or put together, a wedding planner with lots of pocket folders and room to grow. Label separate folders for every vendor you plan to hire—one for color charts, one for fabric swatches, at least one for your fashion ideas, and several more to fill up with inspirational ideas, photos, and magazine tear sheets. Take your binder with you to tastings, tours, and meetings with professionals.

Search the Internet for resources and start a favorites list on your computer to quickly find the wedding websites and blogs that you love. Treat yourself to the books and magazines that you're drawn to; put your feet up, read, relax, and let yourself dream.

Planning Basics

Get started planning your big day by checking these items below off of your to-do list first:

Create Your Guest List	Begin your guest list with your families. This might seem like a given, but they have to eat too, and they'll figure in your head count. If your heart is set on a particular venue, find out how many people the site accommodates before you finalize your list. Focus on people who love and support you; after all, they're the VIPs in your life. Keep in mind that the average wedding costs between $100 and $150 per person.	
Get Organized	Staying organized is the key to event success. If keeping organized is not your strong suit, hiring a planner to help you will be invaluable. Include a timeline, a seating chart, your budget, your guest list, and your priority list in your organizer. Don't forget to refer to your budget and your priority list as you make decisions. Keep copies of all your contracts and deposit receipts in order and in a safe place.	
Get Inspired	Create a collage of images or an "inspiration board" that you can refer to when explaining your wedding style vision to the professionals you're working with. Inspiration comes from an endless variety of sources. Let yourself be inspired by your favorite color, song, or hobby, or take inspiration from your family and faith. Visit wedding blogs and websites and get inspired to create a wedding that's all about you.	
Create an Heirloom	Arrange your prewedding photos, letters, and sketches, including tickets and mementos from favorite dates and trips. Record stories that you don't want to forget. Include kind gestures, helpful advice, and funny things that happen along the way. Showcase the color swatches, fabrics, and fashion and design photos that inspired you. Finish off your scrapbook with a copy of your vows, your signed marriage license, and a picture of your kiss. Create a pretty scrapbook later from the items in your planner.	

© photo by La Ve Photography

if you do, don't worry; we'll give you lots of suggestions for saving money without sacrificing style.

Who's hosting? Traditionally a bride's parents paid for her wedding, but this is no longer the norm. If your parents will be involved financially, ask them to contribute a set amount rather than pay for certain items. It will make it easier for you to allocate expenses. No matter who ends up paying, your wedding is still a family affair. Be sure you take into consideration the desires of those closest to you.

Setting Your Budget

Creating an organized budget is a necessity. Start by determining who will be hosting and contributing to your wedding and then add together all the available resources. Chances are the two of you will pay for much of it with help from your parents, but every family is different, so that is far from a given. Whether or not your parents decide to be financially involved, they may have people they want included in your guest list. Meet with your families and show them your guest list as well as the top three items from each of your priority lists so they'll know what's important to you.

The average wedding in the United States today costs $25,000 and includes approximately 170 guests. That's around $150 per person. You may not flinch at that figure at all, but

Personalize Your Spreadsheet: To stay on budget you'll have to stay organized, so have your budget spreadsheet ready before you begin

On average, up to 50 percent of your wedding budget will be spent on your reception. Other big-ticket items will include your wedding fashions, music, flowers, and photography. Allocate funds for each service, and if you go over on one, subtract from another. Almost half of all weddings go over budget, so take care of unforeseen expenses by building in an extra 10 to 15 percent before you begin spending.

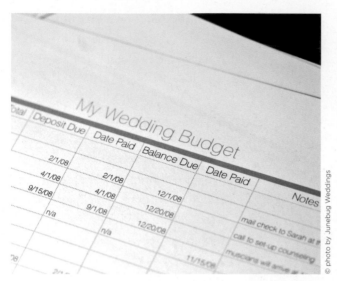

© photo by Junebug Weddings

add to your income instead of borrowing. Use the money management techniques you learn now to build a strong foundation for the future.

Your Traditional Responsibilities

Traditionally the bride and the groom have different responsibilities when it comes to the wedding. In more recent times these distinct roles have often become blended, the lines between them blurred. To help you figure out who traditionally is responsible for what, we've broken it down for you:

You're the Bride: It used to be that a woman had very little to do when it came to planning her own wedding. Her mother would make the arrangements, her parents would invite all of the guests, and the groom did his best to arrive on time. The bride was responsible for buying her husband's wedding band, providing gifts for the members of her bridal party, setting up beauty appointments, and sending out thank-you notes. As a modern bride you'll do all of

spending money. Create a spreadsheet for your guest list and your budget. Keep track of how many people RSVP to help finalize your budget. Set aside time once a week to update your spreadsheets and create an electronic backup of all the wedding information you have stored on your computer.

Manage Your Debt: To stay organized and within your budget, open up a separate bank account for your expenditures and record all of your transactions in a spreadsheet. Update it regularly and review it together throughout the planning process. If you're already homeowners and need a wedding loan, look for a home-equity line with no prepayment penalty before using a credit card. If you do need to use a credit card, search for a low-interest option that offers some sort of reward. Consider creative ways you can

Wedding Loans

If you plan on getting a loan to pay for your wedding, a good rule of thumb is to not spend more than you can pay off in a year. Avoid opening new credit cards, save wisely, and give yourself another reason to celebrate your first anniversary: being free of wedding debt!

that and more. Chances are you'll be involved in almost every decision, from deciding on your wedding date to the flavors in your cake. Your to-do list can quickly become overwhelming.

That's why it's important to set up a support team of professionals, friends, and family members who can help make your wedding planning fun and easy. You'll want to delegate early and often to people who want to help. Your mom and members of your bridal party are the obvious first choices to turn to. If you're hiring a wedding consultant, he or she will be a valuable asset in helping you create a stylish ceremony and reception that runs smoothly. If you aren't hiring a consultant, you'll need to look to family members, friends, and other trusted resources to ensure you have the support you need.

Don't be shy about asking for recommendations and references. Experienced wedding vendors should have numerous current references to give to you, and newlyweds love to talk about what worked and didn't work at their own weddings. Listen to advice gracefully and thank the person giving it, but don't feel pressured to follow every recommendation to a T—and don't give the impression that you will follow it unless you're planning to.

Follow your instincts about what you need to stay healthy, happy, and organized so you can thoroughly enjoy this exciting time!

The Modern Bride: Traditionally brides have been responsible for sending thank-you notes; nowadays your groom needs to get in on the act as well. Include his ring, your bridal party gifts, and your personal stationery in your own

Traditional Family Responsibilities

Your engagement is bound to spark a flurry of excitement and expectations from you, your friends, and your family. Even if you haven't been thinking about your wed-

© photo by J. Garner Photography

ding since your were little, chances are one or both of your parents have, and even the friends closest to you may have preconceived notions of how your wedding will unfold.

To help you navigate the waters between your desires and those of your loved ones, here is a rundown of the traditional family member responsibilities that are often the center of people's expectations (whether they know it or not). These are merely guidelines that are meant to be tailored to the resources and realities of your unique relationships and families.

Keep in mind that your parents may not be able to financially support your wedding planning expectations. Traditional norms have changed rapidly over the years, and now almost 50 percent of couples pay for their wedding themselves. Communicate clearly so everyone, including you, knows what to expect financially.

Here's a roadmap to help you navigate these tricky waters:

The Bride's Family: Traditionally the bride's parents pay for the lion's share of their daughter's wedding, including the engagement party, the dress and veil, all of the expenses related to the ceremony including music, and all of the expenses for the reception except for the beverages (which the groom's family may cover). In addition they'll pay for transportation and the engagement announcement in the newspaper.

Sit down with your fiancé and both sets of parents to discuss their top three expectations for your wedding. Consider how these requests might fit in with your vision. Traditionally your father will walk you down the aisle, make a toast at your reception, and dance with you after your first dance. Your mom will be there to help you get ready, dance with your groom, and be a gracious hostess at your reception.

The Groom's Family: The groom's parents are commonly responsible for the rehearsal dinner, a wedding gift (often a monetary contribution), the beverages for the reception, and their own wedding attire.

Traditional roles may leave the groom's family feeling left out of the wedding planning. Be sure they have an opportunity to contribute and share their wishes. The rehearsal dinner gives the groom's family a chance to show their gratitude and excitement about your marriage. Take their

desires and resources to heart when planning this special event. Honor the groom's family by making sure your photographer covers them thoroughly and takes any special portraits or additional photos they would like.

Communicate: Family members will appreciate a schedule of events for your wedding weekend well in advance so they can plan for parties, pictures, and special events. Pay close attention to time frames and transportation so people can easily get where you need them to be. Start your own wedding website to keep people in the loop as details unfold. Sharing in your process will create a lasting sense of connection.

Delegate: You'll need more than financial support from your families to pull off a great wedding. If you're paying for your wedding yourself, enlist the help of your relatives in other areas. Consider sending out a contact list of all participating members so they can coordinate with one another and plan surprises. A lot of people really want to help, but they can't read your mind. This is one time it is absolutely acceptable to ask for huge favors. Don't be shy!

© photo by GH Kim Photography

budget if your parents are hosting your wedding. "To your own self be true." Don't let fantasies or false expectations take over when planning your real wedding. You absolutely can't please everyone, so just remember to be gracious and recognize good intentions.

Your Support Team: People's schedules and talents differ. Don't expect help; just ask for it nicely and always say thank you. Offer members of your bridal party fun things to do like help you pick out your dress or brainstorm DIY opportunities. Whenever people help you, let them know how much you appreciate them right away. They'll be much more likely to pitch in the next time you ask. Draw on the hobbies and passions of others when delegating responsibility.

Helpful Advice: Contrary to popular belief, wedding consultants can save you both time and money, in addition to making your wedding stress free. But if you do choose to tackle your own planning, just stay meticulously organized. Create a calendar in your PDA or online and post another one where you can't miss it. Consider setting up a "wedding office" in your home or at your parents' home and keep everything in one place.

Trusted Referrals: There's no one like someone who has been through it to lend her advice and provided trusted referrals. Connect with other brides at work and online to "talk shop." Once you've decided with whom you want to work, relax and trust them to do their job. Communicate openly and be direct with your desires. No matter what happens, keep a sense of humor. It's your attitude that determines if a problem is a minor setback or a major disaster.

Creating Your Timeline

(see also our handy timeline chart on page 348)

Twelve to Eight Months before Your Wedding

Among the many details involved in wedding planning are a few foundational elements that set the stage for all the others. Start with these important decisions and you'll be ready to move forward and plan, stress free.

1. Set your date. Ideally, you'll give yourself twelve months or longer to plan your wedding.

© photo by Positive Light Photography

Begin by choosing a date that's easy on you and your guests. Then consider hiring a consultant. Wedding consultants are available for every aspect of planning, from complete coordination to "day of" assistance. Plus, experienced consultants have the knowledge and expertise to help you save time and money while giving you the confidence to pull off a memorable event.

Choose a date in your favorite season, or one of emotional significance, like the day you first met or first kissed. Before you set your date in stone, check with the people most important to you and be sure they're available to attend. If you start planning a little late, or if you're on a

tight budget, consider having your wedding on a date other than Saturday, when locations and vendors will be more available.

2. Book your reception venue. Once you've chosen an overall style or theme for your wedding, you'll want to search for a venue that really shows it off. Your venue will be the key to setting the tone for your wedding day. The cost to rent your reception site, combined with catering expenses, is bound to be your largest expenditure, so don't get overwhelmed. Schedule time for your ceremony and rehearsal, and be sure to add one to two hours to your allotted ceremony time for pictures and unforeseen delays.

Groom's Gospel

Hey ladies, remember: Planning can be even more fun when you get your man involved! This section involves a little work on the groom's part, so go get him from the next room (or away from the TV or off the basketball court or . . . you get the idea!), and go through this together as a couple to be sure everyone's on the same page and the groom has his marching orders. Also, whenever you see the "Groom's Gospel" throughout the book be sure to include your groom in that part of the wedding planning.

You're the Groom: You've popped the big question and gotten the yes you were looking for. Now your journey to the altar has begun. After you've got a good idea of

© photo by GH Kim Photography

what's most important to you and your fiancée and you know what you can afford and who you're going to invite, you're ready to take the plunge into planning.

First, get organized. Approach your wedding like a project manager. If you haven't already, create a spreadsheet with all of your contacts and budget information and make your big to-do list. Once that's done, choose your best man and your bridal party based on friendship, family ties, and common sense. You want someone who is organized, reliable, and excited to help as your best man, and guys you can count on in a pinch for your groomsmen. Communicate to your guys what part you want them to play in your big day, and coordinate your wedding party fashion with your fiancée's. You'll get lots of tips on how dress to impress in the pages ahead.

Once the basics are covered, plan your honeymoon and book your wedding-night room ASAP. Research diligently and get an early jump on the best travel arrangements and the most romantic accommodations. A stellar honeymoon will bring you big husband points and great memories.

Add buying your wedding bands, creating your song list, and getting your marriage license to the list of things you'll need to do together. You'll probably be on your own when it comes to buying gifts, writing your toasts and vows, and arranging for transportation. Start setting up appointments to interview potential vendors, and don't forget to check with your fiancée to find out about other appointments she would like you to make or attend with her.

You're a Lucky Man: Consider writing an engagement announcement that fits your wedding style. A message from you about what a lucky man you are signals your involvement and gratitude for having found the woman of your dreams. Ask her how you can be the most help to her. A little support can go a long way. Write and mail your own thank-you notes, and don't forget to include one to her parents for raising the love of your life.

Set Up Your Support Team: Your best man will have a lot of duties before and during your wedding. In addition to choosing someone reliable, be sure he has the time and energy for the job. If you're having a hard time choosing between your best friend and your brother, etiquette says family first. Cousins and close friends make fantastic groomsmen and ushers. Your ring bearer should be at least four years old and your altar boys at least ten to avoid mishaps.

Start Planning Your Honeymoon: Check all of your reservations, including transportation to and from your accommodations, twice. Don't be fooled by ads and photos. Ask lots of questions, get referrals, and find out if any events or construction may affect your visit. If you're traveling out of the country, arrange for all travel requirements for passports, blood tests, and immunizations before you book. Have dinner reservations ready for the first night that you arrive.

Buy Gifts and Finalize Details: Shop for gifts well in advance, and help your fiancée register for the wedding gifts you'll be receiving from guests. Make a list of everyone you want to thank at your reception, and don't forget to include your wife in your list. Research your state's marriage requirements online many months before your wedding date. Don't hesitate to verify your agreements by requesting written confirmations. Keep all of your receipts in the same place for easy access.

© photo by GH Kim Photography

done, you'll look to your wedding photos for your memories and you'll pass them on to future generations. Don't underestimate the importance of hiring a pro for this important job. Popular photographers' and videographers' schedules fill up quickly, so book them well in advance and be ready to give them a deposit along with your contract to secure your wedding date.

Compare at least three photographers for style, price, and personality. Schedule any additional photography time for your rehearsal dinner or engagement photos when you book your wedding. Create a photo album for your guy that he's guaranteed to love. Schedule a tasteful boudoir photo session and show off your playful,

Popular venues can book up years in advance, so don't delay in making this important decision. Book your officiant along with your ceremony site. Some sites require certain officiants, and some officiants won't travel to perform ceremonies. Conduct site inspections of your locations. Take traffic flow, parking, rental needs, and lighting into consideration. Calculate the distance between your ceremony and your reception site and have a plan for group transportation if necessary.

3. Book your officiant. Find someone you like and respect and who shares your beliefs. Then schedule any required counseling appointments.

4. Find your photographer and videographer. We know that when it's all said and

Consider hiring a consultant. The average wedding takes over 250 hours to plan. If your time is valuable, hiring a consultant can be a highly practical use of funds. Savvy consultants know how to negotiate contracts and cut costs on things you and your guests will never miss. Many couples say that hiring a consultant was their best wedding planning decision. Interview at least three different consultants and consider their professionalism, experience, and personalities.

© photo by La Vie Photography

sexy side. Consider asking your photographer for vendor recommendations; their unique perspectives can be priceless.

Eight to Four Months before Your Wedding

Here's where life gets busy and super fun! You're about to decide what you'll be wearing, how to announce your wedding day, and what you'll be offering your guests, from food to music to atmosphere.

1. Play dress up. Have some fun and dive right into your fashion fantasies to find a dress that makes you feel like a million bucks. Arrange

© photo by GH Kim Photography

to have any necessary alterations started immediately to avoid last-minute hassles. Choose your bridal party and get your girls together to brainstorm their fashions. Get busy putting together the rest of your wedding look, from your shoes to your hairstyle to your accessories, and be sure your man is busy putting his look together as well.

The transformation of a woman into a bride is simply breathtaking. Revel in your moment by creating a look that makes you feel confident, poised, and totally gorgeous. Buy your dress first, then your shoes and your veil. Most wedding dress boutiques require appointments, so be sure to call ahead. Make appointments for day-before mani-pedis and day-of hair and makeup services when you first book your stylists.

2. If you haven't hired an in-house caterer through your reception site, meet with caterers now. Decide on a menu that harmonizes with your style and fits your budget, and be sure you understand exactly what's included in your contract. Order any additional rental items that you'll need like tables, chairs, dishes, dance floors, and lighting.

Once you've sewn up the questions of where, when, and what to serve your guests, choose any and all of the musicians, DJs, and entertainers you're planning on having.

Determine the type of meal you'll be serving based on the time of your reception, and then choose the formality of the service. A

© photo by GH Kim Photography

seated dinner with a full waitstaff is the height of classic elegance, but it's substantially more costly than a buffet-style brunch. Nearly anything is available to rent, so look for stylish options for your dishes, linens, chairs, portable dance floors, and lighting. If you want an elaborate custom cake, book your designer now.

3. Meet with an invitation designer or pick out your paper products online. Remember to mail your save-the-dates nine months ahead to guests who'll need to make travel arrangements.

Meet with at least three designers and bring your address list and details about your wedding style, theme, and colors with you. Ask your stationer if he or she can help you with wording and hand addressing envelopes. Be clear about who will be responsible if mistakes are made in the printing process. Order your invitations along with your other paper decor, from save-the-dates to thank-you notes, to help save time and printing setup fees.

4. Hire your florist. Flowers are an important piece of your wedding decor and your fashion ensemble. Choose someone who is creative and passionate about helping you express your style.

Determine whether you'll need a florist or a floral designer. A florist will provide you with arrangements, and a floral designer will transform your venue with floral decor. Take your color palette, fabric swatches, a picture of your dress, and a list of the flowers that you love with you to your meetings. Communicate your budget requirements up front, but don't eliminate a company that you love simply because the first quote doesn't work. Thoroughly discuss alternatives and options.

© photo by La Vie Photography

5. Book hotel rooms for yourself and your guests. Negotiate a package price for a block of rooms, and if you're having a destination wedding, make these arrangements as early as possible.

Four to Two Months before Your Wedding
In the next few months, you'll be putting the finishing touches on your planning to ensure that your big day unfolds gracefully.

1. If you haven't already, set up a time to taste cakes and desserts. Take your mom or friends with you to add to the fun. If you're not cake lovers, consider getting a small one just for cutting, or choose another sweet dessert alternative. Wedding cakes come in a mouthwatering array of delicious flavors and fillings and an endless array of styles, usually ranging from $2 to $12 per slice. Attend a tasting to try out

© photo by Junebug Weddings

photo by Yours by John Photography

samples of cake flavors and see photos of other cakes the designer has made. To guarantee that your cake is as delicious as it is beautiful, be sure it will be served fresh and never frozen and ask your baker for a list of the ingredients that he or she uses.

2. Pick out your wedding bands and shop for gifts. Make a day of it and have fun choosing these things together. Decide if you'll be buying matching bands or each choosing your own style. While there are good companies online to buy your wedding bands from, it's safest to buy from a reputable local dealer who has at least ten years' experience in business. Allow eight to ten weeks for special-order gifts and engravings.

While your mind is on gifts, be sure to register for items of your own. Give your guests a wide range of options to suit every budget. Check your registry as things unfold to be sure

a wide range of gift options and price options remains.

3. Be sure you have your paperwork in order. Research and complete the marriage license requirements for your state, renew your passport if traveling, and schedule any necessary blood tests or vaccinations. If you'll be changing your name, consider waiting until you get back from your honeymoon. Air travel may require the name used at the time of booking. Make a list of financial items that you'll need to address, including merging bank accounts, mortgage documents, and insurance information. Sit down together and run a complete credit report on each other's financial profiles before you merge your assets. If you have concerns about existing property or inheritances, consider a prenup. They're not just for celebrities.

© photo by GH Kim Photography

Check in with your groom to be sure he's taking care of his specific responsibilities, but don't ask for too many details; there may be fun surprises in the works!

Formal and semiformal invitations should be hand addressed. Send your photographer your invitation so it can be photographed. Set up a wedding website for your guests. Post your wedding schedule, tourist information, driving directions, and fun, personal content.

Two Months to One Day before Your Wedding

You're almost there! As your wedding day approaches, you'll be preparing for your

4. As time unfolds, confirm every reservation and detail. Meet with your caterer, give your DJ your playlist, and send your photographer and videographer a list of important shots. Go to final fittings to ensure you're dressed to impress and make appointments for your mani-pedi, makeup, and hairstyle.

5. Last but not least, send out your invitations. Eight weeks is the perfect amount of time for nearby guests to make arrangements for your wedding. Remember to have thank-you notes ready as your RSVPs and wedding gifts roll in. Addressing invitations is exacting and time-consuming. Consider hiring your invitation designer or a calligrapher to assist.

ceremony and reception, shopping for your honeymoon, going to parties, and getting gorgeous. Have a blast and stay organized!

1. Finalize the details of your ceremony. Meet with your officiant to discuss your schedule and review processional and recessional arrangements. Write and rehearse your vows, confirm musicians and readers, and set aside your programs to be delivered to ushers two days before your wedding day.

Remember to think through your entire ceremony from start to finish and don't forget the ending. Your exit provides an opportunity for a really fun send-off and a great photo op. Choose birdseed, bubbles, sparklers, or bells to give out to your guests. Make a list of extra items you'll need during your ceremony. Include things like your Ketubah, a glass to break, a

unity candle, a lucky penny for your shoe, and your interpretation of "something old, something new."

2. Visualize your reception. Write your toast and practice it, and be sure your best man and other speakers are prepared as well. Schedule dance lessons and take two a week until you're ready to glide into your first dance. Consider buying toasting glasses or a special knife to cut your cake. Make the most of your lighting; be sure it plays up your decor and showcases your reception events.

Double-check that your reception site or DJ will provide the necessary sound equipment for music as well as speeches. Make a list of the extra items you'll need at your reception, like wedding favors, special gifts, a garter for throwing, and a guest book. Give your caterer and venue manager your final head count. Confirm set-up and tear-down details and obtain any necessary permits or insurance.

3. Enjoy your parties! Schedule your rehearsal dinner and other wedding-related events. Have fun at your bachelor and bachelorette parties and enjoy socializing with friends from near and far. Their presence is a gift.

4. Send out your thank-you notes and express your gratitude generously. Do your best to get handwritten notes out within two weeks of receiving gifts, and be sure you have your thank-you gifts wrapped and ready to go. Give gifts

© photo by La Vie Photography

© photo by La Vie Photography

© photo by J. Garner Photography

Show your appreciation by being on time and smartly dressed for all parties and showers in your honor.

5. Remember to pamper yourself every day along the way. Drink lots of water, eat well, take your vitamins, and go to the gym more often than not. Enjoy visits to the spa, get a series of facials, and take care of your hands and feet. Run through your complete wedding day look to be sure you're not forgetting anything. Get rid of tan lines, whiten your teeth, and let yourself smile!

Brides, be sure to take your veil, hair accessories, and jewelry with you to the salon for a trial run-through of your hair and makeup. And for your grooms . . . tell them not to discount the relaxing and rejuvenating power of a good massage or spa treatment. They're not just for the girls! Get plenty of rest the week before your big day, even though there are lots of things to do to keep you extra busy.

CHOOSING A LOCATION

We go into extensive details about ceremony and reception locations in chapters 8 and 9, but it is important to mention them briefly here, too, as securing a location for your big day is one of the first things you'll do. Depending on the availability of your desired location—and some places can be booked up to a year in advance—your entire wedding timeline will fall into place. Securing your location—and soon—will determine if you're in for a short or longer engagement, and you can plan accordingly.

to your bridal party at your rehearsal dinner or wait until you get home from your honeymoon; either is appropriate. Tickets to favorite shows and sporting events are great gifts you can share with your friends. Gifts like good luck charms, jewelry, or watches are reminders of your appreciation that will last a lifetime.

© photo by GH Kim Photography

Ceremony Locations

When planning your ceremony, there are several things to keep in mind. The first is determining if you want a religious or civil ceremony. Many of today's couples choose to get married in a church, synagogue, or other religious location, but truly any space that feels sacred to you can be the perfect place for your ceremony. Religious ceremonies are often held in houses of worship and incorporate rules of faith and require a religious officiant. Civil ceremonies can take place in city hall or any location you love. They require a legal official to marry you, whether this is a justice of the peace, judge, magistrate, county clerk, mayor, boat caption, or even friend ordained online.

Next keep in mind location, size, and space of your ceremony site. How many guests will you invite? Keep in mind that you'll need about eight square feet per guest to accommodate people comfortably. If you're having an outdoor wedding, have a backup plan for wind and rain. One such option is a tent, which can be decorated to look quite beautiful. If you're not getting married in a house of worship, consider some unique alternate locations, such as a golf course, the beach, or even a family member's backyard. Regardless of your location or style of ceremony, to help secure your first choice, try to book your site and your officiant twelve to eighteen months before your wedding day.

Reception Locations

Choosing a reception location will be one of the most important decisions you'll make while planning your wedding. Between the catering and rental fees, the style and ambiance, the reception costs may easily add up to more than

Here's a quick list of suggested locations for receptions:
- Backyards/Private Homes
- Hotel Ballrooms
- Mansions and Historic Buildings
- Private Clubs and Golf Courses
- Gardens and Parks
- Beaches
- Ranches and Country Farms
- Boats
- Museums and Galleries
- Wineries
- Destinations

© photo by GH Kim photography

half of your budget. But don't stress: Remember to look for places that fit the style of the day that you want. Make a list of your must-haves/priorities, consider your budget, and don't be afraid to think outside the box when it comes to finding reception sites.

You'll want to look for a venue with multiple locations for taking photos; remember that every vista and architectural element is a potential backdrop. If you're sharing a location for both ceremony and reception and will have to turn the room from one into the other, be sure you have a place to keep guests entertained during the transition. And don't underestimate amenities. Having spacious getting-ready rooms, extra bathrooms, and plenty of on-site parking can be a godsend on your wedding day.

CHOOSING YOUR WEDDING PARTY

Choosing the wedding party can be one of the most difficult, personal decisions you make. It can also be a point of contention—with some people sometimes getting hurt feelings as a result. Try not to let it all get to you. You want to choose people who are enthusiastic about your engagement and pending wedding and who have the available time to handle all of the necessary responsibilities that come with being part of the wedding party.

Your Maid of Honor

Choosing your maid of honor can be a sweet and challenging experience. Ideally you want to choose someone whom you love and trust and who has enough time and energy to support you throughout your entire planning process. Who's always in your corner? Who reminds you to never put yourself down? Who makes you feel better when you're around her? Chances are whoever that is, she's the perfect choice to be your maid of honor. Blessed with sisters and friends who all fit the bill? Choose your oldest sister first or the friend you've known

the longest. That decision will be easy to justify should hurt feelings arise. Choose out of love, not out of guilt. To make sure both you and your maid of honor are happy with your choice, start off by being clear about what you're requesting. Give her a wish list of things you anticipate needing her help with and give her time to consider it before signing on.

Traditionally your maid of honor will help you pick out your dress and the fashions for the whole bridal party. She'll make sure that the bridesmaids attend their fittings and arrive at the altar looking put together from head to toe. Before your wedding she'll be the hostess of your bridal shower and your bachelorette party, and she'll help you keep track of all the thoughtful gifts you receive. She'll spread the word on everything from where you're registered to what time to arrive at your rehearsal dinner, and she'll help you make dozens of important decisions along the way.

In addition to having her lend a hand as a fashion consultant before your wedding, ask your maid of honor to stay close by on your wedding day to help put on your dress, touch up your makeup, and bustle your gown. It's customary for your maid of honor to pay for her dress, your bridal shower or bachelorette party, and a wedding gift. Keep her resources in mind and don't expect her to go out of her

comfort zone financially unless you're planning on contributing.

During the ceremony, your maid of honor will stand to the right of you, holding his ring and your bouquet during your ceremony. If your train or veil needs straightening, your maid of honor will attend to it before she takes your bouquet. Once your license is signed, your maid of honor will ensure that all your personal items are transferred from the ceremony to your reception. Then she'll arrive ahead of you to alert your venue to prepare for your grand entrance.

> *Your maid of honor is there to lend her support throughout your wedding planning process. While it's thoughtful for her to give you extra time and patience for being the bride, don't forget what's going on in her life. Be supportive of her and you'll stay friends long after your wedding day.*

It's common practice, but not required, that your maid of honor give a toast at your reception. You may also call on her to dance with your groom and his father and to gather the single women together for the toss of your bouquet.

People will naturally gravitate toward your maid of honor and best man to ask questions. Be sure they know all the relevant info your guests need, from where to have their parking validated to the location of the restrooms.

Groom's Gospel

Your Best Man

Choosing a stand-up guy to stand up for you does require some forethought. You'll want someone who you really like and trust, someone who's reliable, knows what's important to you, and has enough time to have your back all the way to your honeymoon.

Your best friend or your oldest brother is an obvious first choice to be your best man. Give your best man a list of the jobs you need help with when you ask him to take on the role. Your best man will plan your much-anticipated bachelor party, and he'll coordinate with your maid of honor to make sure that your entire bridal party has the information they need about important events like your rehearsal. He'll come with you to pick

out your tuxes and help you put together your look, and if you're lucky, he'll have some great advice on what's in style and what can help you stand out from the rest of the guys.

Throughout the planning process your best man will be there to be sure the groomsmen work as a team. Your best man will attend fittings with you and the guys, and if he's extra-organized, he'll show up at the wedding with shoe polish, extra socks, and a sewing kit. On your wedding day, your best man will be at your side to take your calls and be sure that your groomsmen show up on time and on task, perfectly dressed to impress. He'll hold your bride's ring for you during your ceremony, stand next to you while you say your vows, and make the whole thing official by signing your license as a witness.

When the party portion of your day gets underway, your best man will kick off the celebration by raising a glass to you and your bride. Ask your best man to prepare a one- to three-minute toast. If you're at all concerned about what he might share, ask him to omit personal stories and jokes and focus on what he wishes for your marriage.

He'll dance with your new wife after you and her father do. If he's single and naturally sociable, ask him to help keep the single

ladies in your bridal party and family dancing so you can focus on your bride. And, when your wedding day comes to a close, he'll be there to drive you to the airport, take your gifts to your house, and return your tuxes if necessary.

With all the tasks required, being a best man is a true honor and a real responsibility. Remember to thank him for accepting the job and for everything he does for you along the way.

Your Supporting Cast

Choosing your bridal party and contributors to your wedding ceremony provides a fantastic opportunity to honor your friends and family. If you're having a large wedding, there will be plenty of spots for bridesmaids and groomsmen. If you're having a small intimate affair, you'll still need to choose ushers and others to contribute readings or music to your ceremony. For your bridal party you'll want people whom you love to hang out with and who enjoy one another's company. After all, you'll all be together for your shower, rehearsal dinner, and wedding, at the very least. Choose people who

are enthusiastic about your engagement and who have the available time to attend necessary fittings and functions. For your ushers choose responsible friends and family members who are usually punctual and polite.

For your ceremony you may have special readings, poems, or songs that you would like to share with your guests, which is a perfect way to ask family members to participate. Want to add an extra splash of sweetness and light to your ceremony? Then get the little ones involved. There's really nothing cuter than a little boy in a tuxedo or a little girl throwing petals as she makes her way down the aisle.

© photos by J. Garner Photography

© photo by La Vie Photography

pay for their outfits and attend your rehearsal dinner. Teenagers are ideal as ushers. The role gives them something important to do, without requiring too much time or other commitment from them.

Flower Girls and Ring Bearers: To give little ones extra confidence, have them walk down the aisle together. Having a buddy can help calm last-minute jitters. Typically children four to eight years old fill these special roles. Kids who are naturally outgoing and truly excited to participate have a better chance of fulfilling their tasks well on your wedding day. Seating parents in an aisle seat where kids can easily see them also helps them feel safer.

Your Bridal Party: A couple's closest friends and siblings usually compose the bridal party. There are generally two to ten bridesmaids and groomsmen. While it's conventional, it's not necessary that you have the same number of attendants on each side or that his side be all guys, or your side be all girls. Traditionally the members of your bridal party pay for their outfits, wedding gifts, and their lodging, if necessary, and they should be on hand to support you throughout your planning process.

Attendants and Helpful Friends: Ushers are typically male and have the important job of seating guests and escorting mothers down the aisle last. The lucky mother of the bride pictured above has both of her handsome sons at her side. Traditionally your ushers will need to

© photo by GH Kim Photography

A Note on Gifts & Gratitude

The members of your wedding party are your friends, your family, your support systems, and your comic relief. They've no doubt played important roles in your lives, and throughout your wedding planning, they will shower you with sweet gifts and gestures, so it is only natural for you to reciprocate. When the time comes (typically at the rehearsal dinner or after the wedding), showing gratitude for all they've done is important.

Coming up with thank-you gifts that express what the people mean to you can be a superfun and creative project. What does each of them love to do? Show them how well you know them with personalized gifts: a specialty single malt scotch for the connoisseur, a dinner out at a new local restaurant for the foodie, tickets to a ball game for the sports nut, a first-edition book for the scholar, fabulous accessories for the dedicated follower of fashion, or activities you can do together for friends who love to get up and go.

While thoughtful gifts are always appreciated, nothing says thank you like publicly declaring your gratitude, so raise a glass to those who have shaped your life and made

© photo by Junebug Weddings

© photo by One Thousand Words Photography

your wedding possible. A little recognition goes a long way to honor those you love. Here are some ideas for showing gratitude:

Say thanks by treating your wedding party to an activity you want to do together in the days before or on the day of your wedding. Spring for all the guys to play nine holes of golf, eat a great brunch, or get hot shaves at the barbershop the morning of the wedding. Spring for all the girls to get pedicures, get their horoscopes read, or have their makeup done on the big day.

Give a short thank-you speech at your reception, introducing your wedding party and explaining what makes each of them an important part of your lives. The rehearsal dinner is a great time to give out thank-you gifts to the wedding party and family since it will be a gathering just for you and them. Wedding planning is full of small details. Don't let the little things people do for you go unnoticed; small gestures can make a huge impact.

And remember: Thank-you gifts don't have to be expensive; it truly is the thought that counts. No matter what gift you give, accompany it with a card and a message from the heart. Tell the members of your wedding party what their friendship means to you and why you're grateful they're part of your big day.

Gifts for Your Guys: Sterling silver gifts like cuff links, flasks, key chains, Swiss army knives, or money clips are classic and elegant ways to say thank you. Find each groomsman a pair of vintage cuff links that matches his personality and hobbies. Scour thrift stores and Internet auction sites for great selections. Each gift doesn't have to be the same. Your groomsmen are all different, so play to their personalities to find the perfect thank-you gifts you know they'll love.

Gifts for Your Girls: Jewelry to wear on the wedding day is always a welcome gift. Be sure to let them know ahead of time that you've got their jewelry covered. Classic jewelry they can wear for years will remind them of your friendship. Engrave it with a sweet sentiment to make it more personal. Personal stationery customized with their monogram, initials, or another pretty design will never go out of style. Give them something pampering they wouldn't normally buy for themselves.

© photo by La Vie Photography

Man's Best Friend: Dogs are the most popular pets to include in weddings because they are the easiest to train. If you decide to include your pet, have someone designated to take care of him or her throughout the day. Musician Gwen Stefani had her sheepdog, Winston, escort her down the aisle. Actor Adam Sandler had his dog, Meatball, as his best man.

Beware...

If your beloved pet is a member of your wedding party, you're not alone. Increasing numbers of couples are including their pets in their ceremonies, and sales of doggie tuxedos and ring pillows from pet stores have soared. While pets are adorable, you will want to consider the obvious risks when making this decision.

Chapter 2

ATTIRE

࿆

What to wear, what to wear? Perhaps no question looms quite as large as this one when it comes to planning your wedding day. As the bride, you'll take center stage that day, with all eyes on you, so what you wear will set the scene for the day's activities. Will your dress be formal or casual, alternative, or a homage to a specific custom or tradition? Picking your dress can be one of the most fun experiences of the planning journey. Take your friends, family, and soon-to-be mother-in-law with you to help you play dress up. Take their advice and concerns into consideration, but remember that, in the end, you'll be the one wearing the dress, so be sure that you're happy, confident, and comfortable in your choice.

It's not just you who will be carefully choosing an outfit for the big day. So, too, will your groom. And whether your wedding will be formal, casual, or somewhere in between, suits and tuxes help you pull off a modern and stylish wedding day look. Regardless, you want to coordinate the style of your and your groom's outfits, along with the rest of your wedding party.

Enjoy this part of the planning process—it's a time to bond with family and friends and really play up your personal style.

YOUR DRESS

When it comes to weddings, there's nothing more iconic than the image of the bride in her wedding dress. Flooded with history, symbolism, and emotion, your dress is one of the biggest style statements and most fun fashion choices you'll make in your lifetime. To make

© photo by Positive Light Photography

the process of finding your dress a stress-free experience, consider the following: your wedding theme, your color palette, the time of year, and your personal style. Each will play an important role in helping you pick your gown.

Shape

Begin with the basics of dress shape so you're sure to find one that fits and flatters.

Ball gowns are inspired by the most formal and romantic of events and lend an air of fairy-tale splendor. A-line dresses are classic with versatile shapes, their skirts form a simple triangular line, and their waistlines can begin high, middle, or low depending on your frame. Mermaid-shaped dresses are the exaggerated version of a drop-waisted dress, and their body-hugging lines add drama to your look. Sheath dresses are the simplest in their construction, but they can have big fashion impact and fantastic fit.

Try on something from each category to see what flatters your form. Then choose the one dress that has the fit, fabric, and flair to make you truly feel like a bride.

Ball Gown: Ball gowns are made with many layers of fabric and petticoats and can have an overlay of tulle or other sheer embroidered fabric. Some ball gown skirts have varying numbers of "pick-ups," or gathers, in order to make the skirt look fuller and more textured. With the full shape of most ball gown skirts beginning at the natural waist or just below, these dresses look best on brides who want to draw attention to their upper bodies.

© photo by Junebug Weddings

A-Line: A-line skirts create a slimming silhouette that flatters most every body type. An A-line dress with an empire waist beginning just below the bust brings the focus up toward the chest, shoulders, and face and hides an undefined or fuller waist. If the A-line skirt begins at the true

© photo by Junebug Weddings

waist, it shows off a classic and sweetly symmetrical silhouette. Drop-waisted dresses accentuate a long lean body or an evenly proportioned hourglass figure.

Mermaid: Mermaid-shaped dresses bring out the curves in a slim figure. Extra texture can be created and flaws hidden with gathers and ruches in the fabric of the bodice. When trying on a mermaid-shaped dress, walk around a bit to be sure the skirt isn't too tight to move in comfortably. Avoid the mermaid-shaped dress if your body is pear-shaped or heavier on the bottom than on the top.

© photo by Junebug Weddings

embellished fabric with spectacular details for a formal, sophisticated look. The uncluttered lines of a sheath dress make a beautiful base for captivating accessories.

© photo by Junebug Weddings

Sheath: Sheath dresses closely follow the lines of the body and are best made with fabrics that drape well. Bias-cut dresses are slim and sexy and create a glamorous look perfect for a more vintage style. Choose a sheath dress in a simple fabric for a casual, clean style, or try an

Choosing Fabrics

Wedding dress fabrics can vary greatly, so be sure to consider the wrinkle factor if you'll be sitting or traveling in your dress, as well as the weight of the fabric for the season. Look carefully at the construction of the dress, and have your seamstress reinforce pulling seams or loose buttons.

Necklines

Once you have an idea of the dress shape that works best on you, the next thing to consider is the neckline. The neckline is the frame for your face that guides the eye toward your features while giving your dress unique personality.

Strapless dresses are the new classics, and they're designed in every dress shape and style available. Look for a version that flatters your particular build, whether curvy or petite, and be sure it is constructed to stay in place comfortably. V-neck and halter-neck dresses can also be combined with several different dress shapes, and the shoulder straps and neck fasteners that are used to hold them up provide extra support for figures that need it. The right shaped V-neck can either lessen the look of a full-size bust or show off the curves you want revealed. Off-the-shoulder, portrait, illusion, and bateau or Sabrina necklines are feminine, romantic, and graceful, flattering and framing shoulders and pretty collarbones.

Whether you go with a classic shape, square neck, scoop neck, Victorian collar, or asymmetrical design, find the one that makes the most of your features while complementing the shape of your skirt. There's a beautiful dress out there waiting for you to find it!

Strapless and Spaghetti Strap: Slim, angular figures can wear straight strapless necklines, but slight curves, scallops, or sweetheart necklines are the most flattering options. Spaghetti straps look best on petite frames, and wider straps look best on voluptuous figures. The spacing of straps can change a neckline dramatically. Look at several versions to see what you like best. Detailed gathers and folds at the top of a strapless dress are called "crumb-catchers" and add architectural interest to a neckline.

© photo by Junebug Weddings

V-Neck and Halter Neck: V-necks create a long vertical line that draws the eye up and down, creating a slimmer appearance. Deep V-necks can be dramatic and sexy, but only if you feel comfortable and confident and your dress fits you to a T. Halter-neck dresses emphasize lovely arms

© photo by Junebug Weddings

and shoulders and can show a little or a lot of your back. Experiment with the many styles of halter necks to find one that flatters your face and features the most.

Off-the-Shoulder: Off-the-shoulder necklines accentuate beautiful shoulders, collarbones, and arms. Bateau necklines stop right at the outside edge of the shoulder blade and don't fall lower onto the arm. Portrait collars are made of wide swaths of fabric and perfectly frame the face and upper body. All of these neckline options look lovely with cap sleeves, three-quarter-length sleeves, long sleeves, or no sleeves at all.

as higher rounded jewel necks or plunging dramatic curves, with similar or more dramatic shapes echoed in the back of your dress.

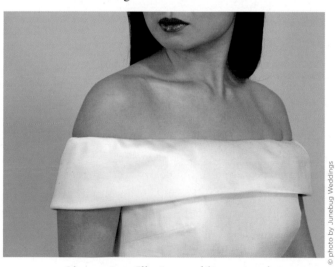

Alternatives: Illusion necklines give the suggestion of sheer fabric but cover you up in all the right places. The one shown top right is double layered over the bust but sheer lace over the back and shoulders. Asymmetrical necklines look ultramodern while harkening back to traditional Grecian style. Scoop necks can be made

Postwedding Care

After the wedding your dress should be professionally dry-cleaned by a specialist and stored in a sturdy acid-free cardboard box or hung on a padded hanger inside a breathable fabric garment bag. Plastic bags won't let air circulate and can trap moisture in the fabric, causing mold, discoloration, and deterioration.

Styles

It's important to pick the style of dress that best matches your personality and your wedding style. Is your wedding black-tie? Classic tailoring, traditional accents, and formal fabrics

© photo by J. Garner Photography

© photo by La Vie Photography

© photo by La Vie Photography

combine to create a timeless look. Having a casual beach affair? Try creative fabrics and playful details that feel as good as they look. Looking for some vintage flair? Evoke an era of romance with an heirloom wedding gown.

Classic Dresses: "Here comes the bride, all dressed in white!" Classic dress styles are timeless and elegant and look beautiful on brides the world over. If your vision is transforming into a modern-day princess at an elegant white wedding, then a classic wedding dress is for you.

> *Wedding dress sizes vary among designers but are usually about two sizes smaller than the average dress size. Don't despair if you are normally a size six but your wedding dress is a size ten. To make alterations easy, go for the larger size if you're on the fence.*

Classic wedding gowns can come in a variety of shapes, though the colors are generally limited to shades of white and cream. Beautiful embellishments like beading, embroidery, sequins, and crystals add formality to these structured, dramatic dresses, and the fabrics used are lush and luxurious.

Wedding dress boutiques and bridal salons specialize in matching brides to their dresses, so their expert staffs can be invaluable resources in helping you find the one dress that is right for you. Familiarize yourself with the basics in fit and style, then make an appointment at a few of your area's bridal boutiques and let the

Considerations

Bring one or two trusted friends or family members along while you shop so you feel supported but not overwhelmed. Don't buy the first dress you try on or feel pressured to buy one the very first day. Returns can be difficult, so sleep on it and be sure of your decision. Most formal wedding dresses are custom made to your measurements, so order yours six to twelve months in advance to allow for construction and multiple fittings and alterations.

professionals work their magic. Experienced salespeople will be well educated in their field and will ask you important questions about what you're envisioning for your big day in order to guide you toward the best dresses to try on. Take their expert advice, but remember to take things slowly. Ultimately you are the expert on what makes you feel fabulous.

Colors: Classic dresses are either true white, natural white, or cream, with subtle colored accents, if any. Look to your shoes and accessories to add hints of color to a classic white dress. Introduce color with a brooch of colored stone at your waist, bust, or shoulder straps. A satin sash in a refined light color such as taupe or pale pink can add a formal touch of color without looking too trendy.

Embellishments: Tone-on-tone beading and embroidery add sparkling embellishments without changing your dress color. Silver, gold, or bronze embellishments are perfect for winter

The Bustle

Ask your mother, maid of honor, or one of your bridesmaids to attend your final dress fitting and learn how to bustle your dress if necessary. Each dress bustles differently, so a little practice will go a long way to avoid unnecessary confusion and loss of precious time.

∾

weddings. Bring along a sewing kit on your wedding day in case embellishments loosen and need repair. Be careful when having your dress cleaned. Beading and embellishments can be damaged by the chemicals, so talk with your cleaning professional about safety precautions.

Fabrics: Popular laces used in wedding dresses are Alençon, battenburg, Chantilly, French, guipure, point d'esprit, and Schiffli. High-quality wedding dress fabrics are mostly made of silk but can also include silk and polyester blends as well as fine cotton. Rich fabrics like satin and taffeta are perfect for the formal beauty of classic dresses. Full skirts in a ball gown or A-line dress may have layers of net, tulle, organza, or chiffon.

Casual Dresses: Casual wedding dresses are for brides who want to give classic wedding traditions their own personal twist. Wear a lovely tea-length dress for your afternoon garden wedding, a ball gown with dramatic black-and-white details for your masquerade-themed gala,

or an ultramodern body-hugging sheath for your urban-chic event. Just use your imagination and discover what represents you most authentically.

There are no color restrictions for a casual gown, and more and more designers are experimenting with shades from pale blue to hot pink and everything in between. Color can be incorporated into the construction of your dress or added on after the fact to add flourish and a fun-loving flair to your look. Embellishments come in all shapes and sizes and aren't limited to traditional materials. The textures of feathers, felt, and unfinished edges combine with formal wedding fabrics like satin, lace, and chiffon to gorgeous effect, and nontraditional fabrics can make wonderfully unique wedding dresses all on their own. Incorporate personal fashion accents, let yourself be inspired by the things you love as well as the style and theme of your wedding day, and you'll have a wedding dress that is anything but ordinary.

Colors: Be bold with splashes of color. The bride in the top photo on page 49 chose a simple white dress to show off purple accents in her hair, bouquet, makeup, and decor. Coordinate your dress colors and accessories with your groom's look and the rest of your wedding party fashion. Choose a champagne, pink, or taupe dress instead of the traditional white. Give a white wedding dress a fresh look by adding colorful jewelry and accessories for your reception.

Embellishments: Ruffles or lace trim at the hem of your dress can finish off your look with flourish. Gathered fabric flowers decorating your neck, shoulders, waistline, or bustle are simple but dramatic feminine touches. Layering sheer and patterned fabrics together is another fun way to create depth, texture, and a sculptural quality to your dress. Ribbon detailing along your neckline and shoulders will add delicate interest and creates a flattering frame for your face.

Considerations

Consider your wedding location and season when choosing your dress. An ultraformal and heavy dress will feel uncomfortable out in the sunshine on a warm day. Play up the theme of your wedding with the style and details of your dress. Trunk shows at bridal boutiques allow you to see the entire dress collection at once and sometimes even meet the designers themselves. Many dress shops have sample sales where you can buy standard-size floor samples at a discount.

Fabrics: Combine fabrics like the lace and taffeta combination shown in the bottom photo on page 49. Wedding dresses don't have to be made of silk; fine cotton dresses in dotted point d'esprit or a sweet summery eyelet are wonderful choices for warm weather weddings. Comfort is the key to an enjoyable day. Move around in your dress to be sure you feel as great as you look. Whimsical embroidery in leaf, floral, and vine motifs can add interest to your fabric choices.

© photo by Stephanie Cristalli Photography

© photo by GH Kim Photography

© photo by Jenny Jimenez Photography

Vintage by the Years

© photo by Cheri Pearl Photography

© photo by La Vie Photography

© photo by Positive Light Photography

1940s and Before: Slinky bias-cut dresses in silk charmeuse that showed off the body's form ruled the 1930s and 1940s. Dresses in the 1920s had looser-fitting drop waists and beautiful beading and embroidery. Dress sizes have changed over time, so pay attention to a garment's measurements, not the size on its tag.

1950s, 1960s, and 1970s Retro: Elegant and mod, the style of the late 1960s and 1970s included long column dresses and empire waists. Cinched waists and full skirts typify a classic look of the 1950s and early 1960s. Buy vintage dresses from trusted, expert shop owners and ask lots of questions about the garment's condition, sizing, and repair history before you buy. Be sure you're crystal clear on the return policy if you buy a vintage dress online.

Vintage Dresses: The romance, nostalgia, and dramatic flair of a vintage wedding dress show off a unique style that can't be compared. From Victorian dresses with regal high collars to the playful retro dresses of the 1950s and 1960s, there are vintage styles to suit every taste.

To find the dress that suits you best, do a little research into dress shops in your area as well as online. Contact the managers of your favorite stores and let them know what you're looking for so they can contact you when a great find comes in. Vintage sizes can be small, and it may take some time to find the dress you're dreaming of, but with a little persistence and creative thinking there are lots of options available.

If you're lucky, the dress of your dreams may already be in your family. If you'd love to wear your mother's or grandmother's wedding dress, there are many ways to alter its fit or update its look so that it looks like it was made for you. If big alterations are what you want, be sure the dress's owner understands your plans and agrees to them. If someone you love allows you to alter her dress to be your own, treat it and her offer with the utmost care. Extend the waist of a short-waisted vintage dress by adding a wide fabric sash to the dress's middle or reattaching the skirt higher up. Seam allowances in the torso can often be let out for a better fit around the rib cage.

Another way to wear the most stylish of vintage wedding dresses is to buy a reproduction dress inspired by the era you love most, or to make a new dress out of a vintage pattern.

Alternative Dresses: A traditional white wedding dress may not appeal to you if you're a bride with a distinct sense of your own personal style, so don't feel pressured to conform. Choose a dress that matches your personality, creates a fashion statement, and makes you feel as beautiful and blissful on the outside as you do in your heart.

Choose colors you have a strong personal connection with or ones that are symbolic of qualities you admire. Cool colors like blues and greens are calming and can represent nature. Warm colors like reds, pinks, and oranges are energizing and can represent romance, joy, and prosperity. If you choose a dress that's less bridal than most, use fashionable embellishments and accessories to add in wedding style. A fabric flower trim or sparkling embroidery across your

---

Vintage-Inspired Reproductions

A vintage-inspired dress gives you a dramatic look without the challenges involved with real vintage clothing. If you're having a custom dress designed, ask your dressmaker to build a muslin mock-up of your dress before he or she cuts into the final fabric. This way you can fix any major issues with the fit first. You're not limited to only vintage wedding dress patterns. Choose any vintage dress pattern you like and use luxurious white fabrics to make it look bridal.

Considerations

Keep an open mind and trust your instincts. No one knows your personal style better than you do! If you buy your dress off the rack, find a good tailor to work with so the fit feels custom made. Wear a bridesmaid's dress in white or another color you love, for a casual yet wedding-appropriate look. Let yourself daydream about your wedding day and take note of the pictures that materialize—that's probably a look worth searching for.

Embellishments: Give a nod to your heritage with ethnically important details, patterns, and embellishments. Both live flowers and fabric flowers can be fashioned onto a sash or clipped to your dress's neckline, shoulder straps, or waistband. Embroidery can be bright and bold or subtle and sophisticated. Use it to add interest and beauty to your dress. Creative construction including pleats, folds, unfinished edges, and elaborate seams add complexity to a simple design.

Fabrics: Silk charmeuse has a lovely sheen and will drape smoothly and dramatically against your skin for a glamorous look. Silk chiffon is soft and airy and looks beautiful gathered and layered—perfect for a Grecian-style dress. Velvet, devore (or burnout) velvet, damask, and brocade make luxurious fabric choices for winter weddings. Linen and cotton fabrics like eyelet, matelassé, organdy, seersucker, and twill are fresh and feminine for summertime weddings.

neckline will add a formal touch and make you stand out in the crowd. Fabrics communicate style and personality with their flow, texture, and feel, so play up your fabric's qualities to purposely soften or strengthen your look. Try on dresses with different shapes and structures to find the style that suits you best. Think outside the box and shop at all kinds of stores to find what you're looking for. You never know where inspiration may strike!

Colors: Who says you have to wear only white to your wedding? Add bold splashes of color like the bride shown on page 51, top left. Choose a little black dress, a rich red ball gown, a patterned mini, or any color dress you love to wear. For a beach wedding wear a sea blue dress that accentuates your surroundings. For a garden wedding wear a floral sundress in tones that match the season's blossoms while highlighting your natural beauty.

Don't Forget: During your dress alteration sessions, bring along your wedding shoes and appropriate undergarments to get the correct hem length and fit. Count on having at least two sessions with your seamstress or tailor for basic adjustments, or more for extensive restructuring or rebuilding.

Lingerie & Underpinnings

Your dress is destined to be the most talked-about piece of your wedding wardrobe, but it's what's underneath that will make it fit and make you look fabulous. Throughout history women have loved lingerie for its beauty as well as its lifting, flattening, and corseting effects that helped them create the desired silhouette of the times. Now it's your turn to define your shape by adding some sweet and sexy things to your wedding wardrobe.

For your big day you may want lingerie that helps smooth and shape you for a flattering look. There are all sorts of strapless bras and body shapers made specifically to wear underneath bridal looks, available at department stores.

Strapless bras and bustiers can add structure and shape beneath form-fitting gowns and help keep them securely in place. Backless and halter dresses need bras with convertible straps or silicone bra cups that adhere directly to the skin. Body shapers are available to smooth any problem areas you might have: tummy, thighs, bottom, back, and more. Take your undergarments with you for dress fittings and alteration sessions.

You don't have to wear just white. If your dress has many layers, sexy, colorful lingerie adds playful personality to your look and can be your "something blue." Anything goes underneath your wedding dress, so have fun with it; no one will see it but you and your new husband. Personalized panties with your husband's name, your married name, or your monogram embroidered or spelled out in crystals are a fun surprise for later in the night.

To have fun with what you're wearing underneath, try a traditional garter, pretty stockings, or colorful, lacy personalized panties.

© photo by Junebug Weddings

© photo by Junebug Weddings

The garter is meant for the groom to throw to your single male guests, so you may decide to wear two: one for holding onto as a keepsake and one to be thrown to determine which man will marry next. When your reception is over, your wedding night will provide the ideal opportunity to have fun with lingerie, so treat yourself to something special that makes you feel sexy and beautiful.

The garter can easily be your "something old" if you have the one your mother or grandmother wore to her own wedding. Long ago it was considered good luck for wedding guests to have a piece of the bride's clothing, so the tossing of the bouquet and garter began. You can wear a garter purely for fashion fun, even if you don't want your groom to throw it during the reception.

Whether it's your first night together or your four hundredth, your wedding night happens once in a lifetime, so make it special with lingerie just for the occasion. A lovely slip or negligee will come in handy for lounging in your hotel room or on your honeymoon. Surprise him with supersexy pieces that you know he'll love to see you in. Choose lingerie that makes you feel confident, sensual, and stunning, no matter what your personal style.

If you're having your wedding dress custom made or altered, a skilled professional seamstress or tailor can often build a strapless bra directly into the bodice. Ask early in the dressmaking process if the fabric and structure of your dress will allow for this handy feature.

VEILS, ACCESSORIES, JEWELRY & MORE

This section focuses on those finishing touches that transform you into the bride. The veil—from full-length to fingertip—completes the bridal look and is a true iconic symbol of the wedding day. You may even choose to have it cover—or veil—your face as you make your way down the aisle to your waiting groom, which helps build up anticipation and add a level of formality and tradition to your ceremony.

While some may think that shoes will always be hidden away under the dress, you may choose to use the shoes to accent your dress or show off your style.

Hair accessories such as jewels, fabrics, feathers, and flowers also show off your personal style and offer fabulous hairstyle accents, which can help maintain interest at the reception after your veil is off. And jewelry that accentuates your beauty lets you sparkle and shine in the spotlight throughout the entire night (particularly that shiny new hardware on your ring finger!). Playing up these finishing touches will make you feel glamorous all night long.

Veils

Wedding veils have been used throughout time to symbolize cultural and spiritual beliefs and wishes. While today some brides wear a veil as a symbol, most brides wear one to make a fabulous fashion statement. Veils come in all shapes, lengths, and styles and act like a little bit of fashion magic as they instantly transform a woman into a bride.

Classic wedding veils can be gathered and fastened at the top of the head, at the back of the head, or at the nape of the neck, depending on your hairstyle and neckline. They come in a wide variety of fabrics, shapes, and lengths and beautifully complement any bride's style.

Depending on the shape and style of your wedding dress and the level of formality of your celebration, you'll want to choose a veil that accentuates your dress's features and adds a finishing touch to your look.

Mantilla: Mantilla veils can be made of lace, tulle, or chiffon and generally have beautifully embellished edges. They were originally made popular in Spain in the 1800s, and they still lend a romantic quality to bridal looks. Mantilla veils are fastened to your hair with a simple comb or hairpins. They are traditionally positioned to lay gently on top of your head with the lace or scalloped edges delicately framing

© photo by Jurebug Weddings

your face and shoulders. Because mantilla veils are embellished with detailed lace, embroidery, and decorative edging, they often look best with simple wedding gowns. Cut in a round or oval shape, they can be any length from shoulder to cathedral.

Fingertip and Elbow Length: Short, full bouffant-style veils add a fun and whimsical look to your day. Elbow-length and fingertip veils are amazingly versatile and are exactly as long as their names imply. The blusher is the layer of the veil worn forward over the face. Traditionally your father will lift your veil as he gives you away, or your groom will lift it just before the kiss. Ribbon, jewels, or other embellishments often line the edges of classic veils.

Full Length: Full-length or cathedral-length veils add traditional formality and grandeur to your wedding look. Full-length veils can have delicate embellishments or embroidery that accentuates their dramatic length and beauty. Most full-length veils create a train that will flow behind you and look wonderful as you walk down the aisle. Consider wearing a full-length veil during the wedding ceremony but trading it for a decorative hair accessory at the reception for ease of movement.

Cage Style: Cage- or birdcage-style veils are retro inspired and made of sheer netting or

Ask your hairdresser to give you extra hairpins to hold your veil in place. With all the activity of your wedding day, your veil may loosen and require extra support. Carry the pins with you or ask your maid of honor to keep them on hand throughout the day.

Photo by Kristen Jensen

tulle. They are dramatic, stylish, and perfect for a fashion-forward bride. Lengths vary, but cage veils generally hit just below your eyes or just beneath your chin. Fabric flowers, feathers, or other decorative hair jewels look great attached to a cage veil where the fabric gathers and attaches to the hair. Small rhinestones or pearls can be added to the veil's edges or to the crossing point of the netting for extra sparkle and glamour. Cage veils look best with vintage-inspired or fashion-forward wedding dresses.

Hair Accessories

Hair accessories offer an infinite variety of fun and fashionable options to add to your wedding day look. From jewels and vintage hair combs to fresh flowers and DIY creations, there are unending options! Use one to add a bit more embellishment to your hairstyle, to wear on its own if a traditional white wedding veil just

isn't you, or for replacing your veil during your reception as a more fun, casual, and party-appropriate accessory.

Wearing a real flower in your hair is a romantic look that will never go out of style. Whether you choose one large flower or a grouping of many small ones, their natural beauty will always enhance yours. Choose flowers that echo those in your bouquet or coordinate with your wedding colors. Each flower has a traditional meaning, so you may want to choose ones that represent qualities you hold dear. Tuck a single large flower like a lily, orchid, or hibiscus behind one ear for an exotic look, perfect for a summer or beach wedding. Daisies and baby roses are often long lasting outside of water and won't easily wilt. Red, yellow, pink, or white roses tucked in or around an updo are classic and romantic and easy to find year-round. Purchase extra blooms and keep them refrigerated so you can replace wilting hair flowers during your reception if necessary.

Traditional tiaras or creative jeweled hairpins are glamorous additions to any hairstyle and can easily be worn with or without a veil. Tiaras sit atop your head and lend a look of royalty, while accessories in all sorts of other shapes and sizes, new or vintage, can be worn to add sparkle and brilliance around your face. Tiaras and jeweled hair accessories are very versatile. They look beautiful worn with a veil and look lovely on their own during your reception once you remove your veil. Consider using a vintage brooch or other piece of sparkling jewelry as a

hair accessory; fasten it securely to your hair with hairpins. Get creative; most jeweled hair clips can be worn in many different positions depending on your hairstyle. Experiment to find the look you like best.

If you're having your dress custom made or significantly altered, find out if there is extra fabric left over that could be made into a simple, elegant headband. Headbands can be worn with long flowing locks, simple updos, or shorter hairstyles and are universally flattering no matter what your hair length or face shape. They can be made of anything—fabric, lace, jewels, or metals—and they portray a sweet and youthful femininity. Add color to your look with a headband that matches your wedding and flower colors. A jeweled necklace could be used as a headband by pinning it to your hair or adding a section of elastic to its ends. Consider headbands for your bridesmaids for a nicely coordinated look.

Creative designs featuring fabric flowers, feathers, beads, crystals, and other beautiful materials are widely available today at dress

A Note about DIY

If you're choosing to DIY your own hair, be sure to still do a hair trial with your veil or hair accessory well in advance of the wedding so that you work out any kinks in your style. Advanced planning now will help prevent any wedding day hiccups later.

shops, online stores, and fashionable boutiques. Making one you love could also be a fun DIY project if you want to get more involved in putting a personal touch on your wedding day fashion.

Fabric flowers can be made more formal by adding sparkling crystals to their edges or centers. For a more dramatic look, long feathers can create height and movement in a creative hair accessory. Explore fabric stores and look at their selections of ribbons, lace, fabrics, feathers, and notions to find creative DIY inspiration. Anything goes! Let your imagination run wild and create something that is as unique and beautiful as you are.

Jewelry

Women's love affair with beautiful jewelry is one that will last forever, and what better day to indulge in your passion for style than on your wedding day?

Classic Style: Classic jewelry is generally made from diamonds, pearls, or rhinestones in elegant shapes that bring to mind classic beauties like Grace Kelly, Audrey Hepburn, or Jacqueline Kennedy. Whether you choose something simple like a pair of diamond solitaire earrings and a single strand of pearls, or ultraglamorous chandelier earrings with layers of dramatic sparkling bracelets, a classic look is timeless. Sparkling diamond or rhinestone jewelry like the bracelet and drop earrings shown on page 62, upper left, are timeless. A simple string of pearls evokes traditional elegance, while multiple strands paired with diamonds or rhinestones create a look of old Hollywood glamour. To keep rhinestone jewelry clean and tarnish free, store it in airtight plastic bags and keep it away from moisture or temperature changes. Pearls should be kept in a soft bag to prevent scratches and gently wiped clean with a damp cloth.

Casual Style: Casual jewelry is often creatively made with freshwater pearls, semiprecious stones, beads, crystals, and metallic wire or silk to create a look that's whimsical, playful, and pretty. Freshwater pearls come in many different colors, shapes, and sizes and create an elegant yet organic look. Semiprecious stones sparkle and shine for far less financial investment than diamond jewelry. Casual jewelry pieces can often be worn in everyday life as lovely reminders of your big day. There's no rule that says you can't mix and match your metals. Different shades of gold, silver, and bronze make a rich and shimmering metallic color palette.

Alternative Style: Play with the shape and scale of your jewelry for an alternative look.

Alternative jewelry styles run the gamut from architecturally interesting, to bright, bold, and colorful and include everything in between. Let your style shine through by choosing nontraditional jewelry that reflects the look you love. The round oversize beads in the photo above look retro and fun, while clean, unembellished, angular lines look modern and chic. If the white of your wedding dress washes you out, wear a pop of rich color near your face in earrings or a necklace to brighten up your skin tone. Be sure colorful jewelry doesn't clash with the tones of your bridal bouquet or bridesmaids' dresses.

Vintage: Wearing vintage jewelry is a gorgeous way to add to your wedding day look. From the intricate filigree work of Edwardian times, to the dramatic angles of the art deco movement, to the more contemporary retro pieces, vintage jewelry adds history and personality that can't

Be careful with your jewelry while you're getting ready on your wedding day. Lotions and hairsprays can cause damage to some delicate materials like pearls and costume jewelry. To be safe, put your jewelry on last, once you're fully dressed and ready.

be beat. You don't have to go vintage from head to toe. Mix vintage jewelry with a modern dress or accessories for a fresh fashion statement that's just your style. Vintage jewelry is always a great ecofriendly fashion choice. Wearing jewelry that belonged to a beloved family member is a great way to keep her memory with you on your wedding day. Purchase vintage jewelry from a reputable and well-educated dealer so you can learn about what you're buying.

The Ring

As it is said time and again, "With this ring, I thee wed." And so we say, "With this ring, you will wed, so find one that matches your style." Here we're including an inspiration gallery showcasing the most popular rings and styles available today. Please flip through to help you pick out which styles, metals, and stones work best for you.

Wedding Bands: The ancient Egyptians were the first to wear wedding rings on the third finger of their left hand to symbolize betrothal. The vein running down that finger was believed to lead straight to the heart, and the circle signified love's eternal nature. These symbols still

endure today in the wedding ring ceremonies of countless cultures throughout the world.

Unlike ancient rings of leather, bone, and iron, today's rings are made from precious metals fashioned to last a lifetime. Strong, durable platinum has remained the most popular metal for rings since the 1950s, but because of its skyrocketing price, white gold and yellow gold are making their way back to the market with lovely results.

While most modern rings are smooth simple circles, many new and custom designs as well as vintage and antique rings feature multiple stones, intricate filigree, or symbolic ornamentation, so no matter what your style, you'll have plenty of options when it comes to choosing the one that's right for you. To ensure you find the one ring you'll be as happy with in fifty years as you are on your wedding day, choose one that complements the size of your hand and the length of your fingers and is as comfortable as it is beautiful.

Gold: Gold rings are imprinted with their karat designation of 24 karat, 18 karat, or 14 karat. Twenty-four karat gold is the most precious, but also the most malleable, and 14 karat rings are less expensive but more durable. Gold rings are hypoallergenic, so almost anyone can wear them with little or no negative reaction. White gold is sturdier than yellow gold and is often used as a substitute for platinum. White gold is available in 18 karat or 14 karat only.

Platinum: The white luster of platinum is beautiful in even the simplest designs. Platinum

Types of Rings

Gold Rings

Platinum Rings

Edwardian Style

Art Deco Style

Creative Cuts

Alternative Colors

Men's Ring: Platinum

Men's Ring: Gold

Eternity Bands

Alternative Styles

Colored Stones

Bands

Nontraditional Shapes

Stacking Multiple Rings

Men's Ring: New Metals

Men's Rings: Alternative Styles

is a rare and durable precious metal that looks lovely with any stone and on any skin tone. Thirty times stronger than gold, platinum rings stand the test of time and don't corrode. Because of platinum's rarity, Louis XVI declared it to be "the only metal fit for a king" back in the 1780s.

Eternity Bands: Eternity bands have a continuous stream of gems around the ring. Wide bands encrusted with diamonds look stunning on long slim fingers, and thin rings with delicate detailing look lovely on small hands. Although all eternity bands are similar by definition, there are numerous styles available; some look modern and some romantic. Some women wear an eternity band instead of an engagement ring or traditional wedding band, while some wear all three.

Alternative Styles: Wide decorative bands make a dramatic impact and can cost far less than a diamond solitaire and wedding band set. Men's and women's wedding bands don't have to coordinate perfectly. There's no reason you can't mix and match metals and stones. Make a

The Power of the Ring

Rings enchanted with the power to protect the wearer have been at the center of folklore throughout recorded history. So it's not surprising that the rings used in today's ceremonies, both Christian and otherwise, are blessed by the officiant, thus continuing the practice of infusing the rings with protective powers.

special date to buy your rings and settle on ones you both adore. If you can dream about it, a jeweler can make it. Play up your jewelry fantasies with a custom ring design.

Antique and Vintage Rings: Choosing an antique wedding ring to represent your marriage commitment is a perfect style choice for the ultimate romantic. Each one-of-a-kind piece has a personality all its own and a long, rich history. The stones were cut to reflect low candlelight; the delicate details were shaped, cut, and pierced by hand; and each ring's originality lives on today.

If your wedding ring is a family heirloom, take it to a jeweler who specializes in antiques to have it cleaned, inspected for damage, and restored the correct way. When shopping for an antique wedding ring, explore the pieces available from reputable jewelers and choose one that speaks to your heart. With antique jewelry, you're investing in more than just the technical aspects of your ring, but you should still ask for independent appraisal documentation to educate yourself about what you're buying.

Ring styles have varied throughout history, and the time period in which your ring was made is a fascinating connection to the past. Changes in politics, economics, and technology led to changes in fashion and standards of beauty. Most antique jewelry available for purchase today begins with Edwardian-style rings from the early 1900s and moves up through the art nouveau, art deco, and retro styles.

Edwardian: Decorative scrollwork, lace-like filigree, flower garlands, bows, and tassels are characteristic of Edwardian designs. The Edwardian period (1901–1910) was named for England's King Edward VII and was also called the Belle Époque. Platinum's strength and light color made it the metal of choice for the popular white-on-white color palette. Old mine-cut and European-cut diamonds, as well as pearls, were delicately set to look like they were floating.

Art Deco: Art deco rings have bold architectural and geometric designs with strong angles and straight lines. The art deco style was popular post–World War I, in the roaring 1920s through the late 1930s. Egyptian, Asian, and Indian motifs; the Machine Age; and modern art like the Cubist movement and the Ballet Russe inspired fashion and jewelry trends. Engagement rings had old mine-cut or Asscher-cut center diamonds, with side accent stones in baguette or geometric shapes.

Colored Stones: Richly colored gemstones like rubies, sapphires, and emeralds were used in rings throughout history. Diamond wedding rings didn't become standard until the mid-twentieth century. Light-colored gemstones like natural zircon, citrine, quartz, and aquamarine make glamorous alternatives to diamonds. Gemstones have always had special meanings. Among other things, emeralds represent faith, rubies represent passion, and sapphires represent intelligence.

Bands: Most antique bands weren't made as part of a set, so have fun with your selections and don't worry about them coordinating perfectly. Antique bands can contain colored stones, or no stones at all, or be sparkling diamond eternity bands. Combining an eclectic mix of antique bands can be a fashion-forward way to wear an old-fashioned style. Antique bands can be so beautifully detailed that they look great even on their own.

> Because the mining of metals and precious stones can wreak havoc on the environment and has been connected to a history of unjust labor practices, wearing an antique wedding ring is a fantastic way to be eco-friendly. You can be confident that no new materials were harvested for its creation.

Alternative Styles: There's no rule that says you need to wear a traditional diamond ring in order to say "I do." Just like your wedding ceremony and celebration, your ring should reflect your personal style and all the wonderful things your marriage means to you.

Take a cue from the jewelry you already wear and love, as well as the demands of your lifestyle. Do you love ultramodern designs with sleek, strong geometric shapes, or do you gravitate toward quirky, creative designs with asymmetric lines and rough-hewn edges? Do you work with your hands and need jewelry that can withstand the elements, or are delicate details right at home in your life?

Also consider different design factors to find the ring that's just right for you. Precious stones can be cut in many different ways, and their looks change greatly depending on the way they reflect light. Metals and stones can have infinite color variations, too. Diamonds come in every shade of the rainbow, and gold and platinum change depending on the other metals they're mixed with and the way their surfaces are textured. Ring shapes can be large or small, traditional or inventive, and stacking multiple rings together allows you to wear your wedding rings in myriad different ways.

Creative Cuts: New versions of rose-cut diamonds combine a vintage sensibility with a modern style. Wedding rings with raw or rough-cut diamonds are interesting and understated alternatives to the classic diamond solitaire. Hand-faceted stones have a soft, organic look, while machine cuts are sharp and precise and give a stone its dramatic sparkle. A bezel setting, where the stone is surrounded by an

even surface of metal instead of prongs, lends a modern look to any ring.

Alternative Colors: Choosing a wedding ring set with colored gemstones you love is a beautifully stylish and usually less-expensive option than a diamond ring. Colored diamonds are a fun twist on the traditional. Yellow gold is making a big resurgence with new looks created by high karat percentages and creative textures and finishes. Gold can be combined with other precious metals to create color shifts. Experiment with shades like rose, apricot, peach, and green gold.

Nontraditional Shapes: Organic shapes that resemble wood, vines, and flowers are alternative yet ultrafeminine. Diamonds can be set in many creative ways. Pavé settings can cover large surface areas, and bezel settings let stones float inside other materials. Wide bands with or without embellishments can be an easy-to-wear option instead of a traditional wedding set. Let your life inspire you. Rings can be designed to resemble everything from magnolia blossoms to microchips.

Stacking Multiple Rings: Stacking multiple small bands gives you flexibility to wear one ring at a time or all of them at once, depending on your activities. Mixing and matching colors, stones, metals, and textures creates a fun, funky, and eclectic look. Stacking sparkling diamond bands creates glamorous high-impact style. Wearing a number of simple bands is a great low-budget option and sets you

Recycled Goods

Recycling materials from old jewelry can be gentle on the environment as well as your pocketbook. Both precious stones and fine metals can be repurposed for new designs, and many independent designers will be willing to collaborate with you to take what's old and make it new again.

up for a romantic future. Start with one now and add more for anniversaries or meaningful milestones.

Men's Rings: Men's wedding rings don't get as much attention as their female counterparts but are just as important nonetheless. They're the items that will physically represent your marriage to yourselves and to the outside world, and for many men they're the only pieces of jewelry they will own. Most men's rings are categorized by their width, ranging from three millimeters to eight millimeters, as well as the materials they're made from. Have the groom try on rings from every category to see which one looks and feels the best to you. For an item that's seemingly simple, there are lots of interesting options available.

Platinum: Platinum became the most popular metal for jewelry in the early twentieth century and remains the favorite today. It's a strong, heavy precious metal that will look timeless even when your children and grandchildren are shopping for their own weddings.

Choose a high-polish finish or a brushed matte finish for your ring, or combine the two looks in one ring for more textural interest. Platinum is very rare and therefore more precious and expensive than gold. Because of its strength and resistance to tarnish, wear, and corrosion, platinum is an ideal material for fine jewelry. Yellow gold and platinum can be used in the same ring, so you don't have to choose one look over the other.

Gold: Gold and white gold are also classics, with white gold being the more popular for modern grooms. Because of the softness of gold, your ring will inevitably get scratched and scuffed. Take it back to your jeweler every few years for a polish or plating that will bring back its original luster.

Yellow gold comes in 14 karat, 18 karat, and 24 karat, getting softer and more richly yellow the higher the karat percentage. White gold is an alloy, made with a combination of 24-karat gold and either nickel or palladium. White gold can be coated with a thin layer of rhodium, a silvery white metal in the platinum group. Pay attention to the heft, height, and inside edges of your ring to be sure it will fit comfortably on your hand.

New Metals: With the prices of platinum and gold on the rise, less-expensive metals have become popular. Titanium and tungsten are both known for their strength and are far less expensive than platinum or gold. They can be difficult materials to work with, so not all jewelers are able to use them. They are usually not able to be sized or engraved, so keep that in mind when you make your purchase.

A tungsten ring is heavier than a super-lightweight titanium one of the same size, and some men prefer the extra heft. Tungsten and tungsten-carbide rings are steel gray in color and are so hard they easily resist scratches and dings. Titanium is extremely strong, as well as lightweight, and is commonly used in the aerospace, sporting goods, and medical industries.

Diamonds

Just like snowflakes and people, each diamond is different. To find one that stands out from the crowd, shop at a reputable store that carries independently certified diamonds complete with warranties and educate yourself about the four Cs.

Cut: The shape of the diamond you choose, whether it be round, square, emerald, or marquise, is a matter of preference. The way a diamond is cut is a matter of skill. Even a moderately priced diamond in the hands of a skilled jeweler can become a stone of mesmerizing brilliance. To ensure your diamond makes the cut, choose a certified stone that's rated good, very good, premium, or ideal.

The most popular diamond today is the 58-facet round. Some jewelers offer finer cuts that have dozens of additional facets to increase light refraction. The depth of a diamond's cut affects its brilliance. Diamonds that are cut too deep or too shallow lose brilliance from the bottom and can appear dark and muddy. Look at your diamond under natural light to see its true brilliance. The artificial lights used in most retail stores can be misleading.

Color: Diamond colors start at the extremely rare and colorless grade D and continue through the alphabet to the light yellow grade Z. The more truly colorless a stone is, the more you can expect to pay for it.

While colorless diamonds are rare and expensive, many people like diamonds in the faint yellow category. Buy in person to ensure you get what you pay for and like what you see. Beware of fancy names for yellow and brown diamonds. They are often used as a sales gimmick to sell diamonds of lower quality. A few very rare diamonds come in colors like pink, green, gold, and red.

Clarity: The clarity of a diamond refers to the impact of its inclusions, tiny imperfections that can affect the way it reflects light. The fewer inclusions, the more expensive the stone. Look at your diamond under a GemScope with 10x magnification and ask if the diamond has been filled to hide imperfections. Diamond clarity ranges from flawless down to several levels of imperfect. Flawless gems are extremely expensive, so keep in mind that inclusions seen only under 10x or greater magnification cannot be seen by the naked eye. Buy based on what you see, not based on what a salesperson tells you.

Carat: The carat is the weight of a diamond. Remember: There is no correlation between the size of a diamond and the happiness of a marriage. For some folks the size of the rock does matters; for others it's the cut, color, or sentimental value. Most grooms buy engagement diamonds for about one to three months of their salary. We suggest you spend whatever you're comfortable with. Be sure to have your diamond weight verified before you make your purchase.

An internationally adopted certification process called the Kimberley Process now ensures diamonds are conflict free in over forty-eight countries, so couples no longer have to worry about buying a "blood diamond" that contributes to global strife. Ask your jeweler if your diamond is "Kimberley Certified" and ask to see documentation. To find out more visit www.diamondfacts.org.

Titanium does not react with the human body, so it's a good option for hypersensitive skin.

Alternative Styles: The designs of alternative rings are limited only by your own imagination. Buy from an independent designer, choose unusual patterns, add diamonds or gemstones, or get in on the design process yourself to create a ring unlike any other.

The top surface of your ring isn't the only area to work with. The side edges of the rings on page 65, bottom row right, have been decorated, and the insides could be engraved. Popular patterns include milgrain edging, hand-hammered surfaces, or braided detailing. Different types of wood can be combined with metals to form unique wedding rings. Diamonds or other stones can be set in nontraditional ways for a casual, quirky, or especially masculine look.

Photo by Kristen Jensen

Shoes

Your wedding dress will most likely be the starting point for your wedding day fashion, but it's easy and fun to add on to your look from there by playing with your accessory choices. Shoes are perfect to liven up your style without straying too far from your comfort zone. They're hidden under your dress but make delicate and dramatic special appearances as you walk down the aisle, twirl on the dance floor, and give a little jump for joy. For the most successful result, consider the look you're going for as well as your practical needs.

If you live in an area where there aren't many shopping options for formal shoes, explore the many online boutiques. Shopping

for shoes online is easy as long as you understand the return policies and are able to send back shoes that don't fit correctly or aren't quite what you are looking for.

If you find the shoes of your dreams, but they pinch or rub in one particular area, visit a cobbler to find out if they can be stretched just enough to fix the problem. Cobblers can be miracle workers when it comes to shoe repair and maintenance.

White satin shoes are available in all heel shapes and heights. Choose a shorter and wider heel for more comfort and stability if you're not typically fond of high heels. Peep-toe shoes look great for summer weddings, and closed-toe shoes work best in cold weather. Wear your heels around your house for at least thirty to sixty minutes prior to your wedding day to soften them up and get used to the way they feel.

Find beautiful shoes that tie into your wedding color palette and add whimsical fun to your look. Colorful shoes can often be worn again, so you can get more mileage out of your purchase and enjoy the memories of your wedding day each time you wear them. If fabulous shoes are important to you, find a pair in navy, royal, baby blue, or turquoise and let them be your "something blue."

Sparkling jeweled pumps and sandals can be coordinated with your jewelry and hair accessories for a whole new level of glamour and

For added comfort and support while you're on your feet, buy soft pads for the insides of your shoes. There are a wide variety of pads available to invisibly cushion the balls of your feet and underneath your heels or to keep your heel straps from rubbing and slipping.

style. Make any shoe jeweled with shoe clips, vintage costume jewelry brooches, or clip-on earrings. Shoes made with metallic leathers and fabrics are a good middle ground if you don't want pure white or colorful shoes. They're modern and stylish in neutral tones that look great with all shades of white.

If you never wear high heels in normal life, starting with your wedding can be quite uncomfortable. If you feel most confident and pretty in flats, go for it! To keep your look formal, stick with shoes made of satins, delicate fabrics, and sparkling embellishments instead of thicker leathers or canvas. Save your feet so you can celebrate all day long. Wear delicate-looking flats for your ceremony and change into heeled party shoes for your reception.

Something Old, Something New
The Victorian-era English saying "Something old, something new, something borrowed, something

blue, and a silver sixpence in your shoe" is a good luck tradition that many of today's brides still follow. Each part of the poem has significance, and interpreting it your own way can add sweetness, creativity, and a little extra magic to your day.

"Something old" signifies a connection to the past, including your family values and family history. You may want to wear a piece of heirloom jewelry or your mother's wedding veil as a sign of this bond, or you may choose to incorporate into your ceremony a favorite photo, childhood story, or song that has sentimental value to you and your family members.

"Something new" indicates hope and an optimistic look at the road ahead. This can be represented by any new item you purchase or be a gesture of what you hope for the future. Maybe you would like to start your own new tradition. Think of new and creative ways to honor your friends or support your favorite cause.

"Something borrowed" denotes the respect you have for others who have been role models in your life. Choose to borrow something of significance from someone who exemplifies the traits of a good partner and let a little of their wisdom "rub off" on you.

Switch it up

Consider switching it up for your reception, whether it's an outfit change, a hairstyle change, or adjusting a few accessories.

~

"Something blue" is a sign of fidelity and true love. For many years before the white wedding dress came into vogue, brides were married in blue as a symbol of their purity. Nowadays brides wear just a touch of blue to finish the charm, often incorporating the color into their garters, shoes, lingerie, or wedding bouquet. No matter what you choose to do, make it fun and make it meaningful.

© photo by La Vie Photography

Something Old: Look to your mom, his mom, and your grandmothers for lovely jewelry and accessories that have family significance. Carry a picture from your parents' wedding or a love letter from your father to your mother in your purse. Wear your mother's wedding dress or veil, or carry a purse or compact mirror she used on her wedding day. To break away from fashion for a minute, your "something old" doesn't have to be something you wear. Introduce your "something old" by making your getaway in a vintage Rolls Royce or holding your reception at a beautiful historic site.

Something New: Wear new shoes, choose a new perfume, or buy a new shade of lipstick. Have a new cocktail recipe invented and named after you and your partner. Serve it at your reception with a recipe-card coaster. Buy new earrings or a charm for your charm bracelet that can be passed down to future generations. Ask your guests to bring a wish or a small token to add to your "time capsule box" to be opened on your silver wedding anniversary.

Something Borrowed: Borrow a special item to wear from one of your closest friends and ask her to help you put it on. Borrow a passage, song, or special prayer from the wedding ceremony of a couple you admire. Get married at the home of a relative or spend your honeymoon at a family member's vacation property or time-share. Use a pearl-handled knife or decorative cake cutter that you've borrowed from a friend, or put your parents' cake topper on top of your cake.

Something Blue: Tie a light blue ribbon around your garter or have one woven into the handle of your bouquet. Incorporate forget-me-nots, larkspur, delphinium, or love-in-a-mist blossoms into your bridal bouquet for a romantic touch of blue. Buy yourself some lacy blue underthings or other fun blue accessories. Have your cake decorated with blueberries and other fresh fruits and flowers, or serve blueberry pies and tarts as an alternative to your wedding cake.

© photo by J. Garner Photography

© photo by John and Joseph Photography

WEDDING PARTY ATTIRE

So now that we've got your attire picked out, it's time to focus on your supporting cast—your wedding party. This group will be a very important and central part of your big day, so it's important that everyone dresses the part. Some brides choose to be matchy matchy, with all their girls wearing the same style and color dress, and that's completely fine. Other brides choose simply the color and let the bridesmaids pick the styles and cuts that best suit their bodies, and that, too, is completely fine. Still other brides choose to be a little funky and allow their bridemaids to wear a variety of colors and styles that somehow all tie in to the overall theme. And, yup, that's fine, as well. It's all about how you want the overall look and feel of your wedding to be.

Beyond bridesmaids, you'll also be deciding on outfits for groomsmen, attendants, and any kids in the wedding party. When it comes to fashion and attire, it's all really about the look and style you want—there are plenty of choices out there to fit every need and desire. So enjoy this section and have fun with it! This is a time to enjoy bonding with very important people in your life and a time to walk the wedding planning journey together.

Style for the Girls

The colors, shapes, fabrics, and details of your bridesmaids' fashion will make a huge impact on your overall wedding style, so have fun coming up with their looks and creating the wedding style you're dreaming of.

Many classic and casual dresses will be available from a single bridesmaid's dress designer or boutique. If you're in charge of ordering the dresses for each of your bridesmaids, have them try on the store's sample dresses to choose the best size. If they are out of town, get their bust, waist, hip, and waist-to-floor measurements, as well as their regular dress and bra sizes, to give to your dress salesperson. If the correct size is in question, opt for the larger one. It's always easier to take a dress in than to let one out. Alterations will probably be necessary for a proper fit and hem length, so be sure the dresses arrive in plenty of time to be finalized without a rush.

Bridesmaids traditionally pay for their own dresses and accessories, so be conscientious of what you're asking of them financially, especially if they are also traveling to attend your wedding or hosting parties in your honor. If you have your heart set on a dress that is above their budget range, meet them halfway and contribute to the cost.

The dresses are only one part of your bridal party's look. Shoes, jewelry, purses, flowers, hair accessories, and other stylish extras are all up for your unique interpretation and give you a chance to explore your fashion vision. Choose luxe gold shoes for a glamorous modern affair, fresh flowers for their hair at your seaside beach wedding, or a sparkling art deco rhinestone brooch for their necklines at your vintage-inspired soiree.

Groom's Gospel

All About the Groom

With so much focused on the bride on the wedding day—and with wedding planning—isn't it nice to have a section all your own? Yes, it is your big day, too, and yes, you do have some responsibilities to attend to! First and foremost will be to make sure that you—and any of your supporting cast—look good. Selecting your suit can be a fun, but sometimes overwhelming, process. There are many styles and selections out there to choose from. Thankfully, we've broken it down for you here so that you can move forward with all the right knowledge in hand to pick the outfit that best . . . suits . . . you.

Tuxedos & Suits

Everyone loves a man in a suit, and your wedding day gives you the opportunity to put together a truly spectacular formal look to woo your bride, wow your guests, and make you feel like a million dollars. There are many options available for men's formal wear, from the most formal white-tie tuxedo to the most casual linen suit, so consider your event's theme, location, time of day, and time of year to find the perfect look for you.

Both formal and casual suits are very popular for modern grooms and their wedding parties, as they are still appropriate for this kind of special occasion but leave a little more room for alternative style. Most tuxedos and formal suits are available to rent, but a purchased one that's tailored to fit you will be the best quality. If you think you'll have the opportunity to wear it three or four times a year, or if you want it as a special memento of your day, consider buying instead of renting.

White-Tie: White-tie is considered the most formal classification of menswear and brings an aura of history and glamour to your event. Unlike other styles of menswear, where you can be a little creative with your choices,

© photo by John and Joseph Photography

© photo by GH Kim Photography

white-tie is extremely traditional and the guidelines of what is appropriate are very specific. Worn only after 6:00 in the evening, white-tie consists of a black tailcoat, black trousers worn with suspenders, a white winged-collar shirt, a white waistcoat, and a white bow tie. The white-tie tailcoat has a horizontal, cutaway front that leaves long tails in the back. It looks double breasted, but it doesn't actually fasten in the front. The white bow tie and waistcoat are made of matching materials, typically cotton pique. The daytime version of white-tie is called morning dress. The most noticeable difference is the cut and color of the coat and the use of a necktie or cravat.

Black-Tie: Black-tie is the most common level of formal wear. It consists of a classic black tuxedo or a modern variation. In the summer months or in very warm climates, a white dinner jacket can be worn with a simple black cummerbund and bow tie, reminiscent of James Bond or Humphrey Bogart in *Casablanca*. Traditional collar options on a

tuxedo range from the long rounded shawl collar and the sleek and elegant notch lapel (as shown on the left) to the more dramatic and angular peak lapel. Bow ties and formal neckties should match the fabric of your tux lapels. If you wear a cummerbund, its pleats should face up. The daytime equivalent of black-tie is called the stroller and is very similar to morning dress, except that a necktie is nearly always worn and the coat has no tails.

Formal Suits: These men below are wearing black suits, which creates a formal and cohesive look. Single-breasted suits usually have two or three buttons. Two-button jackets have a longer vertical shape and flatter most body types. Three-button jackets have a broader shape and look best on large or tall men. Suits are made from wools that are categorized by numbers like Super 110, 120, or 150. Generally the higher the number, the finer and softer the wool.

© photo by GH Kim Photography

Mix-and-match suits offer a sharp, semi-formal look but allow for a more unique interpretation. Combine different colored pants and jackets, go jacket free, or play with the colors and patterns of your shirt, tie, or other accessories.

A nicely tailored neutral-colored suit looks great paired with your favorite colors. Play up your wedding color palette or the color of your eyes. Experiment with a patterned or boldly hued tie like the one shown below. Wearing tan slacks with a navy blue blazer looks classic, clean-cut, and slightly nautical. To make any suit more modern, opt for flat-front trousers and a nicely tailored, slim-fitting jacket. Black or dark gray trousers look good with most any color combination.

Casual Suits: Navy and tan suits look more casual than their black or dark gray counter-parts. In a well-fitting suit, your shirtsleeves should extend about half an inch beyond your jacket cuff and your shirt collar about half an inch above your jacket collar. Light-colored linen, poplin, and seersucker suits are cool, comfortable, and casual during warm summertime weddings. A suit worn without a tie or with a sweater vest underneath is a fun informal menswear option.

Alternative Attire

If your wedding theme has a personal twist, why not let your wedding fashion reflect the mood of the day? Lighten up the fashion rules for your wedding day and wear a creative alternative option that perfectly matches your style, your wedding theme, or your environment.

For a casual wedding on a warm beach or near the sand, a heavy wool suit obviously just won't do. Adopt the laid-back

feeling of a tropical vacation and incorporate breezy fabrics and unstructured shapes into your wedding day wardrobe, or take a classic outfit and relax the details so you feel right at home at the beach. Go without a tie, roll up the sleeves of your crisp white shirt, and choose dress pants made with a casual fabric.

As on the gentlemen above, linen drawstring pants and lightweight shirts are breezy and perfectly beach appropriate for a casual tropical wedding. Pair a lightweight cotton suit with leather sandals for a ceremony in the sand, or skip the shoes altogether and celebrate barefoot! Don't go so far with this look that your outfit seems sloppy. Strive to look fresh, clean, and casually polished so you look fantastic standing next to your glowing bride.

If honoring your family heritage is important to you, consider incorporating aspects of your national dress into your wedding day attire. In fashion etiquette, traditional dress from any culture is considered a welcome alternative to formal wear. If it reflects who you are as an individual, it will add wonderful personality, history, and pride to your celebration and be perfectly appropriate for your wedding.

The most popular version of national dress in the United States is the kilt, worn by those with Scottish or Irish heritage as well as those without. Auspicious colors can be added to modern formal wear as a symbol of your heritage. A red cummerbund, vest, or pocket square could symbolize good luck. Men of African descent might wear a dashiki suit or a grand boubou, and men with Latin American heritage might wear a guayabera dress shirt.

Military dress uniforms are near and dear to the hearts of the many people throughout the world who have worked hard to earn the honor of wearing them. Each branch of the

U.S. military has its own version of dress uniforms appropriate for formal occasions. They have long and interesting histories with special names, classifications, symbolism, and decorations that represent ranking.

Military dress uniforms are also known as "full dress," "mess dress," "mess uniform," or "mess kit." According to fashion etiquette, a military dress uniform is appropriate to wear at occasions of any level of formality, even the most formal white-tie events.

Finishing Your Look

No matter what kind of menswear you choose for your wedding day, your accessories will add personality and put the finishing touch on your look. Gone are the days of ultrastrict fashion etiquette except in the most formal of settings. Outdated rules like never combining navy with black and never layering patterns have fallen by the wayside in favor of tasteful, individual fashion freedom. Embrace the opportunity to play with these details, and give yourself permission to have a little fun with fashion!

Suits and tuxedos are made up of more than just pants and a jacket. Everything from your shirt and tie to your vest, cummerbund, belt, shoes, and coat will need to be chosen, and each piece offers an opportunity for creative self-expression. Men's jewelry includes classic staples like cuff links, shirt studs, and watches, all of which can be either formal or funky. Choose high-quality pieces that will stand the test of time to be handed down as heirlooms to future generations, or choose trendier items to add an element of fun.

Classic dress shoes will never go out of style. Wear shiny black patent leather dress shoes with a tux or formal suit and simply shaped and nicely polished dress shoes with more casual suits. Sleek belts should be worn with suits, but tuxedos should be tailored to fit or held up with suspenders. In cold weather a topcoat is the appropriate coat to wear with a tuxedo or formal suit. The most classic version is the velvet collared Chesterfield topcoat.

Cuff links worn with French cuffs are a must for men's formal wear. They can be brightly colored and modern, vintage and full of history, whimsical and humorous, or customized with your initials, monogram, or other favorite detail. Wear a dressy wristwatch or carry a vintage pocket watch in

your jacket or pants pocket to keep time on your wedding day. Shirt studs with matching cuff links look sleek with a tuxedo.

Ties don't have to be black, white, or gray. If you're wearing a suit, experiment with incorporating your wedding colors into your shirt and tie combination. A little color can go a long way. To stay formal, add small splashes of color with your boutonniere or accessories. For a more casual look, the sky's the limit, so have fun with it! A pocket square adds a vibrant splash of color or a complementary pattern for texture and depth.

Adding color and other fun extras to your ensemble is one of the easiest and most powerful ways to change up your style. They can be incorporated into nearly any aspect of your attire, and there is no limit to what combinations will work. Coordinate with your wedding colors and the fashions of your wedding party, but be sure to wear something individual to stand out as the man of the hour. Take your time, enjoy the process, and really make your look your own.

Instead of traditional black dress socks, go goofy and wear brightly colored or patterned socks with your groomsmen. Boutonnieres can be made of more than just flowers. Interesting ferns, feathers, fabrics, jewelry, and even tiny toys can be used to make a one-of-a-kind accessory. For guys who are sporty at heart, classic Converse sneakers are a playful choice paired with a suit. How about a hat? Visit a specialty hat store to try on dressy options.

© photo by Positive Light Photography

© photo by La Vie Photography

© photo by La Vie Photography

© photo by Positive Light Photography

Classic Style: Full-length dresses are the most formal choice for bridesmaids and look elegant and timeless at black-tie weddings. Matching dresses in the same shape and color make a dramatic impact, especially with large wedding parties. Look for dresses in fabrics like silk taffeta, charmeuse, organza, or chiffon for the most classic look. Shoes should match the color of the dress or be a sparkling metallic or jeweled shoe with a mid-heel or high heel.

Casual Style: Let your bridesmaids choose their own neckline and dress shape from a selection of dresses made from the same fabric. You'll get a uniform look with some fun variety, and your maids will feel superconfident in their favorite style. Tea-length dresses add a playful quality to the wedding party look and can show off newsworthy shoes. Fabrics can have slight patterns or textures within their weave or be made of casual materials like cotton or linen.

Alternative Style: Want to include a guy on your side of the wedding party? Give him a shirt, tie, pocket square, or other accessory to coordinate his fashion with the ladies'. Give your bridesmaids an idea of the level of formality you're looking for and color swatches of your wedding color palette, and then send them off shopping for a unique dress that's all their own. Choose an array of tones for the bridesmaids' dresses and create a multicolor effect.

Fun Extras: Honor your maid of honor by styling her to stand out from the rest with a special dress, sash, fresh-flower corsage, or brooch. Shoes can be the focus instead of the accessory. Choose simple little black dresses for your bridesmaids and brightly colored shoes that steal the show. Give your gals a little guidance as to the style of jewelry you would like them to wear. The right jewels can easily dress up or dress down a simple gown.

Style for the Boys

There's nothing like a group of well-dressed men to make a big fashion impact. The styles you choose for your groomsmen will add personality to the overall wedding style and help define the level of formality of your event. Classic suits and tuxedos say romance and sophistication, modern suits with creative accents express fashion-forward style, and alternative attire like kilts shout creativity.

If you and your wedding party are renting suits or tuxes, come up with a game plan for how to get everyone fitted. If some of your guys are out of town, consider renting from a national chain so they can arrange their rental from their own hometown. If you want to work with a local shop, find out exactly which measurements they require to determine each man's size and have your friends visit a professional tailor to have their measurements taken correctly.

If you would like your wedding party to purchase matching suits, let them know well in advance, since fittings and alterations can take time and they may have to save up some funds. Nice suits can be big investments, so be considerate with your financial expectations and think about pitching in to help with costs if appropriate.

Classic Style: Classic tuxes look best if every member of your wedding party is coordinating his details. Rent from the same resource or tell your guys what lapel shape, tie size, vest, or cummerbund fabric to look for. Whatever kind of tux you're wearing, your groomsmen should follow suit with the same style and color. Bring extra cuff links, studs, ties, and pocket squares in case someone's goes missing. A lint roller works wonders to clean up dark suit fabric.

Casual Style: Ask each groomsman to wear a black or dark gray suit, then add color or interest with their shirts, ties, pocket squares, and boutonnieres. Many tuxedo rental shops also rent suits. Visit a few in your area to see their selections. If your guys are scattered across the

country, find their shirts and ties in an Internet shop and send them a link so they can purchase online. Specify if they will need shirts with French cuffs for cuff links.

Alternative Style: At ultracasual celebrations like the beach wedding on the bottom left, your groomsmen don't have to wear suits just because you are. As long as they coordinate, you'll all look great. If you wear a military uniform, your

guys will look great in coordinating tuxedos or dark suits. Your whole wedding party doesn't need to be Scottish to wear kilts with their formal wear. If it's a look you love, go for it and get one for each of your guys.

Fun Extras: Choose wild ties for your groomsmen and give them to your guys as gifts. If you all wear something truly out of the ordinary, like sneakers with your suits, surprise socks, or unusual matching cuff links, don't forget to capture them on film. At a Hawaiian beach wedding, groomsmen look handsome in traditional *kukui* nut necklaces instead of boutonnieres. Mixing and matching colors and patterns can create a sophisticated and dapper look.

Fashion for Kids & Attendants

Having children in your wedding party can add joy and sweetness to your day and be a great way to honor the little ones you love. When choosing fashion for young children, comfort is key and each child has a different level of tolerance when it comes to clothing. Communicate with their parents about the clothing they normally gravitate toward and how they have done in the past with dress-up situations. Choose items you think they'll enjoy wearing and schedule the day so that they don't have to be in formal wear for too many long hours before the ceremony and reception.

For older children, make the experience of being part of your wedding extra special by involving them in picking out their outfits. Spend a little time with them and let them choose from a couple of options that would both look wonderful, or let them decide on some of their accessories. Just the time spent with you and your partner will make their experience that much richer.

For junior bridesmaids and ushers, choose styles that will coordinate well with the rest of the wedding party so they'll look and feel like part of the group. When planning each outfit, think of how everyone will look together in a large group portrait.

Flower Girl: Choose a dress that is pretty but comfortable so the flower girl will fully enjoy the experience. Look for soft fabrics and trims, and bodices, necks, and armholes that aren't too

© photo by La Vie Photography

tight. Add a dash of your wedding colors with a sash or ribbons for her hair. If she's carrying a basket with flower petals down the aisle, give it to her early with extra petals so she can practice and play.

Ring Bearer: A suit or tuxedo matching the men in the wedding party will always look sharp. Many tuxedo rental shops also carry children's sizes. Give him a boutonniere or other accessory that's just like the big boys' in the wedding party. Traditional ring bearer outfits with knickers,

shirts, and vests have a classic, romantic charm and come in colors to match your wedding color palette. Choose a ring pillow or other ring box that's easy for a little one to carry.

Junior Bridesmaids: Junior bridesmaids are older than flower girls but younger than bridesmaids, so choose age-appropriate dresses they'll feel comfortable but still fancy in. Choose dresses in a shape or color similar to the bridesmaids', but

give them a slight variation so they stand out as their own important group. A special gift, like jewelry to wear on the wedding day, will add to their look and be a sweet treat for a young girl.

Ushers and Attendants: At a formal wedding the ushers and other attendants should wear

the same tuxedos or suits as the rest of the wedding party, with a stylish variation in their accessories. Special boutonnieres, ties, pocket squares, or vests will differentiate them from the groomsmen. At a casual wedding ushers and attendants don't have to be as dressed up as the groomsmen, but they should coordinate with one another in some way so they can be identified as honored members of the wedding party.

Teenagers and preteens in your wedding party will probably be organizing their own clothing for your wedding day but may not have much experience with dressing up for formal occasions. Give them a checklist a few weeks ahead of time of the clothing and accessories they should be sure to bring along.

Fashion for Moms

Modern mothers of the bride and groom have many choices when it comes to their wedding fashion. The ultratraditional rules from years ago are gone, so most mothers now opt for dresses and accessories that truly represent their own personal style as well as coordinate nicely with the style and formality of the day.

To be sure your mothers feel confident with their choices, it's smart to let them know if you have preferences for the styles they choose or to make it a project you can work on together.

Shopping with your mother or future mother-in- law can give her the chance to easily follow your lead and learn which options you think will best complement the style of the event.

Traditionally the mother of the groom defers to the mother of the bride when it comes to choosing the appropriate fashion for the wedding. At the very least the moms should communicate about the dresses they are planning to wear so their styles won't compete but will look gorgeous together. There will most likely be important family photos with both sides of the family together, so similar colors and levels of formality for the mothers will look best. Their outfits should also complement the colors and styles of the rest of the wedding party.

Moms should enjoy this opportunity to have fun with fashion and embrace their roles as honored guests of the day. Whether it's a custom-made formal gown, a simple black cocktail dress, or a playful outfit for a casual affair, your mothers' looks should be age appropriate but not matronly. They should give themselves lots of time to find the perfect dress and choose something that makes them feel beautiful, confident, and special.

Classic Style: With a sleeveless dress, a matching bolero jacket like the one shown on page 88, top photo, will show respect during a traditional ceremony and warm bare arms later in the evening. Full-length dresses are appropriate for formal events at any time of day. For a daytime event, the dress should stay simple and

© photo by Positive Light Photography

© photo by Positive Light Photography

© photo by GH Kim Photography

sophisticated without extra embellishment. For an elegant evening celebration, glamorous jewelry and accessories or a gown with more intricate detailing can liven up a look.

Casual Style: A cocktail-length dress is perfect for most casual weddings and can be dressed up or dressed down with fresh flowers, shoes, jewelry, a purse, and other accessories. Items from a favorite designer are more likely to be worn again for other special occasions. The style of the wedding, venue, the time of year, and the theme of the wedding can all inspire the fashion choices of your mothers and grandmothers.

Alternative Style: Moms can have fun with wedding themes, too. Fun colors and accessories are the easiest ways to turn a classic look into a thematic look without going over the top. At a beach wedding, a flowing lightweight summer dress will be the most comfortable. If it's a winter wonderland theme, look for fabric and accessories with a sparkling metallic sheen. Even if the bride isn't wearing a traditional dress, no one, including the mothers, should wear white to the wedding.

Fun Extras: If your mothers will be wearing pinned-on corsages, they should be informed so they can choose their dress fabric and bodice shape accordingly. Hats can be fabulous fashion accessories for events like weddings. They should be tried on with the dress ahead of time and taken to the hairstylist on the day of the wedding. Family heirloom jewelry and accessories lend a bit of romance and history to the wedding day and honor those who came before.

Fashion for Fathers

The roles of fathers evolve as their children grow up, but no matter how much things change, one thing is certain: Your wedding will be a big day for them. Honoring their importance in your wedding planning is a great thing to remember, and even small details like their wedding day fashion can work wonders to make them feel like the special family members they are.

Most fathers play an important role in the wedding itself—walking you down the aisle, acting as host, giving a speech, or greeting family and friends—so their attire should fit in with the look of the event and make them feel fantastic while they're in the spotlight. Tell them what the rest of the men in the wedding party will be wearing and what you envision for them. If they're uncomfortable in formal wear, or even if they're really excited about it, you can offer to go shopping and work on it with them. If the groom and groomsmen are all renting tuxedos, inviting your dads along for fittings can help get them involved, make them feel welcome, and give them confidence that their look will be exactly right.

Classic Style: If the men in the wedding party are wearing tuxedos, the fathers should wear them as well. Dads can update a classic tuxedo they already own with a new shirt, tie, shoes,

© photo by GH Kim Photography

© photo by GH Kim Photography

© photo by Yours by John Photography

Something Old . . .

Is there something special your dad wore to his own wedding that would still look great today? Whether it's his handkerchief or his cuff links, it's the little mementos like that, full of charm and emotion, that can start a family tradition of your own.

∽

and other accessories. The fathers' tuxedos can be rented along with the rest of the groomsmen's so they will be the same or nicely coordinating. Communicate with both fathers early on about what they will be expected to wear so they have plenty of time to prepare.

Casual Style: If the men in the wedding party are wearing dark formal suits, the fathers should wear them, too. Next to the groom and groomsmen, the fathers should be the most dressed up men at the event. Casual suits come in many colors—navy, tan, light gray, dark gray, or patterned—and many dads already own at least

one. The father of the bride and father of the groom should check in to be sure their casual looks are harmonious.

Alternative Style: If the groomsmen are wearing something truly unique, give the same outfit or accessories to the fathers to tie the family's look to the wedding party's. For any alternatively styled wedding, the fathers should be given a little fashion guidance so they'll feel like they fit in on the big day. If the father of the groom is in the wedding party, be sure the father of the bride's outfit coordinates or is given equal thought and attention.

Fun Extras: Family heirloom accessories like a pocket watch or cuff links are a great addition to a father's wedding day style. Fathers can wear a pocket square or tie that corresponds with the colors of the wedding party so they look like part of the gang. Special boutonnieres for the fathers and grandfathers will honor their importance and show off their position in the family to guests who haven't yet met them.

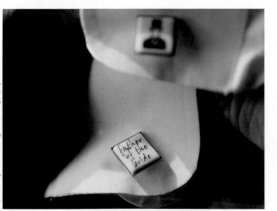

© photo by Positive Light Photography

© photo by La Vie Photography

Chapter 3

Hair, Makeup & Beauty

&

You've undoubtedly seen endless photos of wedding day hairstyles and beauty in bridal magazines and on wedding websites, and—even when you count out those cringe-worthy styles from the 1980s that are still on many sites—it can be extremely overwhelming to click on page after page after page of hairstyles, all commingled in under headings such as "Long Hair" or "Curly Hair." Who has time to sort through such a collection of images? And even if you love every single picture and can see yourself in each of them, how do you know which styles would truly work best for you?

Well, just as your wedding gown has to fit your wedding style and shape, your hairstyle—and beauty style—has to "work" with many factors for your best look. These next few pages will help you decide between a glamorous updo, romantic flowing curls, a classic and elegant chignon, a playful ponytail with a gardenia accent, a fun and flippy shorter hairstyle, or movie-star hair made fuller and more dramatic with fabulous extensions. These next few pages of inspiring photos will also help you pick the perfect makeup to complete your look.

Here's one insider bit of information: Some brides are spending more on their hairstyles than they are on their invitations! Some are spending more on their manicures than on their wedding day shoes! And consider this: The average bridesmaid spends $65 on her hair, $32 on her manicure, and $30 on her pedicure, not to mention money spent on tanning, teeth whitening, and other beauty regimes.

Now you might be among the brides who have neither the wish nor the budget to hire professional hair and makeup artists for yourself and your bridesmaids on your wedding day. For you, we have easy, step-by-step, do-it-yourself (DIY) advice to create that lovely updo, the perfect, chic chignon, celebrity-style spiral curls, and many other beautiful bridal looks all on your own.

Looking gorgeous on the wedding day, and at each special wedding event from showers to the morning-after breakfast, is a high priority for brides. Before you spend the money on your hair, makeup, nails, and other beauty treatments, you must first think through your overall vision for how you want to look.

Photo by Kristen Jensen

GETTING GORGEOUS: THE GAME PLAN

You're going to look gorgeous on your wedding day! Your hair, your makeup, your smile . . . all will be perfect and completely stunning, putting your groom and all your guests in awe of how beautiful you are. They always knew you were beautiful, of course. You've just taken it to a whole new level! Your wedding day calls for your best look ever, and that is exactly what you will achieve through the inspiration and advice in this book.

Get ready to be transformed from head to toe, from updo to pretty pedicure, and fulfill your wish to look "like you, only better" in every

area—hair, makeup, skin, nails, smile, and that inner well-being that turns up your beauty dial to level ten—make that twelve. (Your groom will say twenty!) Get ready to hear, "You look amazing" a few hundred times, and get ready to look in the mirror on your wedding day and breathe, "Wow, I do look amazing!" This section discusses the basics you need to know to get the look you want on your big day.

Suit Your Wedding Style

You know that certain wedding gown styles suit the formality of a wedding. A ball gown says formal. A knee-length, flowing sundress says outdoor casual or beach wedding. A sleek, sheath dress shows off your curves for a city-chic wedding. The same rules apply to your wedding day hair and makeup.

Your look makes the best impression when it's suited to the style and formality of your wedding. Think about it: Would you walk into your ultraformal wedding in a lavish ballroom wearing an elaborate beaded gown, carrying a lush bouquet of formal white roses and gardenias, with your hair hanging down over your shoulders with just some flowing, natural waves in it? No, that's too informal. Guests would think you just hopped out of the shower, air-dried your hair, and popped a tiara on top of your head.

At an outdoor wedding, would you show up with heavy foundation and dark-rimmed eyes? No, you wouldn't, because you'd look out of place, overdone, and severely lacking in beauty wisdom. To start planning your overall beauty, begin with the best beauty vision to match your level of formality, your location, and your wedding's style. This sets the foundation for every beauty decision you will make from here on out, allowing you to perfect your wedding day look.

Styles for a Formal Wedding: Both updos and half-up/half-down hairstyles work perfectly for formal weddings. Look to celebrity and iconic formal wedding styles and beauty looks from elite events like the Oscars. A formal updo has amazing structure, pinned-in curls—notable detail that has taken effort to create. A formal daytime or nighttime wedding calls for a polished makeup style with either eyes or lips making a statement with color.

Styles for an Informal Wedding: An updo is also appropriate for an informal wedding but should be more relaxed, with natural curl and perhaps pinned-in florals. Loose and flowing hair is the most popular style for an informal wedding, with polished waves and curls creating the ideal effect. Choose natural shades of makeup, with just a bit of extra shine on the lips only.

Styles for an Ultraformal Wedding: The ultraformal wedding calls for a dramatic upsweep of the hair. The most popular choice for ultraformal hair is an elegant upsweep with

a mass of structured curls on top. A tiara and headpiece are the stars of an ultraformal look, dazzling with jewels, and hair is its setting. Ultraformal weddings take place at night, the time when dramatic eye makeup and darker lips work perfectly.

Styles for an Outdoor Wedding: Outdoor weddings may be either formal or informal, so use prior tips to guide you. Being outdoors, you'll contend with breezes and perhaps humidity, which make the slicked-back ponytail or chignon ideal for comfort. Bridal hair is beautifully accented with fresh flowers or sparkling crystals that catch the natural light outdoors. Being out in natural light calls for a fresh, dewy complexion and neutral-to-light makeup shades with just a bit of gloss.

Photo by Mary-Anne Conner

93

Be sure you have your wedding gown selected and ordered before you begin exploring your beauty style. Once your gown fits the formality and style of your wedding, both you and your professional hair and makeup experts can match your beauty look to your dream dress.

Matching Your Wedding Dress

You've chosen your dream wedding gown to accentuate your shape and fit your dream image of how you wish to look on your wedding day. Your hair and makeup will need to work with your strapless neckline, the elaborate beading on your bodice, the plunging back that shows some skin, or the simple and unadorned style.

An updo, for example, elongates your neck and shows off your shoulders and collarbone,

Photo by Kristen Jensen

which allows the upper part of your gown to shine without any coverage or competition from a loose and flowing hairstyle.

A low neckline creates open space from your neck to your chest, perfect for an updo with plenty of volume. A straight-across, strapless neckline works well with both an updo and down styles. A high neckline requires an updo so that hair doesn't cover gown details, or get stuck in accent beading. If you have lots of crystals in a line across the top of your bodice, provide a subtle amount of crystal accents in your hair to coordinate.

If your dress is ornate, with lots of tiers and crystal-pinned draping or a beaded bodice or pleats, a simpler or slicked-back hairstyle ensures that your dress—and your face—steal the show, while your hair still looks elegant and beautiful. Your entire look—from head to toe—needs to coordinate and be balanced so that you don't have too much going on. A dress that is formfitting on the top and wide at the bottom looks best with hair that has more volume on top to balance. A sheath dress looks lovely when hair is slicked back into a chignon accented with big, dramatic flowers. A column or A-line dress welcomes either up or down hairstyles. The most popular hairstyle that works with most dress silhouettes is the half-up/half-down style.

You make your initial impression when you walk down the aisle, but you're in view from the back throughout most of the ceremony. Your hairstyle in the back is in full view, even through your veil. If your veil has multiple layers and your hair is hidden during the ceremony, the "reveal," when you remove your veil, impresses at the reception. Be sure that the patterns of curls, braids, or accents in the back do not compete with the back of your dress.

If your dress has any color to it, such as a blush- or deep-colored sash, incorporate that same color in your eye makeup. If your dress has colored beading, such as a line of pink gemstones at your neckline, use the same pink for your lipstick shade. A romantic, flowing dress calls for softer shades of makeup. Sleek or sheath dresses invite more dramatic makeup in rich matte or glossy shades.

You'll need to assess each element of your wedding gown—neckline, silhouette, and the view from the back—to help you determine how much detail you'd like your hair to have, all to give your look brilliant balance and allow the right elements to stand out. Beware of competing dramatic effects! You wouldn't do dark, dramatic eyes and dark, dramatic lips in any makeup style that's not happening on Halloween. The same goes for coordinating with your gown. Place the drama on either the gown or the hair, never both.

Flattering Your Face

You probably already know which hairstyles look best on you, but perhaps you are one of those brides who hasn't yet discovered the hairstyles that really look great, styles you haven't yet tried because your visits to the salon are usually just to freshen up your existing look.

In short, you might have no idea that you look amazing—and five pounds thinner!—with some volume on the sides of your head or with a bob that reaches just below your jawline.

The perfect hair length and style can transform your face, accent your best features, and play down those features you're not wild about. And that's exactly what a great wedding hairstyle achieves . . . you, only better.

Consider the shape of your face and the hairstyle rules to follow for your best and most beautiful look. Professional hairstylists cringe when a bride insists on a hairstyle that is the exact wrong style and shape for her face, chosen because that's the one in the photo she likes. Don't marry a hairstyle before you consider the shape of your face and your facial features. Countless brides thank their lucky stars that a trained eye brought to light a solution that made them look slimmer in the face.

Your first step is to determine what your face shape actually is. Are you round or oval? Heart shaped or triangular? Assess your shape in the mirror and ask your stylist for his or her expert opinion as well. Remember to be open to your stylist's honest assessment of your face. His or her trade is to make you beautiful.

Round Face: Brides with round faces should never pull their hair back, as this makes the face look even rounder. They should also avoid hair fullness on the sides of the face, which also magnifies the circle of the face. Instead, they should choose long layers and natural waves, not

Photo by Kristen Jensen

full-volume curls, that reach to below the chin, elongating the face. If you have a round face and like the look of a bob, make sure the ends reach two inches below chin level.

Heart-Shaped Face: Long layers detract from the look of a pointy chin. Bobbed hair needs to reach below the chin to balance the

Photo by Kristen Jensen

pointed-down angle of the jaw. A heart-shaped face is appropriate for pulled-back hair. Look at pictures of Reese Witherspoon, your heart-shaped-face style icon. Copy her long and straight or long and bobbed styles.

Triangular Face: Your goal is to create the illusion of width at your chin to balance your facial features. Avoid an updo with a lot of curl and volume at the crown of your head, which will only make your chin appear narrower. If your hair is short, above the shoulders, create fullness at your temples to balance your look. Sweep your bangs to the side to create a visual direction that narrows your forehead in balance.

Additional Face Shapes: If you have a long face, choose a style that is long on the sides and has less height on top. If you have a diamond-shaped face, full or gently sideswept bangs narrow the forehead. If you have a square face, keep hair at the sides sleek and pulled back fully or loosely, avoiding the illusion of extra width. Use moderate height at the crown of your head. An oval face works well with virtually all hairstyles, especially with pretty bangs lightly swept to the side.

Matching with Your Bridesmaids

Do you want one unified and identical look for yourself and all your bridesmaids? Some brides love the idea of their circle of friends all sharing the same dramatic updo style. From the upsweep to the romantic curls—and even the

Photo by Kristen Jensen

pinned-in crystal accents—everyone's hair look is the same. It makes for a stunning effect in person and is captured forever in photos of same-coiffed bridesmaids encircling the bride.

Some brides, however, think that everyone having matching hairstyles would make the entire group look like a cheerleading team or a dance troupe—not the ideal effect, they might decide.

The good news is that you get to choose just how matchy matchy you'd like your bridesmaids' hairstyles to be. And part of that decision is asking yourself if you're the type of bride who enforces a hairstyle rule to the bridesmaids. Some brides out there will actually tell their bridesmaids to start growing out their hair in order to have that identical updo, and some—shockingly—admit that they have left friends

out of the bridal party because they didn't want a bridesmaid with supershort hair ruining their plan for identical dos. Chances are, you're stunned that any bride would dream of requiring a set hairstyle, and that puts you among the 99 percent of brides who opt for a coordinated hairstyle plan.

Formality, of course, is the number one issue, as your bridesmaids' hairstyles need to work with your wedding's style and formality level, just as your own hairstyle does. The second issue also borrows from your own beauty rules: The bridesmaids' hairstyles must flatter their diverse face shapes, as well as the style of their dresses. This means they can look at the guidelines and images in this book to decide on the hairstyle they like best that also happens to beautifully coordinate with your style.

If all your bridesmaids will wear identical updos to match yours, have your stylist choose the right height and volume to flatter each. Consider whether or not your bridesmaids have the hair texture to hold an updo; superfine hair is not a good candidate. If you require that the matching updos be done by a pro, it would be good of you to pay the entire bill. You can set yourself apart by having beautiful crystal accents in the back.

For a coordinated formal look, you can wear a dramatic updo with curls at the crown, and they can pull their hair back into elegant chignons. They can customize their chignon by going sleek and flawless, or by pulling out some strategic pieces for effect. Each bridesmaid can wear an identical chignon accent, such as crystal pins or a floral band. To set her apart, your maid of honor can wear an accent of a different, yet coordinated style.

If you will wear an embellished ponytail, it's ideal for your bridesmaids to wear them as well. Choose a uniform level for the ponytail—low or high. The bridesmaids will achieve uniformity with matching ponytail accents, all in the same color. To set yourself apart, your ponytail accent can be white while theirs matches their dress color, or yours can be larger and more dramatic, such as a gardenia to coordinate with their stephanotis.

Bridesmaids with long hair can wear ponytails with a side barrette, while those with short hair wear the same barrette style to coordinate. Long-haired bridesmaids can wear a gentle upsweep, while the others sport the same waves or pin curls. Decide on a uniform part and then have all your bridesmaids wear their hair wavy. Give your bridesmaids matching headbands, either plain or with a floral or silk accent, and allow them to choose their own styles.

Perfect Timing

In order for your hair to look its best on your wedding day, you need to have perfect timing. Your cut, color, highlights, trims, and deep-conditioning treatment all need to be done at the right intervals—and the right number of days (or weeks)—before the big day so that your style is at its peak of perfection when you walk down the aisle.

Here you'll find out how to time your hair preparations. This is especially important if you're like many brides who try to grow out their hair to achieve their dream updo or dream length of curly, loose natural hair.

It's a good idea to meet with a professional hairstylist—hopefully your wedding day stylist—a year before the wedding (or right now, if you're less than a year away!) to get an expert assessment of your hair's true texture and personality, discuss your hair color and highlighting preferences, and to start a conditioning regimen to bring out your hair's healthy shine and bounce.

Use the detailed Beauty Countdown on page 354 along with these guidelines to pre-schedule all your hair appointments now. That way you don't have to keep track of how many weeks it's been since your last cut and color. Beauty salons and experts say they book bridal clients' appointments as far as two years in advance. To make this even easier on their clients, many salons have online appointment bookings, complete with reminder e-mails that are sent out close to upcoming appointments.

Timing Your Hair Color: If you're one to change your hair color with the seasons, decide on a hue for the season of your wedding. Plan to get your hair color touched up professionally every four to six weeks. If you only do highlights or lowlights, have those freshened every six to nine weeks. Have your last color one or two weeks before the wedding, and boost your shine and color with a professional glazing three days before the wedding.

Timing Your Haircuts and Trims: Have your hair cut and styled right before you get your engagement photos taken for that perfect, fresh-from-the-salon style, volume, and shine. Consult with your hairstylist to create a customized plan for your haircuts and trims during the months leading up to the wedding. Schedule regular trims to eliminate split ends and keep your layers fresh. Schedule your final haircut for two weeks before the wedding, or your final trim for one week before the wedding.

Growing Out Your Hair: Nightly scalp massages stimulate blood flow and encourage faster hair growth. Hair grows half an inch per month, so

be patient. Use hair products containing algae proteins to naturally speed hair growth. Tame your growing-out hair and keep those short sections under control by wearing a headband.

Hair & Makeup Trials

The day before your big day, you attend the rehearsal to do a few trial runs of your ceremony. After all, it's important that everything goes perfectly on the big day. The same goes for your hair and makeup, although your trial runs should happen far more in advance than the day before.

Your trial-run appointments with your hairstylist and makeup artist are among the most exciting tasks on your to-do list, as it is at these appointments, as you sit in the stylist's chair and look into the mirror, that you watch yourself transform into the beautiful bride you're going to be.

Even though these trial runs are a task, and you have to make important decisions, you will get the VIP bride treatment. At some salons, brides visiting for their trial runs get the royal treatment: champagne, berries, and cappuccino. It's a big deal!

Before you can get your cappuccino or champagne, however, you need to find the right stylists—the perfect hair and makeup artists who will bring out your best beauty and perfect your wedding day transformation. The success of your look depends on whose hands you're in. Here is where that search begins, and where you find out the do's and don'ts of your trial runs.

Ask your regular stylist if he or she does wedding hairstyling; not all hair experts specialize in event styling. Ask your stylist to recommend the in-house wedding hair specialist who does your planned style. Consider asking recently married friends if they would recommend the stylist who did their wedding day hair. Ask your wedding coordinator or other wedding vendors who they recommend in the area; local wedding experts all know each other's work.

Ask to be introduced to the in-house makeup artist at your salon, and make a consultation appointment. Ask recently married friends to refer you to their wedding day makeup artists. Don't forget that Sweet 16 party guests of honor get their makeup professionally done, so ask family friends if they'd recommend their daughter's makeup expert. Your wedding

coordinator and other wedding vendors, again, are the ideal sources for referrals to the best makeup artists in town.

Bring a photo of your wedding gown to your initial consultations so your stylists can assess your style and formality. Bring five to ten photos of looks that you like. Be open to your stylists' input on each. Don't bring just one photo; a range of photos will better convey your personal tastes. Tell your stylist how your hair behaves, or if your skin gets blotchy with oil-based makeup. This information helps the pros decide if your wished-for look will do.

Don't attempt to save money by skipping trial hair and makeup sessions. Your hair and beauty experts need to assess how your hair holds a style and how your skin reacts to foundation. They need time to try out several

Photo by Kristen Jensen

different looks to find the one that is perfect for you. Your day-of styling will likely fail without trial runs.

Ideally you'll meet with your hairstylist a year in advance of your wedding to allow plenty of time for a hair-health plan and growing-out time, if necessary. Also, visiting with your stylists a year in advance allows them to see what your hair and skin look like in the season when your wedding will take place. Schedule a trial run closer to your wedding date—approximately three months prior—so that your hair is close to its wedding day length. A makeup session three months prior to your wedding day allows your stylist to see your look in season.

HAIR

Let's face it: Hair is a big deal. This next section discusses some hair-raising questions: To updo or not to updo? Waves or curls? Chignon or the more casual ponytail? And how does that whole veil thing come into play? On your wedding day, you want your hair to look its best and to be the most flattering style for you. Since sometimes it's easier to tell from a photo whether or not you like a hairstyle rather than from, say, lots of cumbersome, descriptive text, in the next few pages we've included plenty of inspiration galleries for you to look through to help you decide what look works best for you.

Hairstyle Basics

Your hair is one of your most important accessories for your wedding day, and there can be a great number of ways to wear it, depending on its length and thickness. Look to the general style of your wedding for inspiration, as well as specific fashion items like your wedding dress, jewelry, veil, or hair accessories.

Practicality can also play a part in your hairstyle decision. If you're getting married in a hot climate, you may not want to wear your hair down on your neck; if you'll be somewhere breezy, choose a natural style that will look nice a bit tousled.

In the midst of your wedding planning, remember to take care of your hair and make appointments for all the maintenance you'll need leading up to your big day. If you color your hair, have it freshened up a week or two ahead of time, and unless you're really daring, don't go for any major changes right before your wedding.

Have fun experimenting with different looks, and ask a friend to take photos of you from different angles if you're trying to decide between options. Take photos of your look once you've decided on it so you'll have an easy reference point for other fashion purchases.

Classic Hairstyles: A low chignon at the nape of your neck, as shown on page 102, upper left, is universally flattering and an eternally classic look. If your hair isn't very long, but you'd like an updo, try temporary natural hair extensions or hairpieces. A simple updo at the crown of your head looks lovely with a veil placed either above or below it. A French twist is another classic

© photos by Junebug Weddings

hairstyle that looks beautiful from every angle and can accommodate many different types of veils and hair accessories.

Casual Hairstyles: Wear your hair down in smooth waves for a naturally romantic look, or go sleek and straighten your hair to add a modern edge. Wear your hair half up and half down for an option that's pretty but not too formal. To look most like yourself, try a twist on your everyday style. Choose your favorite look and

add a little extra polish. Add the finishing touch to your casual do with an antifrizz serum or shine spray.

Vintage or Retro Hairstyles: A 1940s-inspired updo with rolling waves and dramatic shape like the one shown on the bottom left creates a fun backdrop for sparkling hair accessories. Finger waves with a bob or shorter haircut is a look inspired by the 1920s. Find your favorite vintage look and work with your hairstylist to

If you'll be getting your hair professionally styled, schedule a trial run at least a few weeks before your wedding day. Be sure to take along your veil or hair accessories and a photo or description of your dress so your stylist knows what will work best.

create a flattering updated version. For subtlety, balance a modern wedding dress with a vintage hairstyle, or a vintage dress with a modern do.

Alternative Hairstyles: A little height in a hairstyle can make a simple look more dramatic. Ponytails are playful and can be worn high, low, or off to the side. Let your chosen hair accessory or veil inspire a hairstyle that you will absolutely love. Be careful not to choose something too trendy that will quickly look dated. No one wants to look back on their wedding photos years down the road and wonder what they were thinking.

Updos

Formal weddings most often call for an elegant upsweep of hair, and the shape, height, and patterns of the updo can vary in so many ways according to your wedding vision mixed with smart hairstyle selection. Here and in the following pages, you'll refine your hairstyle selection by exploring different options within up, down, half-up/half-down, and shorter styles to find the perfect placement and patterning

of your hairstyle's most eye-catching elements, such as curls, twists, braids, pleats, and other artistic styling.

Ponytails & Chignons

The ponytail is one of the most popular wedding day looks for brides who don't want the upswept Cinderella look. The chic and elegant ponytail provides a smooth, polished look that serves as the basis for formal and informal looks. Ponytails can be accented or stylishly simple, and they're appropriate for both indoor and outdoor settings. The ponytail is the equivalent of the A-line wedding dress—a foundation style that can be dressed up or down according to your personal style.

Chignons are one of the most popular styles for weddings, since a smooth, chic chignon says "elegance," while a loosely gathered, "messy" chignon says "effortless beauty." Both styles are in demand because they are beautiful and quite easy to create on your own. Brides who want a pretty hairstyle but don't have the budget for a professional stylist often choose the chignon as their wedding day hairstyle, and they start practicing their technique months before the big day to perfect that smooth sweepback, the twist, and the pinning into place.

Loose & Flowing

Curly hair provides a fresh, soft, ethereal look for wedding day hair, and more brides are selecting the all-over spiral-curled look for their formal weddings. The mass of loose and flowing

Romantic

The Height of Glamour

Symmetrical Curls

Curls Rising from Your Tiara

The Gentle Fall of Looser Curls

Constructed, Tighter Curls

The Gentle Fall of Ringlets

Looser Curls and Your Tiara or Veil

The Loose Upsweep

The Loose Upsweep with Waves

The Loose Upsweep with Ringlet

Chic

Side Part

Showing Off the Top

With Curls

The Straight Back

The Side Pull

The Out-There Style

Traditional French Twist

Accented French Twist

The Single French Braid

Informal French Braid

© Surkov Vladimir / Shutterstock

Photos by Kristen Jensen (unless otherwise noted)

Ponytails

Low Ponytail, Straight Hair

Low Ponytail, Wavy Hair

Low Ponytail, Medium Hair

High Ponytail with Straight Hair

High Ponytail with Curled Hair

Chignons

The Round Wrap Chignon

The Modern, Formal Chignon

Accenting the Chignon

The Casual Chignon

Adding a Dash of Color

Loose & Flowing

Tight, Symmetrical Curls

Curls with Accents

Tiara and Headpiece Matching

Loose and Flowing Curls

Loose and Flowing Waves

Flowing Curls Accents

Gentle Wave

Tiara and Headpiece Perfection

Half Up / Half Down

Romantic Curls on Top

Tight Spiral Curls on Top

Half Tiara

Full Tiara

Headpiece and Veil

Straight Up, Straight Down

Straight Up, Curl Down

Braid or Twist Up, Curly Down

Straight Up, Straight Down
(Medium Hair)

Straight Up, Curly Down
(Medium Hair)

Photos by Kristen Jensen

Long & Sleek

Long Hair au Naturel

Long Hair with Clips

A Polished Look

Gentle Waves

Waves with Jeweled Barrettes

The Sidesweep and Part

The Rounded, Straight Blowout

Curled-Up Ends

The Finished Look

Headband

Photos by Kristen Jensen

Short Hairstyles

The Sidesweep

Angled Bob Style

Waves

Straight Bobbed Style

Pin Curls

Pinned-In Accents

Pixie Cut

© Lev Olkha | Shutterstock

Flippy Layers

© Carlush | Shutterstock

Tiara

Half Up/Half Down

Highlights

spiral curls works with just about every wedding gown type—from simple and sophisticated to more ornate, beaded dresses to sleek and modern unadorned sheaths and satiny A-line gowns.

Half Up/Half Down

The half-up/half-down style—in which the front and sides of your hair are gathered up into a pretty clip or curls and the back of your hair hangs down—is quickly becoming one of the most popular styles for brides who like both the up and down look. And the style works equally well for formal and informal weddings, indoors and outside. This style also has the added perk of showing off your earrings beautifully.

Long & Sleek

It's not just curly hair that looks romantic for weddings. The smooth, superstraight look has become another of the most popular styles for both formal.

While a superstraight hairstyle may seem like an option only for brides whose hair is baby fine, it is in fact possible for brides with almost any hair texture to achieve that elegant flow of smooth and silky hair falling beautifully over their shoulders or down their back. Today's improved smoothing serums and hi-tech styling tools can magically erase frizz and waves, even turning ultracurly hair into a silky effect. Superstraight hair works for any style of wedding.

Short Hairstyles

If you have gorgeous, gamine hair—sleek, soft, and shiny, and the perfect frame to show off your face—you're not left out of the bridal hair conversation. In fact, you have gorgeous hairstyle options of your own, ones that perfect that gamine look you love on yourself and have seen supermodels transformed into on *America's Next Top Model*.

Accents

You might decide to include flowers as beautiful bridal accents to your whole wedding day look. A few fresh flowers pinned into your updo become a beautiful reveal when you remove your veil for the reception, or flowers in your hair can take the place of a traditional headpiece and veil. This is a lovely bridal look and can save you huge amounts of money, with veils and headpieces sometimes costing more than the gowns themselves.

Brides whose floral dreams include something different for their look often incorporate tiny flowers as jewelry pieces such as bracelets, necklaces, and even floral pendants that hang down to showcase a plunging backline showing off the brides' best assets. The advent of florals

Photo by Rich Penrose

Accessory Ideas

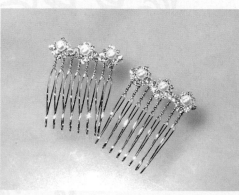

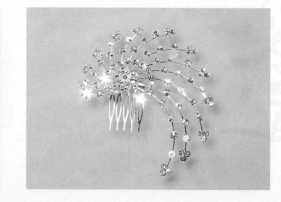

Photo by Kristen Jensen

Photo by Kristen Jensen

MAKEUP

Just like hair, makeup is also a big deal. Since you'll have so many photos taken of you on your wedding day, you want your makeup to look fresh—and continue to look fresh—throughout all of the day's events. Deciding on the style of your makeup depends a lot on the time of day and location of your wedding. If you're having a day ceremony and reception, for example, you might go a little lighter and more natural with your makeup. However, for a night-time affair, you might choose to play it up with smoky eyes and more dramatic lips. This next section will provide you with all you need to know to have the perfect look.

Oh, and since more and more brides are choosing to do their own makeup these days (it's a good cost saver, too), we've included plenty of DIY tips to help you out.

Makeup Basics

Whether you love beauty products or rarely wear any at all, finding great makeup and the best way to wear it on your wedding day can really complement your look. If makeup is your thing, then have fun doing it yourself; get expert advice at your local makeup counter and through online video instruction and forums. If your interests lie elsewhere, a professional makeup artist can be an invaluable investment. With his or her technical know-how and artistic abilities, he or she can create a look that's both beautiful and practical and makes you feel like the very best version of you.

in pendants now means you can create a fresh accessory for the front or back of your wedding gown.

Flowers are the new accessories for brides, and they work for both formal and informal weddings, indoor and outdoor celebrations, and at-home and destination weddings. Especially if you have a very simple, classic, elegant gown with a minimum of embellishments, a few well-placed flowers can turn your classic bridal look into an ethereal, floral wonder, all for just a few dollars, rather than what you'd spend on expensive jewelry.

© photos by Junebug Weddings

You will be photographed all day, so you need to choose products that will look great on film and hold up to long hours of wear. Outdoor weddings are photographed in natural light, so you'll look best with more natural-style makeup, tones that complement your coloring, and nothing too extreme. Indoor weddings often require flash photography and artificial lighting, so avoid products with SPF, as they may reflect light in an artificial-looking way. Camera flashes can also bring out redness in lighter skin, so be sure to create a good base and cover up any redness in your skin with the proper tones of concealer or foundation.

Glowing Skin: Your makeup will look best if your skin is happy. Finish beauty treatments twenty-four to forty-eight hours prior to your wedding day to allow time to ease any redness. If you have sensitive skin, look for products made with natural ingredients and that are hypoallergenic or noncomedogenic. Be sure to moisturize well before applying your makeup. Start with a concealer or light base to even out your skin tone and cover up blemishes.

Classic Makeup: Lightly line your eyes in black or brown or use a liquid liner to create a more defined line and give a slightly vintage effect. Brown eye shadow in the crease of your eyelid and a lighter shadow highlighting your brow bone will accentuate your eye's natural shape. Simple pink cheeks and a classic red lip will never go out of style. Try out different shades of red lipstick to find the shade that complements your skin tone.

Casual Makeup: Show off your natural beauty with makeup that looks barely there. Gently shimmering products can give your skin a little extra life, but overdoing it may make you appear shiny in your photos. Pinks and earth tones are nice warm neutrals that will give you a rosy, healthy glow. Play to find the shades that work for you. Choose a creamy lipstick that enhances your natural lip color, or go for a simple translucent lip gloss.

Dramatic Makeup: Smoky eyes with gray, brown, or even rich plum or navy liner and shadow are dramatic statements for fashion-forward brides. False eyelashes add instant glamour and definition in photographs. Use a short strip of graduated-length lashes on the outer half of each eye, or add a few individual lashes for the most natural look. Choose one area of the face to focus on so you never look overdone. Go for a dramatic eye with a neutral lip, or vice versa.

Your eyebrows help to frame your face; giving them the correct shape can make a huge difference in your look. Get your eyebrows professionally shaped well before your wedding day to be sure you like them, and then have them retouched one week before.

Eyes

While most brides choose to get their makeup done by a professional on their big day, there are many brides who choose to do their own makeup—fearful to trust another with their face on their most important day. For the DIYers, we've included lots of tips on eye makeup. If you plan on getting your makeup professionally done, use the photos on page 118–19 as inspiration to help guide your professional.

Daytime Romantic: Makeup for a daytime wedding needs to be soft and natural, showing off your best features and bridal glow with lighter colors, neutrals, soft pinks, and pastels. This rule applies for a daytime wedding in any season, when natural sunlight will showcase your face both indoors and out during your arrival, your dash to the car, and outdoor photos.

Daytime means extra light on your face, calling for a softer touch and appropriate tones.

The key to a lovely daytime eye is using the best soft tones to bring out your eye color and framing your eye with a softer yet still appealing liner and mascara look. Eyes may be matte or shimmery in this daytime romantic category, and, yes, faux lashes are possible without crossing the line into overdone theater makeup that's too heavy or too dark. Those are the mistakes made by brides who think they have to overdo the eye makeup a bit in order to stand out in photos, which is not the case.

Your eye-makeup brushes are key to your best look—longer bristles give you a wash of color, while shorter bristles apply more eye makeup to a specific area, like the lining of your upper lids.

Dramatic Smoky Eyes: An after-sundown wedding calls for a more dramatic makeup look that suits the formality and style of your celebration, and that means creating a makeup plan with added flair, deeper colors, smoky eyes, and shimmer that suit the later hour.

Again, you're just focusing on your eyes here, looking at ways to give yourself those sultry, smoky eyes that will floor your groom and make you look like a supermodel. It's you . . . only better—an extraordinary transformation from your everyday neutral look to sexy siren of your wedding day. With deeper tones and model-perfect lined eyes, thick and fabulous lashes, and that confidence that shows when you know you look amazing, your dramatic eye-makeup plan will perfect your look for the later hours.

Of course your degree of sexy, dramatic eyes is completely up to you and your personal comfort level. If your makeup artist overdoes it, and your thickly dark-rimmed eyes make you unrecognizable, that's a wedding beauty mistake of the largest proportion. You always want to look like your best you. So experiment with dark, smoky eye designs at your trial-run sessions with your makeup stylist. Try different tones of shadow, and you might agree that a medium powder shade is fabulous on you, with the drama created with just a slightly thicker smudge of deep liner or faux lashes.

With dramatic, smoky eyes for evening, blending has never been more important. Darker jewel tones have to blend into one another flawlessly, and eyeliner has to be even in shape and thickness on both sides, so consider blending to be the most important element of your look.

Lips

Like with eye makeup, many brides choose to self-apply their lipstick. Here are some great DIY tips to help you look fabulous—and stay looking fabulous—on your big day.

Natural, Romantic & Neutral Lips: Natural lip colors work with your skin tone and hair color for a soft touch of hue and shine, achieving a barely there sheer wash of color. Brunettes look

Daytime Romantic

Photos by Kristen Jensen

Apply light, neutral tones such as taupe, honey, beige, brown, light gold, or light plum on the lid only to crease level, not over the entire eye area. Brown-eyed brides look best with pastel colors; blue-eyed brides look best in lilacs; and green- or hazel-eyed brides look best in soft plums. Powder eye shadows can look chalky, so instead dab translucent cream shadow only on your lids up to the crease line. Use shimmery eye shadow sparingly for just a hint of sparkle.

Use a medium, color-coordinated tone just two shades darker than your lid color. Use a tapered blending brush to apply crease powder from the outside of your eye crease halfway to the inner, and blend well. Don't go up too high onto your brow bone; stay in the crease itself with highlight powder in vanilla or champagne under the brow and in the tear duct area.

Photos by Kristen Jensen

Flattering colors include neutrals such as brown, dark green, plum, sapphire, and bronze for a metallic sparkle. Blend in liner pencil on upper and lower lids using the sponge on the end of the pencil. As an alternative to liner pencil, dampen a stiff, thin brush, dip it into your darker eye shadow, and apply from your outer to inner lash line. Use two different liner shades: a darker brown on your upper lid and a slightly lighter brown on your lower lid.

Waterproof mascara is essential, since tears of joy will flow. Choose a mascara in a tone that matches the darker shade of your eyeliner. Deeper tones of brown are most flattering on all skin tones, but many brides love to accent with darker plum or deep green to coordinate with their eye color. Avoid the ultradramatic thickening mascaras that can make your lashes look too thick; just one pass of quality mascara and one coat of clear are all you need.

Smoky Eyes

Photos by Kristen Jensen

Apply a lighter base eye shadow color in a neutral tone or a light shimmery tone on the lids just to the brow bone, to provide contrast for that dark, smoky eyeliner and lash color. Create the smoky look on your lid by using an eye shadow brush to blend in a darker shade, such as a deep brown, deep gray, or deep purple, along the lash line and then blend upward. Sweep a line of deep color below your bottom lash line to encircle your eye and create that smoky look.

With a smoky eye you won't be using traditional slightly darker colors in your crease. The contouring color is swept along the upper lash line in a quarter- to half-inch- thick line. Blend your darker eye shadow color into your upper lid eyeliner. Top colors for providing that smoky eye effect are violet, brown, plum, deep green, and charcoal or slate blue gray.

Photos by Kristen Jensen

Traditional eyeliner colors for a sexy, smoky eye are black, brown, and gray. For a more creative smoky eye, use deep jewel tones such as purple, dark green, teal, dark sapphire, or navy. Line the upper and lower lash lines with an eye pencil starting thin at the inner crease and getting twice as thick moving outward. Sweep a same or slightly lighter shade of powder in a one-eighth-inch line directly under your bottom lid to the pupil, and blend well.

The deeper colors of your eye shadow "line" and smudged liner provide a great amount of drama. Create thickness to your lashes without overdoing it and making "spider lashes" with the wrong mascara formula. Use volumizing mascara to give lashes some extra thickness. If you've lined your eyes with a brown, gray, or jewel-tone liner and shadow, choose a darker shade of mascara in the same color family, which often looks better than black.

Photos by Kristen Jensen

best with a coral-colored neutral, and olive- and darker-skinned brides should avoid pinks and use reddish browns instead. Blondes look best with soft peach tones on their lips, or warm pinks. Redheads look best with an apricot tone, and if they have a fair complexion, peach or soft brown pinks.

Lip liners give your lip shape more definition. Never use lip liner in a darker shade than the rest of your lip color. This is the number one lip design mistake, as it can make you look ten years older. For a natural look, line and fill in your lips with a matching shade of lip liner pencil. Or, put a tiny dab of foundation on a concealer brush and carefully trace the outline of your lipsticked lips to create the perfect finish.

Neutral lips attract attention when you give them a bit of sheer gloss. Experiment with sheer and opaque glosses to achieve the right amount of shine and perhaps a touch of tint. Always plan to wear a neutral lipstick to provide lasting color, rather than counting on endless touch-ups of shaded gloss. After you apply your lipstick, touch a small dab of lip gloss at the center of your bottom lip for perfect shine.

Natural Romantic Pink Lips: Experiment with different shades of pink lipstick; pinks may have undertones of blue or even orange that may clash with your skin tone. If you have small lips, a lighter shade of pink will make your lips look larger, while darker shades will make them look smaller. A pink lipstick with gloss containing shimmer provides that pretty, natural bridal look. If you have dark or olive skin, your pink tone may be more in the darker rose family, with perhaps a lilac undertone.

Choose a lip liner that is the same shade as your lip color for the most natural effect. Before using lip liner color to fill in your entire lip, moisturize your lips with a quality lip balm. If lipsticks bleed outside your lips due to fine lines, line your lips with a flesh-colored lip liner before applying your color. Practice often if you're not used to lining your own lips; a steady hand is essential to look your best.

Your gloss color doesn't have to match your lipstick color, so try a slightly lighter shade over your chosen pink tone for a custom hue. Rather than gloss your entire lips, just dab a bit of gloss on the center spot of your lower lip for pretty, subtle shine. A new trend is to wear a lighter, sheer gloss for your daytime ceremony hours, and then touch up with a slightly richer rose-colored tone for the evening hours.

Passionate Palette: If pale or pink lips is not the style you're after, you probably want a stunning red kisser for your dramatic wedding day look. More brides at formal, evening weddings are choosing the bright or berry red lip look, to coordinate with their lipstick red bouquets.

Try exploring a variety of colors—from cherry red to merlot—and choose the tones that work best with your coloring and your vision of a brighter lip look. Not every red looks fabulous on every person, due to undertones of blue or orange that might be revealed with a swipe of

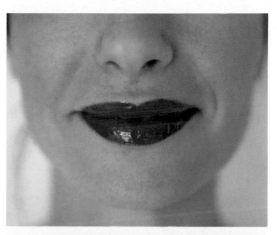

Photos by Kristen Jensen

a red lip color that looked amazing in the tube. When you blend a lip hue with your lips' natural color and add in your skin tone, you want an ideal effect. Your beauty expert will assess your skin tones and undertones and try out different shades on you, and your research will leave you well prepared to talk tones with him or her.

Red lipstick looks lovely in matte or a soft gloss, depending on your preferences. And, of course, the neatest of applications and touch-ups are required with so bold a hue. After all, your lips own your look, so your eyes should take on a more neutral and softer shade.

Who shouldn't wear red lipstick? Those who have small lips, since brighter red tones will only make small lips look smaller and more severe. And don't try to trick the system by applying red liner outside the lip line. That's a recipe for a clownish look.

Skin

Here is where you'll envision your complexion, your foundation, that flawless, fresh face that your groom will look upon with pure love and that will look celebrity gorgeous in person, in photos, and in your video. Movie stars' beautiful looks are created by teams of aestheticians and makeup stylists, and you too might choose to have a team of face-focused beauty experts guide you to your loveliest look.

It all starts with healthy skin that enjoys a regimen of cleaning, exfoliating, moisturizing, and—especially—regular sunscreen application so that your face becomes the perfect canvas for the next steps of bridal makeup magic. When your skin is moisturized, fine lines disappear and your skin plumps, ready to show off your chosen form of foundation to give you that youthful, glowing complexion that every bride desires.

Dewy Foundation: Using sheer products creates a natural effect that allows your skin to show through and still gives you a glow. Dewy skin shines on the cheekbones and temples and very lightly along the bridge of the nose and keeps its moist effect along the jawline. Shine is a no-no for the hollows beneath your eyes, however, so keep those gently powdered or blotted. Tinted moisturizer provides a healthy glow with a subtle touch of pigment.

Dewy doesn't mean oily, so make sure your shine is planned and placed correctly on your face. Too much shine on your nose and above your eyes makes you look greasy, so use blotting papers on those areas. Beware of going too matte on your T-zone, which can make your skin look dry and chalky next to your dewy cheekbones. Powder foundation brushes onto your T-zone for coverage and helps moderate shine as a touch-up product.

Choose your ideal foundation hue by sampling colors near your jawline. The best tone will disappear into your skin and provide coverage, not a change in color. The dewy look shines when you use a water-based liquid foundation and a cream blush—not a powder blush—to keep the shine uniform. To maximize dewiness,

Photo by Kristen Jensen

translucent sparkle that still lets you be a radiant bride. Matte is not usually a look for older brides with drier, crepey skin, because matte foundations and powders can be quite unforgiving. Whatever your age and dry-skin levels, you must have healthy, moisturized skin beneath this type of makeup.

Look for products labeled as "mousse matte foundation." Matte liquid foundation should be tailored to your skin type, such as a formula for oily or dry skin. Cream-to-powder foundations smooth on in moist form and then dry to a flattering matte powder. Airbrushing can deliver a matte look with your makeup stylist's expert selection of a matte foundation suited to your skin type.

dampen a fresh foundation sponge applicator with a little bit of water before using it to apply and blend in foundation.

Matte Foundation: The matte look eliminates shine, creating a flat, flawless face. You do need to guard against looking too dry or chalky, however, which can make you look older. Be sure to choose products specially formulated as matte coverage, because they do produce the slightest touch of sheen in a carefully created scientific method. Trying to "matte up" your face by applying layers of powder or using powder blush where it doesn't belong is an enormous, unflattering mistake.

If you have an oily complexion, you will likely find that the matte look gives you that fine, movie-star finish, with mineral makeup granting you exceptional coverage and a bit of

Use a lightweight matte product if you have normal skin. Use a powder foundation if you have oily or combination skin. Use oil-control makeup labeled as "no shine" if you have oily to combination skin. Loose powders, especially loose mineral powders, provide the most coverage in a true matte layer when applied with a fluffy dome brush.

Blotting papers will be your salvation, so pack lots of papers in your wedding day beauty emergency bag. Sweep your dome brush over mineral powder, shake off the excess, and apply light layers as needed. If you overapply touch-up powder, buff off excess with a clean makeup sponge or clean puff. Don't apply touch-ups with a puff swiped over a solid powder or creamy powder in a compact; scratch a bit of powder onto the mirror half of your compact and apply with your dome brush.

Beauty

Achieving the perfect look for your big day goes beyond just hair and makeup. As the bride—and therefore the center of attention—you want to be sure that everything else is also flawless—from skin to nails, even to your teeth! This section helps you out and gives you some great pointers along the way.

French Mani-Pedis

For years brides wore their nails in traditional French manicure style for their big day. It was the manicure of choice, and you rarely saw bridal nails in any other style. Now brides count the French manicure as being just one of many choices of nail style, with some sporting bright red nails to match their lipstick and the luscious red roses of their bouquet. Personal style extends from the gown to the hairstyle, to makeup and now to the nails.

The baby pink French manicure is no longer your only option. You can go pink, or you can go tan. That telltale white stripe at the ends of your nails can be whisper thin or it can be a bold thick stripe that really garners attention and maybe

even makes your fingers look longer and more delicate.

If you already go for your mani-pedi on a regular basis, the information here will help you bring your nail style to a new level. You may discover that a new tone or new band width gives you a more modern look.

Trial sessions aren't just for hair and makeup! Schedule a style consultation and a few practice sessions with your manicurist to select the best look for your big day and embark on a hand and foot smoothing and softening regimen for perfect skin on your big day . . . and the honeymoon!

A neutral-colored mani-pedi features pale shades of tan, sand, beige, and champagne. Neutral-colored nails provide the softest contrast with the white French manicure stripe. If you're planning to wear neutral shades of

Photo by Kristen Jensen

Do-It-Yourself French Manicure

Your DIY plan for creating your own French manicure should be inspired by the pros' attention to detail, use of the best products, and practice, practice, practice to get those noticeable accent lines just right and polish perfectly applied.

Begin by planning a few evening "spa" sessions at home for you to line up your French manicure supplies bought fresh from the beauty supply store, soak your feet, slough your heels with a Ped-Egg, and practice your French manicure skills on your fingernails and toenails. Many brides plan girls'-night spa get-togethers at which everyone sips Bellinis or sangria, snacks on spa fare such as veggies and hummus, and everyone does their own nails.

Next, follow these steps to begin your lessons in painting the perfect French manicure for your wedding day look and remember to take it easy on the caffeine—and the champagne!—on the morning of the wedding, or your hand-painted French manicure is doomed!

Preparing Your Nails

Soak your nails in warm, soapy water to soften them. Using a cuticle-shaping tool gently push your cuticles back but do not cut cuticles on your own or you might risk infection and finger injury. Next, shape your nails with an emery board followed by a gentle buff with a buffing block. Dab a bit of cuticle oil on your cuticles, let sit, and then use an orangewood stick to gently clear any dirt or nail dust from underneath your nails.

The First Coat

Apply an even clear base coat on each nail to fill in ridges and create a flawless surface for painting. Let the base coat dry fully; a too-quick application of the white-tip paint can blend or smudge. If you smudge base on the sides of your nails, wait until your nails are dry, then use a cotton swab for nails dipped in acetone nail polish remover to remove it. If your base coat comes out uneven, with some areas thicker than others, remove and start again.

Creating the Light Line

Experiment ahead of time with those little, white curved strips. Since they can leave ridges of color when removed, hand painting the white line is the preferable method. Use an ultrathin brush to give you control over your fine-line application. Dip the brush into the white polish, dab it on the bottle mouth to remove excess polish, and then draw a single line across the edge of your nail in your chosen thickness.

Polish and Finishing Coat

Allow the white line to dry, then use a cotton swab dipped in remover to carefully remove any white polish from the sides or front of your nails. Apply a thin coat of shaded polish on each nail, and allow them to dry fully. Apply a second coat of polish, let dry, then apply a layer of SPF-formula topcoat that protects your manicure from chipping or fading in the sun. Allow at least ten minutes of drying time

Photos by Kristen Jensen

Nail Colors

Photos by Kristen Jensen

Exercise & Nutrition

Most people could always do a bit more to be healthy, but with your wedding approaching, there has never been a better time to take great care of yourself and enjoy a big dose of TLC. A healthy diet and regular exercise will give you the energy and clarity of mind to be creative and keep track of details as you plan your wedding, and when your big day arrives, you'll feel fit and fabulous when all eyes are on you.

Treat yourself to a healthy diet, which revolves around loads of water, fresh fruits, vegetables, lean proteins, and whole grains. Look for brightly colored fruits and vegetables, which are rich in heart-healthy antioxidants. Protein keeps you fuller longer, so start your day with eggs, yogurt, or tofu in your breakfast. Dark green vegetables like kale, chard, broccoli, and green beans are packed with vitamins, high in fiber, and low in calories, so you'll stay satisfied longer. Get quick energy from powerful carbohydrates in whole grains like brown rice, wild rice, whole wheat, and oatmeal. Approach desserts and alcohol with moderation, and take a multivitamin or vitamin supplements if you feel that your diet is lacking in nutrients. If you want to make a big shift in the way you're living, talk with your doctor or nutritionist to be sure you're on the right path for you.

Get active, have fun, and make yourself feel good! Make time to take a dance class, take a walk, get to the gym, or play your favorite sport, even if your schedule seems unmanageable. The

makeup, neutral-colored nails will complete your soft, ethereal look. If you're planning to carry pastel- or bright-colored flowers, neutral nails look soft and bridal in comparison, especially in those close-up photos. Short fingernails look best in paler shades of neutral, as opposed to brights.

French mani-pedis in pink range from barely there blush pink to a brighter cotton candy pink. Keep pink shades on the pale side, because brighter color shades contrast too harshly with the white French stripe. If you're planning to wear pink shades of makeup, your pink French mani-pedi coordinates perfectly with the soft, romantic princess look. If you're planning a bouquet of white flowers or a collection of pink flowers, a pink-based manicure coordinates your look in person and in pictures.

Photo by Kristen Jensen

not make it a team effort? Teach each other the activities you love and grow your common interests for a long and fun future together. Biking, rollerblading, and hiking are great activities to do as a pair. Just getting outside and throwing a Frisbee or taking a walk will get you moving and let you spend quality time together. Staying active together is a great way to connect, especially now when you have so much to celebrate. It's also a great way to start healthy traditions that you can continue to enjoy all the way through your marriage. Encourage each other to get enough sleep. Being well rested supports physical and emotional health in a big way.

Savvy Skin Care

Everyone's skin is different, so no two people are guaranteed to love the same products. Finding the skin-care system that's right for you can be a fun and pampering process. Its success goes hand in hand with your healthy lifestyle choices, so take good care of yourself, inside and out.

The same things that are good for the body are also good for the skin. Regular exercise

time spent being active will give you energy for all the things on your to-do list. Yoga will strengthen your body as well as calm your mind during this busy time. Use exercise as a stress reliever if your schedule begins to feel overwhelming. Think about the areas of your body that your wedding dress is going to accentuate and target your strength training so you'll be excited to show them off. Take small stretching and movement breaks throughout your workday to maintain good circulation, posture, and strength and to ward off fatigue. If you could use some motivation and moral support, find a "bridal boot camp" or fitness class for brides to be. There's nothing like good friends to help you reach your goals.

Exercising on your own isn't the only way to go. You both need to feel your best, so why

Everyone knows by now that tanning the old-fashioned way can lead to serious skin damage. If you want a sun-kissed look on your wedding day, experiment with sunless spray tanning in the months leading up to the big day to see which system works best with your complexion.

pumps blood to the skin, the body's biggest organ. Good nutrition and lots of water also keeps the body looking healthy and hydrated. Getting enough sleep gives the skin time to repair and rejuvenate, and steering clear of cigarettes and too much alcohol is a necessity for a glowing complexion.

Beauty products abound for every purpose under the sun. Cover your bases with a complete basic regimen. Washing your makeup off every night keeps your pores from clogging. Washing too often, or with water that's too hot, can strip natural moisture from your skin and dry you out. Find a great cleanser to gently remove makeup and toxins morning and night, an exfoliation system to encourage new cells to shine through, and a moisturizer to soften your skin and create a smooth base for your makeup. Gel-based cleansers do a better job at removing makeup, but cream-based cleansers are more moisturizing for dry skin. A deep-cleansing facial can work wonders, but leave at least a few days for your skin to recover before your wedding day. After the daily cleanse you can focus on any issues that you want to improve. From acne and psoriasis to redness and irritation, there are products and information out there to help treat any issue.

A regular exfoliating routine will help you look your best and glow with happiness on your wedding day. Gentle scrubs with tiny particles and microdermabrasion are great for removing dead cells from your skin's top layer. Alpha and beta hydroxy acids and retinoids go one step

further, exfoliating as well as helping with the production of collagen. Use toners that act as humectants, which help your moisturizer penetrate your skin. Avoid products that contain alcohol.

For daytime, choose a moisturizer with SPF 30 to protect your skin from everyday sun damage. Apply a vitamin- and nutrient-rich moisturizer before going to bed. Two-thirds of the body is made up of water. Drinking at least eight glasses of this elixir a day is a must for healthy, hydrated skin. If you live in an extremely dry climate, use a humidifier in your home to add moisture to the air.

Treat acne on your shoulders, chest, and back with an acne-fighting body wash or body "facials" so you'll feel fabulously confident in your wedding dress. For serious issues and the

© photo by Junebug Weddings

best advice, visit a dermatologist to formulate a skin-care plan. Stress can wreak havoc on your skin. Find nourishing ways to relax and enjoy this exciting time. Love is a powerful beauty treatment. As the one getting married, you're guaranteed to look stunning on your wedding day, no matter what!

Additional Beauty Tips

In addition to all the basics that we've covered in this section—from eyes to lips to skin—here are a few more things to consider when prepping for your big day.

Waxing: Waxing has long been a popular method of removing unsightly hairs from the face and body, and because your wedding day calls for flawless skin, you may be among the many brides who seek expert wax treatments.

If you've done your own waxing using home kits, you might decide to stick with your DIY method, or you might choose to indulge in a professional aesthetician's flawless work as part of your pampering plan. An experienced waxing professional at a salon has training with the method and the ability to "read" your skin, assess it as dry or sensitive, and tailor the method and materials to produce better results than you may be able to produce on your own.

Another reason to consider expert waxing when you've used home wax strips with good results: Sometimes a wax strip can pull off some skin along with hair, leaving an ugly red wound on your lip or eyebrow. For this important day,

and for the honeymoon to follow, you might decide to seek the services of a professional you have tested out far before the wedding day to assess his or her technique and results.

Never wax the day of or the day before the wedding, because redness or irritation can occur, even if you've been waxed a hundred times before. Plan your waxing session for at least a week before the wedding—some pros suggest two weeks.

Teeth Whitening: Your smile will warm your groom's heart and dazzle your guests, not to mention be captured for all eternity in your wedding photos and video. So make sure your smile shows off pretty white teeth by treating yours to an easy whitening process.

Many brides are surprised to find that their teeth are actually not as white as they could be. Certain shades of lipstick will make nearly white teeth look yellow, too, so guard against a tooth-shade disaster by taking a close look at your pearly whites to make sure they're not stained.

Your possibilities range from simple whitening toothpaste to strips to more extensive treatments offered by your dentist. And beauty salons now offer revolutionary processes that can brighten your smile after just one or two visits. So there is a way to get a brighter smile that fits your budget, time, and comfort level.

You want your smile to shine for each and every event leading up to your wedding weekend—including the taking of engagement photos, bridal showers, and bridesmaid get-togethers, so it's never too early to start your tooth-whitening regimen.

Certain healthy, natural foods can help you whiten your teeth. Snacking on apples, celery, broccoli, strawberries, and spinach increases your saliva production, which can clear away stains, and you get healthy nutrients from them, too.

Self-Tanning and Bronzing: Baking out in the sun is no way to get a tan. You risk deadly melanoma at the worst, surgery and scarring if you get another form of skin cancer, or sunspots and dark patches. Plus, too much sun exposure can cause premature aging of the skin.

You don't want to be a tangerine bride, nor do you want the stress and distress of a tanning nightmare right before your wedding day. So proceed with caution, and vow to take safer steps to getting that golden glow. Always investigate ingredients in self-tanning lotions and ask plenty of questions at salons if getting spray tanned or using a tanning bed.

Sunless tanning products have been on the market since the 1960s, and those earliest formulas have since been vastly improved to deliver natural-looking tanned skin. These are still chemicals, though, so be very careful about which brands you trust. And be aware that although tanning pills are on store shelves, they have not been approved by the FDA for safe use; some have even been linked to hepatitis and yellow deposits in the eye, and because a pill is absorbed by the body, the chemicals do work their way through the internal organs. Simply put, there is no magic pill for getting a tan.

Emergency Fixes

Didn't your mother always tell you it's better to be prepared in life than not prepared? The same advice goes for the wedding day itself. As Murphy's Law predicts, sometimes the worst thing that could possibly happen does happen. (But don't worry—it usually doesn't!) So this section will help you take all the precautions to fix any possible glitch that might come up during your otherwise perfect big day.

Photo by Kristen Jensen

Wedding Day Survival Kit

With all the hustle and bustle a wedding day brings, there are sure to be moments when you need some helpful supplies to assist with the issue at hand. Thinking ahead and either purchasing or putting together a good collection of beauty, health, and emergency items to have available on your wedding day will save you lots of worry and may, in fact, save the day!

A lot of thought has gone into getting your look just right for your wedding, but if your day begins early and your celebration ends late, you will probably need to freshen up your hair and makeup at some point to stay looking your best. Just a few beauty basics can really come in handy.

If you're getting dressed and ready at a hotel or another location away from home, you may miss some of the everyday items you keep in your medicine cabinet but rarely think about as important. To ward off headaches, settle the butterflies in your stomach, file a broken nail, moisten dry contacts, or take care of any other common occurrences, keep a collection of "emergency" supplies available for the both of you, your family, and your wedding party.

As you're planning the schedule for your wedding day, don't forget to consider what you're going to eat before your reception. Your wedding day is no time to run on an empty stomach! Make yummy snacks for everyone part of the

Freshening Up	Basic makeup supplies like concealer, powder, blush, and lip gloss always come in handy for touch-ups. Pack small bottles of hairspray, bobby pins, barrettes, and hair bands in case someone's hairdo needs a little assistance. If your wedding is in the hot summer months, have simple folding paper fans available to help keep everyone cool. Bring along your toothbrush, or at least some breath mints, so you're confident when it's time to kiss.
In Case of Emergency	"Emergency" extras like pain relievers, antacids, feminine hygiene products, and deodorant are all worth having nearby, just in case. A collection of various supplies like tissues, cotton swabs, eyedrops, nail files, and drinking straws are smart additions that are nice to have when you need them. Just a touch of clear nail polish can stop pantyhose from running and the ends of ribbon from unraveling. Pack Band-Aids, sports tape, or moleskin to help ward off blisters.
Take Care of Yourself	Have plenty of water on hand for the two of you, your family, and your wedding party so no one gets dehydrated. Plan to have food available, but put someone else in charge of transporting it. Even if nerves have made you lose your appetite, eat anyway to help maintain your energy. Be extra careful not to go overboard with your alcohol consumption if you're enjoying celebratory drinks.
Your Sewing Kit	A simple sewing kit containing needles, scissors, and both light and dark thread can be a lifesaver for loose buttons, broken straps, and falling hems. Safety pins in numerous sizes are multipurpose tools for fashion or decor hiccups. White chalk can be used to temporarily color over many stains on a white wedding dress. Double-sided tape is helpful for keeping plunging necklines and loose straps under control.

fun of getting ready, and you'll have a wedding party that's happy, with energy to spare.

Straps break, buttons fall off, and invariably a groomsman forgets his socks. Be sure you have a basic sewing kit on hand as well as other supplies like pins, tape, stain remover, and, of course, black men's dress socks, for easy fashion fixes.

Flat & Floppy Hair

You have the most gorgeous wedding hairstyle in the world at ten in the morning, but by the time the midday sun and summer humidity hit you, your hair has turned flat, floppy, and wilted. Those glamorous curls are now barely waves, and that sidesweep of bangs now lays lifeless against your cheek.

How do you fix flat and floppy hair on your wedding day? You're about to find out. On these pages you will learn the first of many emergency fixes.

With a great plan in place—including a plan B style that you can sweep your hair into for your reception if your hair is determined to lose its height and curl—you won't have to spend hours at your computer, obsessively checking the temperature and humidity predictions for your wedding day. You'll know you have all your options considered—that your smart style plans made ahead of time will deliver you from the stress and worry of what the weather is going to do to your wedding day beauty.

At your trial-run session, tell your stylist about your concerns regarding your hair going flat and try out upswept styles that don't depend on volume. A half-up/half-down style eliminates fear of frontal flat and floppies. A sleek chignon, ponytail, or elegant French twist pinned into place is by nature floppy-proof. Choose a realistic second style for the later hours of your reception, perhaps letting down that deflated updo and sweeping your hair back into a ponytail accented with a jeweled clip.

Bring your hair stylist photos of your styled hair taken a few hours into a prior event you attended, and also create a voluminous updo before your appointment so that he or she can feel and see how your hair holds. Knowing your hair's "personality" helps your stylist devise a flop-prop plan for your hair.

When you know your hair gets floppy after a few hours, plan for structural support. Ask your stylist to use extra bobby pins to hold underneath layers and curls. Experiment with undersupport products such as Bumpits that are placed underneath your held-up crown hair. Back-combed hair—also known as teased hair—creates volume in your style, so touch up your volume by teasing your hair gently with your fingers throughout the day.

Use volumizing shampoo and conditioner in formulas specified for your hair type and thickness. Use large hot rollers to give your hair extra volume naturally, and—most important—allow each one to cool completely so that it will hold the curl and volume perfectly. Apply root-lifting spray to your roots to add extra oomph to your crown. Too much product will weigh your hair down, so ask your stylist how you can achieve lasting volume without too much spray.

For on-site fixes, use your fingers! Running a brush through your hair will not only pull out your curls and separate smooth sections, it can make your hair frizzy and dry looking. Spritz on styling spray and give your hair a few quick hand squeezes all over to refresh your volume, waves, and curls. For an upsweep or high ponytail or chignon, push your hairstyle forward—lifting that crown volume again—and apply hairspray to firm the hold. Enlist a bridesmaid to use your curling iron or flatiron to freshen your curls.

Frizzy Hair

When hair frizzes out, it's going to show in person and in photographs, and professional photographers say that frizzy hair is one of the hardest—if not the hardest—flaws to correct in photos. For any bridal style, you want smooth, flawless hair, not a mass of flyaways and frizzies that make you look messy and out of control.

For this style danger, the key is preventive action—and lots of it. Tell your stylist that your hair tends to get frizzy during hot or humid weather, or any time at all, and together you'll create a plan, including defrizz products and treatments, to get your hair in shape.

Even if you've had frizzy hair forever, you might not be aware what's causing it. It's not just the weather. It's the way supertiny slivers of your hair arch away from the hair cuticle and hair shaft, creating the unwanted texture of frizz. When your hair is dry and not adequately conditioned, or it's been overheated with a blow-dryer or curling iron and flatiron, it's a disaster waiting to happen when humidity adds to the problem by removing even more moisture from your hair shafts.

Photo by Kristen Jensen

Here's how to beat frizz and form a pretty plan for your wedding day hairstyle. Frizzy hair is also the result of damage and breakage to the hair shaft caused by the things you do to it. Start wearing your everyday ponytails looser, and never pull a ponytail in two sections to tighten its hold. Also, show your stylist the brush you use, since the wrong brush may be what's causing your hair shafts to split.

Every style can be affected by frizzies, so there isn't any one style that is the cure-all. If you have frizzy hair, avoid sleek, slick-backed hair, as the smooth texture will show any frizzies and flyaways. A half-up/half-down style can be your rescue for frizzies, since smoother parts lead to the headpiece and the down style left curly can be most flattering. If your style has given in to the frizzies, take down your updo and get out your frizz-smoothing ceramic or tourmaline-plated curling or flatiron to create your fresh second look for the reception.

Use a humectant product to promote moisture retention. Humectants attract water from the atmosphere and bind the moisture molecules to the hair shaft. Use antifrizz shampoos, conditioners, and styling sprays and serums to coat your formerly frizzy hair for a softer, smoother style. You don't have to buy expensive salon products, since many everyday brands like Suave, Dove, and Pantene offer antifrizz products that pro stylists say work well for your hair-care ritual.

An up or down do designed to complement a dramatic headpiece may reveal only a fraction of your hair. If you're worried about frizzies, plan to keep your veil on during the reception to lightly obscure your back lengths. If frizzies burst out of your sidesweep, borrow a celebrity secret and pop on a stylish headband to sweep up and hold your hair. A sideswept bang that has gone frizzy gets a rescue with the fresh accenting of a jeweled barrette.

Pulled-Out Pieces

Uh-oh. Your magnificently sculptured updo took a bump when you climbed into the limousine, and now there's a curl out of place. Or, you and your bridesmaids wrapped your arms around each other for a prewedding photo, and someone's ring got caught in your sleek chignon sweepback, pulling a strand right out of that perfect style.

Photo by Kristen Jensen

While some brides have the benefit of their professional stylist staying with them until the moment of their walk down the aisle, most brides are on their own. When your hair is so elegantly and painstakingly styled in a flawless flow and a graceful updo, every hair literally needs to remain in place for the big moments of your ceremony and reception. After all, they will all be captured forever in memories and in photographs.

If your hair falls apart during your big day, that's what everyone will be looking at. That is what will detract from your beauty in your wedding photos and video. So make a style rescue plan now, and rest easy on your wedding day knowing that you can put any fallen pieces back in their perfect positions.

Practice makes perfect, so do your own trial runs of sweeping your hair up into a ponytail or twist, picking out a small hair escapee, and practicing with your supply of small bobby pins to get your hair-hiding method perfected with confidence.

A wide-toothed comb (what we like to call the "Tool That Saves") allows you to smooth that piece and recapture your original, sleek hairstyle. A spiral curling iron can turn a side or back escapee into a style-flattering ringlet to match the others in your style. A narrow-plated flatiron can reflatten that pulled-out piece for a smooth, invisible tuck-in. Small bobby pins that match your hair color are your number one style saver and securing tool for fixing pulled-out pieces.

Spritz some medium-hold hairspray on your fingertips and smooth that escaped section before pinning it back in. Hair-smoothing gel is not going to help you smooth that piece back into place. A tiny, tiny dab of styling wax can help you finger wave that lock back into your wavy updo. A fresh, all-over spray of medium-hold hairspray will coat your entire style and set that returned piece into your do.

A pretty jeweled barrette or clip will turn that troublesome short piece into a style spotlight. If you've placed accent snaps and screw-ins throughout your style, secure a pulled-out piece with one of the extra screw-ins or snaps from your beauty emergency bag. Sweep the pulled-out piece to the side using an "alligator clip." Use a splay comb that features many

crystals on wires in a pretty arch as your second look for the reception.

Lipstick Fixes

Whether or not you'll have your makeup professionally done, you're on your own when your lip color fades or smudges throughout your wedding day. Or, if you are your own makeup stylist on your wedding day, these lip-color application mistakes need professional-quality fixes immediately. After all, lipstick smudges outside the lip line are tough to remove fully and can cause panic, and you don't want telltale patches of pink or caked-on cover-up announcing to your guests that you flubbed your makeup application.

Ask a bridesmaid to alert you when it's time to touch up your lip look. And, of course, repair any lip color smudges or disappeared gloss right

Photo by Kristen Jensen

Photo by Kristen Jensen

this new layer over the smudge. If your lipstick turns out too dark, apply a beige or peachy pink shade to soften. If your lip color turns out pale, apply a slightly darker lip liner color and fill in your lips with it, then reapply your original shade.

Applying just enough lipstick and gloss to create your look, and blotting away extra, will keep color off your teeth. Open your mouth only slightly as you apply lip color and you'll apply the right amount to your lips, rather than to the inside

before your photographer calls you over to take pictures so that your wedding day photos show only lip perfection.

If you slip outside your lip line with lip pencil, don't try to even it out by copying the line on the other side, thinking it will look balanced; remove your first try and start over again.

If your lipstick smudges or bleeds, remove it with a dampened angled-end cotton swab, and reapply. For light-colored smudges, clean your applicator in makeup remover, dip into foundation, dab excess onto a tissue, then swab

of your lips. After applying lipstick and gloss, stick one finger in your mouth, press your lips around it, and pull your finger out to remove any lip color from your inner lips.

Apply a small dot of gloss onto your bottom lip and spread with a fingertip. If lip gloss feels slimy or looks too shiny, switch to moistening lip balm that stays longer. Keep a lip gloss in your handbag and touch up from time to time when you're at your table. If shaded lip gloss is ruining your lip color, remove all of your lipstick, reapply foundation and lipstick, and switch to a clear gloss.

Chapter 4

PHOTOGRAPHY, VIDEOGRAPHY & ENTERTAINMENT

With so many lovely memories unfolding before your very eyes on your wedding day, it's important that you have someone reliable on hand to help you capture them. Picking the perfect photographer—and videographer, if you so choose—will be an important part of your wedding planning process. The same goes for picking the entertainment for your day. These three items may seem like a bit of "behind the scenes" work in the grand journey of wedding planning, but you'll find that both during and after your wedding they will be the basis of your memories from your day.

Whether you choose a DJ or a band to play music at your ceremony and/or your reception, your photographer and videographer will be there to capture the joy your guests have in being entertained by them. It's important to find entertainment that suits your needs—be it funky and lively or more formal and classical—and will be there to stir your guests into a frenzy and make moments happen on the dance floor.

Your photographer should be someone who you feel comfortable with, and who understands your overall vision. Be sure your photographer is well prepped ahead of time with a list of "must get" shots, the important players, and a general timeline of when the important events, such as the cake cutting, are to take place. Same goes for your videographer.

While you may want to cut cost corners with these three items, be careful not to

© photo by Positive Light Photography

sacrifice quality for cost. If you think you'll save money by cutting the DJ or band and replacing it with an iPod or MP3 player, think through this decision carefully—your entertainment plays a big part of your overall wedding day, and you want to be sure you're fulfilling your guests' (and your) needs. And while it may seem cost-effective to hire your best friend who also happens to be gifted with a camera as your photographer, again, think twice. You'll want your friend to be able to enjoy your day as a guest, not an employee. It just might be better to leave these three items to the professionals. This chapter provides you with all the information you need to be sure you're hiring the right ones for your needs.

DETERMINING YOUR VISUAL STYLE

When it comes to picking your visual style for your photos and videos, there are several choices to make, from choosing classic photography or photojournalism, or perhaps a mix of both. This next section differentiates each style for you and provides you with photo examples of each type so you can pick the perfect visual look for your perfect day.

Classic Photography

When your wedding is long over, your pictures will remain to remind you of your big day and the important people who shared it with you, so schedule some time in your day for classic photography that focuses on families and the two of you together.

While traditional photography has given way to photojournalism over the last few decades, today's classic photos are a new kind of gorgeous, and traditional arrangements are still expected by most members of your parents' and grandparents' generations. If you have a large family, your wedding may provide a rare opportunity to get everyone together for a complete family photo. What an excellent time to also get beautiful portraits of your parents and grandparents, and what a beautiful way to show them how much they mean to you.

In addition to capturing people, classic photography also captures places, from country meadows to urban cathedrals, from beautiful ballrooms to family backyards. After all, where you choose to have your wedding is important to you and is bound to become more so once

© photo by J. Garner Photography

you're married. A great wedding photographer will be able to create artistic classic photos of the people and places that made your wedding special and provide you with heirloom images you'll treasure.

When you're having your picture taken, have fun, relax, and breathe. You'll feel better and look better. Your favorite wedding portraits are priceless, so be sure you have copies made of them. Store them in an archival box between sheets of acid-free paper. If you feel uncomfortable in front of the camera but you want a classic portrait, let your photographer know. He or she should have lots of ways to put you at ease.

A well-posed shot doesn't have to be boring. A good photographer connects with people and creates photos with personality. Chances are your family portrait is the one you'll still have hanging on your wall when you celebrate your golden anniversary. To create your family photo list, write down your immediate family members and grandparents first. Talk to your photographer about the time necessary for those photos, and then add other family members according to your schedule.

Bridal party photos are where classic portraiture gets really creative! Photographers feel more inclined to be playful when they're taking photos of your bridal party. As you're having your photo taken throughout the day, stand up straight and smile, but don't hold your breath or

© photo by La Vie Photography

© photo by J. Garner Photography

lock your knees. Be sure to let your photographer know if you want individual portraits with members of your bridal party, and then factor those into your schedule.

© photo by J. Garner Photography

Every posed portrait you request will take your photographer five to ten minutes to set up, depending on the size of your group. Very large family groups can take substantially longer. Schedule your photography time accordingly and consider how much time is too much for you or your guests.

Landscape and architectural photography add yet another dimension to classic wedding photos. Large backdrops like territorial views and landmarks, and small backdrops like stairways and bridges, set the stage for classic portraits. It's become commonplace for photographers to take photos of couples in various locations prior to their wedding and during the time between their ceremony and reception. Let your photographer know if you have some special spots where you would like to stop for photos along the way.

Photojournalism

Photojournalistic wedding photography tells the story of your wedding day and allows you to see through a lens why there is nothing more beautiful than real life and real relationships. After all, what could be more precious than your dad crying, your grandma groovin', or your getaway car being decorated with tin cans and pink polka dots?

An outstanding photojournalistic photographer understands how important your special moments are and captures them for you to keep for the rest of your life.

As part of their photography package, most photojournalists will begin shooting while you're getting ready, to capture the anticipation and beauty of your transformation into a bride. They'll take a low-key approach with their involvement and know where you are throughout your day, although you may not notice them until you need them. By observing and anticipating, they take photos at what famous

© photo by Positive Light Photography

photographer Henri Cartier-Bresson called "the decisive moment."

Some of the most special photos of your day will be taken when you put on your dress and see yourself as a bride for the first time. Don't rush this moment! If you have a photography team, or enough extra time, get coverage of the guys getting ready as well. Let your photographer know if there is anything you don't want photographed. Authentic photojournalism doesn't have to include pictures of you in your underwear with your hair in curlers.

The joy and tears of your wedding day are the subjects of emotional photojournalistic photography. In addition to reminding you of your most emotional memories, a good photojournalist will show you moments at your wedding that you never had a chance to see. If you know that your brother is going to bust a move on the dance floor and that your maid of honor

---

Look for Experience

Photojournalism became all the rage in the 1990s when fast-speed films and digital photography allowed any photographer to capture images on the run. Experienced photographers began to take more spontaneous artistic shots, and amateurs jumped into the field by the thousands. Be sure your photographer has extensive experience and personal references.

© photo by La Vie Photography

© photo by GH Kim Photography

his or her candid shots with emotion and makes posed shots look spontaneous.

The picture on the left of the bride dancing with her father discreetly captures the joy, trust, and love in their relationship. The best documentary shots happen when you don't know they're being taken. If you're not posing for a picture, keep your eye off the camera and enjoy your day. Once your reception begins, a photojournalist will melt into the background. You will need to request any posed shots you want throughout the night.

Alert your photographer ahead of time if a special surprise will be part of your ceremony or reception. Passionate photojournalists don't let a little rain, or even a big lightning storm, get in the way of their photography. If you're into being out in it, they'll capture it. Life is full of the unexpected, and your wedding day is no different. With the right photographer, your unexpected moments will become images to treasure.

Videography Styles

Today's leading videographers capture your day as it unfolds, then edit the moments to create a moving story of the most important highlights and events. Unlike still photographers, they're able to capture the sights and sounds of your wedding day and add music to create atmosphere and transitions. A skilled and talented videographer can create a truly artistic short film that will make you laugh, cry, and watch it again and again.

is going to weep during her speech, let your photographer know ahead of time.

For the best coverage, choose a photographer who mixes classic photography, photojournalism, and commercial photography techniques. Look for a talented artist who fills

Classic-style videographers usually set up vignettes, interview guests, and include footage of your entire ceremony from the processional to the recessional. More photojournalistic videographers usually do not include posed shots. They edit for overall artistic impact and don't always present an entirely linear chain of events. However, almost all videographers will present you with a DVD that is forty-five to ninety minutes in length, including easy-to-navigate menus that take you from one part of your day to the next.

Classic: Classic videographers often interview guests and family members. Some add montages of the bride's and groom's childhood photos to the final product as well. Ask that there be at least two cameras operating during your ceremony and reception to cover events coming and going. Be sure your videographer uses wireless microphones so all of your ceremony will be recorded. Expect to wait several months for your video to be edited and ready.

Photojournalistic: A photojournalist will be with you as the day goes by. You may catch his or her eye occasionally, but for the most part he or she will be invisible. Try to forget that the camera is on you, and the footage will show off your authentic personality. If you have favorite music you want included in your video, let your videographer know before your wedding. It may actually inspire him or her to create something that complements it perfectly.

Photo by Kristen Jensen

© photo by La Vie Photography

DECIDING THE DETAILS

Believe it or not, there are a lot of details that go into figuring out the photography and videography for your wedding. First and foremost is to sift through the list of photographers and videographers in your area to determine who will work best for you. We suggest you get recommendations, from friends, family, or other vendors. Many hires often come through word-of-mouth referrals, so if your cousin mentions that her photographer was "amazing," then it's worth your while to check him out.

Be sure to write down things that are important to you, or any and all questions you might have, before you visit the potential hires. This will make the meetings efficient and ensure that you get your questions answered. We also recommend tailoring your list of people to see, culling the list to about three people per position. This way you're not overwhelmed with the list, and you can make informed, calm decisions based off of your needs.

Fashion & Details

By combining fashion and commercial photography techniques, a great wedding photographer creates images that showcase your look and the details that compose your wedding style. You'll spend tons of time choosing your dress, your shoes, your jewelry, and your bridal party fashions, so why not have some photos that really highlight your choices?

Fashion-forward photos focus on the shape, texture, color, and details of garments and accessories—and the attitudes of the people wearing them. Makeup and hairstyles are highlighted and backgrounds are carefully considered even when photos are not posed. Your photographer will probably require extra time before your ceremony to take fashion and bridal portraits, so be sure to add time to your schedule. If more time isn't possible, just remember to keep your shoulders back, your face relaxed, and your smile at the ready, and you'll get lots of stylish photos that happen naturally.

To add the finishing touch, your photographer will focus on the important details that make your wedding unique. From your cake to your calla lilies, from your grandmother's charm bracelet to the vows you keep practicing again and again, a truly outstanding photographer will have your wedding covered from beginning to end.

Group Style: The photo below focuses on the style of the bridal party and looks like it came straight out of a fashion magazine. Rather than lining everyone up in a tight line that obscures the edges of dresses and suits, the photographer arranged this bridal party in a way that highlights their attire. Notice how the background was carefully chosen to complement the style of the wedding and the color of the fashions worn.

© photo by GH Kim Photography

Personal Style: Does being a fashion model sound like fun to you? Then go for it and strike a pose! For a flawless finish, have a trial run of your hair and makeup and consider having your

© photo by Yours by John Photography

website that features real weddings, details will play an important part in telling the story of your wedding day. Send in lots of photos with your submission.

Sentimental Details: Mail your invitation, programs, and other paper products to your photographer prior to your wedding so he or she can photograph them in advance of your day. Photos of invitations, Ketubahs, and vows make great opening page shots for your album. Be sure to let your photographer know about

teeth whitened. While fashion has become an integral part of today's artistic wedding photography, boudoir photography is now also on the rise. Many brides are having tasteful photos taken of themselves in luscious lingerie to give to their groom on their wedding night.

Fashionable Details: Special jewelry and sentimental accessories can be photographed on or off your body. Your photographer will use detail photos to add interest and style to your wedding album. If you're interested in having your wedding published in a magazine or on a

> To ensure your photographer captures the things that are most important to you, you'll want to create a comprehensive list of the images you're looking for. Keep in mind, though, that your photographer can only capture these images if the people and items in them are willing and available.

any items of significant sentimental value to you that might get overlooked: a family heirloom, a special gift from your groom, a personal memento. Ask him or her to capture them creatively.

Hiring a Pro

With so much to cover on your wedding day, how do you find the one photographer you're looking for, the one with the style, personality, pricing, and packages that will exceed your expectations? Begin by searching the Internet and asking for recommendations from friends

© photo by Yours by John Photography

and family. Pick at least five photographers whose style you adore, then meet with each one to see how well you connect. Ask to see portfolios of several full weddings so you get an idea of how each photographer will capture your day and how he or she interprets each wedding differently. Ask lots of questions and be absolutely clear about what you're paying for: how much time, how many prints, and what extras are included in each package, as well as whether he or she will be shooting digital, film, or a combination of both.

Make sure you get a signed copy of your contract from your photographer when you make your final decision. Ask what equipment your photographer works with, how much backup equipment will be carried, and what guarantee will be provided if he or she is unable to shoot your wedding due to an emergency.

Extras, like albums, enlargements, and additional photos, can add up quickly. Ask your photographer to let you know how much an average client spends on these items.

Your photographer will probably spend more time with you on your wedding day than anyone else you hire. Be sure you enjoy being around this person and trust him or her to capture you the way you want to be seen. Having engagement photos taken is a great way to connect with your photographer, get comfortable in front of the camera, and get great shots of the two of you before you're married.

Wedding photography has become a wildly popular career choice of late. No matter what style, process, or package you're looking for, you're bound to encounter a wide range of pricing and photographic quality that ranges from amateurish to truly artistic.

© photo by Junebug Weddings

Digital versus film is a debate that has been going on since the late 1980s, and over the last thirty years technology has changed dramatically. Early on there was no question that film was of superior quality, but with the advent of new top-of-the-line cameras, lenses, and software, there is now little or no practical difference in the quality between digital and film. In addition, most digital photographers offer client galleries on their websites where your friends and family can view your photos And

© photos by Junebug Weddings

because digital photographers have the option to edit and print only the best shots through a process devoid of chemicals, it's a less wasteful and cleaner option for the environment.

Digital photography allows photographers to take thousands of photos in a day and instantly see the results. To print beautiful quality digital prints and enlargements, you need high-resolution files. Find out if high-res files are included in your package or if you'll need to purchase them separately. As in film photography, the processing and printing of an image helps determine its quality. Good digital photographers are highly skilled in "digital dark-room" techniques.

Many artistic wedding photographers own large- or medium-format that produce large negatives. These are still the preferred choice for enlargements beyond 16x20. Safely store your film negatives in archival acid-free sleeves, out of direct sunlight, and in a cool place where the temperature and humidity are not likely to

dramatically change. Some people just love the idea of film. It simply appeals to their nostalgic, romantic side.

Narrow your search down to at least three videographers whose work you love. Ask the other professionals you've hired who they would recommend. Your photographer and wedding consultant should be particularly helpful in this regard. Don't rely on online examples to make your decision. Be sure you see at least three full

© photo by La Vie Photography

wedding DVDs. Watch for quality throughout and smooth transitions, and eliminate anyone with inconsistent camera or audio work.

While it may be tempting to ask a close friend or family member to capture your wedding video, here are two big reasons not to: You'll want them to enjoy your day as a guest, and the editing that goes into finishing a quality video can take substantial amounts of time and skill.

Albums & Enlargements

With a seemingly endless array of options and prices at your fingertips, choosing your wedding album can be almost as challenging as choosing your photographer. Look for an album that will stand the test of time while showing off the style of your wedding day.

Classic, timeless wedding photos look right at home in traditional albums filled with matted pages and covered in leather or high-quality fabric. Couples and their families usually work with their photographer to choose the photos included in these heirloom-style albums. The couple's names and wedding date are often engraved on the front or back cover.

Making your own album can be a fun way to create a one-of-a-kind heirloom and save money at the same time. If you're savvy with publishing software, you can lay out your own album and have it printed. Or, if you're good

with your hands, you can create and bind an album with fabrics and notions found in framing and craft stores.

In addition to, or instead of, an album, many couples design creative displays of their wedding photo collections to romantically adorn their bedrooms or to add portraits to their wall of family photos to carry on a sentimental tradition.

When it comes time to make your enlargements, you will need the high-resolution digital files or film negatives. Be sure you understand if these items are included in your photography package.

Traditional Album Styles: Today's albums tell the story of your wedding day, even if they're filled with classic photos. Whether your photos are film or digital, most photographers prefer to use a mixture of black-and-white and color photos to make your album more interesting.

© photo by Junebug Weddings

© photo by Yours by John Photography

© photo by Yours by John Photography

For most of the last century, classic albums had a vellum overlay on each page to protect photos from dust and scratches. Some people still prefer that design for its protection and formal look.

Flush-Mount Albums: In recent years flush-mount or "magazine-style" albums have become popular with couples and photographers. Usually the photographer or an album-design company creates artistic page layouts that include single or multiple photos per page. The images are printed directly on the finished pages, creating a bound album that makes a perfect coffee-table book you can leave out for guests to enjoy.

Digital photographers are more likely than film photographers to offer flush-mount albums, but these albums are available for both mediums. Flush-mount albums can look simple and clean, or be full of collages and manipulated images. Think carefully before ordering an album that will look dated later. Albums are priced by overall size, page count, and the quality of materials and craftsmanship. Book-bound albums range from several hundred to several thousand dollars.

Alternative Albums: Parents and relatives love to have their own small albums to share. Consider ordering extra "parent albums" to honor their contributions to your wedding. An increasing number of online companies are making it easy for you to design your own album from prints or digital files. Accordion displays, standing photo screens, decorative photo boxes, and multiple photo mats are just some of the options available at framing stores.

Many photo labs offer choices of photo borders on enlargements. A white border lends a more vintage look. Displaying your wedding photos in your bedroom can be a sweet way to remind yourself daily of your love and commitment. Be sure to mark where you want your photos cropped when you order your enlargements; otherwise the lab may crop them in a way that doesn't work for you.

Some artistic videographers still work with Super 8 and 16mm film that they subsequently transfer to a digital format. This creates a timeless, film-quality look. If your reception site is dimly lit, be sure your videographer has sufficient lighting to capture it. Videography has changed dramatically in the last few decades, with new technologies constantly arising. Ask your videographer to let you know what equipment he or she uses and when it was last updated.

ENTERTAINMENT & MUSIC

One of the most memorable parts of the wedding, both ceremony and reception is the music. It's what friends and family—and you—will be dancing to throughout the night. For ceremonies, from lifting solos to regal arrangements, music sets the tone. You might choose to go the traditional route with string instruments or perhaps a harp, or your church—if you're marrying in a church—may have an accomplished organist or piano player. Or you can go casual with an acoustic guitar or other out-of-the-norm instrument.

The standard choice for the reception music is to hire either a live band or a wedding DJ. There are benefits to both, and there isn't really a wrong choice to be made. Rather, it's about choosing the group or DJ that most jibes with your style and requested "feel" of the night. This section will help you sort through the choices.

Wedding DJs

If you're planning on having recorded music played at your reception, then choosing a DJ will be one of the most important planning decisions you make. While you may have heard some horror stories of DJs who are too obtrusive or too corny, there are many more stories about great DJs who have made the night for brides, grooms, and their guests. So don't despair and don't forego hiring a professional to bring your event to life.

To find an experienced DJ whose personality and playlist complement your own, begin by doing a local Internet search and asking friends and coworkers for recommendations. Experience is crucial, as most seasoned DJs have learned to reflexively read a crowd and make the necessary changes in tone and tempo to keep your night unfolding as planned, so choose someone who has at least fifty weddings under his or her belt. Ask for at least five references from couples who have worked with the DJ in the last twelve months, and contact them all for feedback. Check with your other vendors to see whom they would recommend as well.

Once you've found a few DJs you're interested in, meet with them to find the one whose personality and playlist fit your style. Bring a list of songs that you would love to hear and those you would rather not. The latter is important because it lets your DJ know more about your style and ensures you won't find yourself doing the hokey-pokey or dancing the Macarena (just in case the idea gives you pause).

Make your final choice, then meet again two months before your wedding to go over the ages and musical tastes of your guests and create a final playlist that you all can be truly excited about.

© photo by Barbie Hull Photography

Classic: Today's classic wedding DJs provide an eclectic range of music for crowds of all ages and are experts at transitioning from one event to the next. Your DJ should have high-quality audio equipment as well as backup equipment in case something fails. A classic DJ will wear a suit and tie or tuxedo to your wedding. If black-tie attire is important to you, be sure to specify that on your contract.

Casual/Alternative: Many casual DJs focus on getting your guests to their feet and keeping them there with the latest dance tunes and club lighting that furthers the party atmosphere. Dance DJs mix music to seamlessly move from one song to another and build momentum throughout the evening. If you're looking for something hip and new, visit your favorite local clubs and see if a DJ there can spin for you. Be sure the DJ is willing to modify his or her behavior for your reception if necessary.

An experienced DJ should have almost all your selections on hand. A short playlist is a sign of inexperience. Expect to pay a deposit of up to 50 percent to secure your date. Ask for a signed contract that outlines the company's policy regarding overtime and substitutions. Read the fine print on your contract and insist on meeting the DJ who will be present at your reception. Some large companies have been known to surprise couples by substituting DJs without their consent.

The iPod Wedding: Think twice before replacing a DJ with an iPod unless you have a trusted, outgoing friend who can act as your MC and a professional sound system to play your music over. Ask your friends to help create a playlist for every part of your reception. Put plenty of extra music in each one, in case you need to change your tune. Double-check that you have all the necessary adapters to hook your iPod up to the PA system.

Live Bands

Treating your guests to a live music performance brings an extraspecial touch to your wedding reception. Whether you hire a single musician to play background music during your cocktail hour, or a twelve-piece band to keep everyone dancing late into the night, there's nothing like live music to make a party feel special.

Once you decide on the style of music you want for your big day, start asking around for referrals from friends, family, recently married couples, and wedding professionals you trust. As with most things, word of mouth and personal recommendations are the best bets for success. Skilled professional musicians have busy schedules and are in high demand, so it's smart to try to book them at least six months in advance.

In many areas you may work with a talent agency that represents many different bands and musicians. Be sure to get audio- or videotapes of the exact musicians you're thinking of hiring and that their names are specified in the final contract.

Live music contracts should also list their fees, the day's schedule, overtime charges, cancellation policies, liability insurance, meals, transportation, any special attire you want them to wear, and how many breaks they'll need so you can plan for other music during those times.

Classic: Traditional wedding bands are generally made up of five to ten members with larger bands ranging up to twenty members. Check with your venue to see if there are size, power, or noise restrictions for larger bands. A great bandleader will have the personality to act as MC and make announcements when needed to keep the party flowing smoothly. A great band will be willing to learn a song they don't know as long as sheet music is accessible.

Casual: Sometimes unusual combinations are great as casual bands. A cello and double bass can interpret rock in a whole new way. Just like with a DJ, you should supply your musicians with a do-not-play list. Be sure your band plays a mixture of fast and slow, current and classic songs so parents and older guests who may not be into tearing up the dance floor will have their chance to join in and enjoy the music.

© photo by GH Kim Photography

Alternative: If there's a special cultural dance you want at your reception, ask if your band knows the tune or is willing to learn it; if not, arrange for recorded music to be played. Have a favorite local band? Find out if they ever play private events. Honor your heritage with the appropriate music: Hire a bluegrass band, salsa band, Middle Eastern ensemble, Irish folk music group, or traditional Scottish bagpiper to serenade your guests.

Find out if you need to supply any equipment to your musicians, like chairs, music stands, lights, or speakers, and check with your venue to see if those items are available on-site. A full band may not be needed for the cocktail hour. Sometimes one or two musicians from the band can be booked to play together before the rest of their crew joins in. Personality plays a big part in performance; hire musicians whose personalities match what you're comfortable with.

Ceremony Music

To find ceremony music that you'll love from your walk down the aisle to your exit, look for songs that fit your location and create the emotion you're looking for. If you're getting married in a church or synagogue, you will need to consult with your officiant and the music director. You may discover there are restrictions on your selections and that recorded music is not allowed. Musicians may be provided or you may have to hire musicians to perform your choices. Don't worry! Chances are you still have many lovely options from which to choose.

© photo by La Vie Photography

If you're getting married at another location or by a nondenominational minister, you'll most likely have an open field when it comes to your choice of music and whether it's live or taped.

Regardless, you'll want to choose music for your prelude, processional, interlude, recessional, and postlude. The prelude should begin

Check 'em Out Ahead of Time

Many bands play professional gigs around town as well as weddings and events, so ask if they have any upcoming performances the two of you can check out before making your final decision. Have fun and make a date night out of going to see them play.

∿

© photo by John and Joseph Photography

Classic: Your church may have an accomplished organist, pianist, or even a gospel choir you can hire. Songs performed on the harp are perfect for classic, fairy-tale weddings. Pieces from Mendelssohn, Handel, Mozart, Bach, and Pachelbel are classic ceremony choices that can be played by a live music duo, trio, or quartet. Some churches will allow secular music during your ceremony. Check with the clergy if you would like more flexibility in your musical choices.

Casual: Acoustic guitar, fiddle, and mandolin are all lovely instruments for country casual weddings. Be sure that your music is loud enough to be heard well in your location. Choose songs from your first date together, your most memorable trip, or your favorite band, or pick cultural songs that honor your family backgrounds. Have a favorite song with some words that don't quite fit? Rewrite them and create your own version.

thirty minutes before your ceremony and set the tone for the rest of your ceremony. Your processional (or big walk down the aisle) should be a dramatic tune played at a tempo you can gracefully walk to. This song is meant to convey openhearted anticipation, and it can be quiet and reflective or joyous and exciting, depending on what best fits your style.

The interlude takes place during your ceremony, so look for songs that symbolize your love and/or faith. If you have a friend or family member who's musically talented, this is a great time to get him or her involved.

Once you're married, your recessional will be all about joyously celebrating your new life together. Whether your tastes lean more toward Beethoven or Bon Jovi, have fun choosing music that's unique, triumphant, and uplifting for this part of your day, and follow it with postlude music that plays until your last guest has made an exit.

© photo by La Vie Photography

Alternative: Gospel choirs or other music ensembles are dynamic additions to any wedding. Choose Latin jazz, Caribbean steel drums, or a voodoo lounge–style band. They make great alternatives to classic ensembles, and you'll have a blast dancing your way out at the end of your ceremony. Choose a fun theme and create a score you love that's all from the Beatles, the 1920s, or the latest indie rock group.

© photo by GH Kim Photography

Considerations: Choose your ceremony musicians early; sought-after musicians are often booked up a year in advance. Pay special attention to the acoustics of your site and choose music that will fill the space without overpowering it. If you're getting married outdoors, be sure there is available electricity and adequate coverage in case of rain. For help finding the right music, ask your vocalist, bandleader, or wedding consultant for advice.

Fun Entertainment Ideas

Your wedding reception is the perfect time to get your guests involved in fun activities that fit in with the style of your celebration. From signing an interactive photo guest book, to watching dramatic performances, to learning a new dance, as long as you keep the pace of the party moving, your guests will be up for all kinds of fun.

Kids and adults alike love jumping into photo booths to get their pictures taken. These days there are options to rent the old-fashioned filmstrip photo booths or brand-new digital booths that show the photos on a screen for all to see. Many photographers can also work with you to set up a photo booth area as part of your photography package. Old-fashioned photo booths are nostalgic and fun for everyone. Be sure there is a technician available during your event in case anything needs fixing. Ask guests to take some photos home and leave some behind so you both have mementos. Digital photo booths offer online photo sharing, which means everyone gets copies of all the fun photos. Include props like hats, sunglasses, and feather boas so guests can ham it up in front of the camera.

Kids can easily get bored at grown-up receptions, so create a supervised kids' activity area where they can let loose with friends their own age and parents can feel comfortable leaving their little ones to play. If there are special kids' meals for dinner, let them eat together so they won't get antsy sitting with the adults.

© photo by La Vie Photography

Select the best photos of the two of you throughout the years and those that show the progression of your courtship for a photo slideshow. If you had recent engagement photos taken, include a few to represent the current versions of you. Set your slide show to music to add to the emotion and impact. Be careful to keep your presentation short and sweet; the energy of a party can suddenly fade if guests are forced to sit for too long.

Performances like skits, songs, and professional dancers and singers bring an unexpected addition to the party and can keep guests entertained during the party's transition periods. Traditional ethnic dancers and belly dancers can be exotic, energetic, and dynamic performers for a crowd of high-energy guests. If you love opera, hire a local professional to serenade your guests before the dancing begins. Dear friends

Depending on the ages of the kids, have a special performer you think they'll love, like a face painter, magician, storyteller, or caricature artist. Hire a babysitting service to watch over the kids' area so parents can relax and enjoy the party knowing their kids are safe and having fun. Provide activities that the kids will love, like craft making, coloring contests, dress up, or sports games.

© photo by La Vie Photography

© photo by Positive Light Photography

© photo by GH Kim Photography

Dance Lessons

Your much-anticipated first dance will kick off the party part of your reception and set the tone for the entertainment to follow. Whether you're an avid dancer or a somewhat more reluctant participant, you can ensure that your time in the spotlight feels comfortable and looks fabulous to your guests by choosing the right moves and music.

To get started, choose your first-dance song at least three to six months before your wedding date. Pick five tunes each that fit the style of your reception, then choose the one you both love the most. While old standards are popular at formal events and pop tunes are frequently heard at semiformal affairs, your choice of music can be as unique as you are. Think outside the box and have fun finding a song that really resonates with the two of you.

Once you've decided on "your song," you'll want to practice dancing to it several times, or consider taking dance lessons to help you wow your guests and put your nerves at ease. Many couples today are taking their first dance to a whole new level by learning to tango, fox-trot, or break dance. What a fabulously romantic date idea and a great way to bring fun to your future!

who are professional performers themselves may be willing to sing a song or two during the reception. Give them the contact information of your DJ or bandleader so they can arrange what they need in advance.

If you two are passionate about swing, salsa, or ballroom dancing, but many of your guests are not, hire a few professional dancers to attend the dance portion of your reception so they can give casual dance instruction, dance with your guests, and get everyone involved in the fun.

It's in the Details

Since all eyes will be on you on the dance floor—at least part of the time—these are some things you should consider to help enrich your experience.

Classic First Dances: Follow in the footsteps of thousands of lucky couples before you by choosing a classic song like "As Time Goes By" from *Casablanca*, "Unforgettable" by Nat King Cole, or "The Best Is Yet to Come" from

available in most cities. Do a local search for options near you.

Casual First Dances: New classics are evolving all the time from the latest new music releases. Choose something from your favorite new band. Want to put a smile on your guests' faces and even make them giggle? Try dancing to James Brown's "I Feel Good" or Frank Sinatra's "Ain't That a Kick in the Head," or choose a song from your favorite romantic movie and ham it up. Learn to salsa, line dance, or tap dance to add an alternative touch to your reception.

Parent Dances: Include your parents in the song immediately following your first dance. Begin by dancing with your father and having your groom dance with his mom. Then dance with your groom's father and have your mom dance with your groom. Add grandparents, brothers,

Frank Sinatra. Waltz or tango your way across the room to bring a formal touch to your first dance. Finish your dance with a big dip to end on a classic note. Ballroom dancing lessons are

and sisters according to their ages. Choose a sentimental tune that everyone can dance to, like "Turn Around" by Harry Belafonte or "What a Wonderful World" by Louis Armstrong, and keep your handkerchief handy.

Cultural Dances: Few dances kick off a reception with as much joy as the classic Jewish hora, where couples and parents are lifted in chairs above the heads of circling guests. When you choose an ethnic dance, you honor your parents and grandparents and let guests in on what makes your background special. Cultural dances can represent regions as well as nationalities. Choose a line dance or Texas two-step if you're from the American Southwest or the Hustle if you're from New York City. If you're beginning your reception with an ethnic dance like the Jewish hora, the Greek kalamatiano, or the Italian tarantella, designate members of your bridal party to help guests learn the steps quickly, or have your DJ give a short description then call out the first few moves so everyone feels included.

Lighting & Dance Floors

To get your guests up on their feet and having a great time, you'll need to have a safe and appropriate-size dance floor that's dramatically lit for maximum appeal. If your venue already has a dance floor, you'll want to make sure that it's level and has plenty of room for all your guests. If you'll need to provide your own dance floor, look to local companies that specialize in

dance floor rentals and setup. Plan for one out of every three people to join in, and allot each person four square feet of space. You'll need to have subflooring, too, unless your space is completely flat, dry, and firm.

Portable dance floors and subflooring are available through specialty rental companies in almost all urban areas. Most come in panels that range from 1 x 4-foot squares. Solid and checkerboard laminates and wood parquet floors are the most readily available options. If you're having an average-size reception of 150 guests, you'll need a 200-square-foot dance floor.

© photo by La Vie Photography

Once you've found a dance floor that works for you, look for lighting that can transform it from just fine to simply fabulous. String paper lanterns or twinkling lights across the ceiling to create DIY accents that really make a difference, or go all out with a professional lighting company that creates dramatic lighting to show off your decor and transform your dance floor. Whether your lighting is subtle or dramatic, be sure your dance floor is well lit for your first dance, when all eyes and cameras will be on the two of you.

If you're planning to use candles, check with your location to be sure they're allowed. Candles placed against or on top of mirrors add subtle romantic light and make large rooms appear smaller. Choose colors that complement skin tones, like magenta and gold. Stay away from green, which can make you and your

guests look pasty. Disco balls and track lighting create a club atmosphere, while chandeliers and candelabras create a chic ballroom effect.

There are four types of commercial lighting techniques commonly used in reception lighting: pin spots, color wash, gobos, and LEDs. Pin spots are used as highlights to directly focus light on a small area, while color wash lights blanket large areas with colored light. Gobos, used in the photo on the right below are stencils made of steel or glass that are placed over lights to project a pattern or design that can be simple or elaborate. LEDs, or light-emitting diodes, use less electricity and create less heat.

Luminarias and strings of wireless LED lights project just enough light to safely steer guests on their way. Your photographer may be able to use nighttime lighting to create romantic slow exposure images. Tiki torches are the classic accents for beach weddings of all kinds. Add a twist by purchasing colored oil to match your color palette. Solar lanterns are available in a wide range of styles and make great green gifts for guests to take home.

© photo by La Vie Photography

© photo by John and Joseph Photography

Chapter 5

FLOWERS

∿

You're about to design one of the most gorgeous aspects of your wedding day! Brides say that choosing their bouquets, centerpieces, and floral decor is one of the things they have dreamed about from girlhood through their pre-engagement days. Flowers make the wedding scene, after all! They're a romantic, beautiful part of your big day, and now you're in the enviable position of creating your own floral designs.

Before you take your first steps into the wedding floral world, you must first develop a vision for the overall presentation of flowers in your wedding. At the start of your flower planning, you might have visions of a sea of white roses on every guest table, a glorious bouquet filled with gardenias and stephanotis, and radiant white calla lilies in your bridesmaids' hands. You've seen plenty of beautiful floral photographs in the bridal magazines, and you're thinking, "I want that!" Before you decide on that all-white bridal bouquet or the pink rose centerpieces, take a moment to think about the bigger picture of your wedding and which style

of flowers would work best for your grand wedding day scheme. Are you a traditional bride, wanting all-white or pastel flowers, or are you a city-chic, trendy bride with an eye for bright colors and unexpected touches? Are you planning a destination wedding at a tropical locale? Do you want an indoor or outdoor wedding?

Your wedding flowers set the stage for your dream wedding, and they have to work with the flavor of your day. They also have to work with your budget. So don't decide on anything until you have a set style for your wedding.

This chapter covers bouquets, personal flowers, and centerpieces, and we touch lightly on ceremony and reception flowers. For more on decorating your ceremony and reception, turn to pages 309 and 329. Also, because there is plenty of opportunity to make your own floral pieces, we've included plenty of DIY sidebars to help you along.

THE LANGUAGE OF FLOWERS
Believe it or not, each flower has a meaning, often deeply rooted in our world's past beliefs.

© Jenetta/Dreamstime.com

If keeping to custom is important to you—or even if you're simply mildly interested in these floral statements—this section breaks down, flower by flower, what your bouquet, centerpiece, or boutonniere is really saying.

Roses

Although we live in modern times, we still cling to several Old World beliefs—especially in regard to weddings. One of those beliefs comes from the Victorian-era tradition of the language of flowers, which maintains that different types and colors of flowers hold symbolism, conveying sentiments that can add very personal touches to your day.

In bygone days a gentleman courted a lady both openly and secretly (such as when the lady's family either didn't approve of the match or the parents hadn't been approached yet) by sending her a flower or bouquet. The particular flower he chose might have symbolized everlasting love or said to her that she was precious to him. The lady in question might have returned a message to the gentleman by wearing a symbolic flower in her hair, or carrying one in her hand, for his view and a message of her own the next time he saw her. Flowers, then, played a large part in the ritual of courtship, as love letters in bloom. The language of flowers grew from a secret form of communication to our modern practice of sharing that symbolism for all the world (and all the wedding guests) to see.

You may wish to give your own bouquet a depth of symbolism, incorporating heartfelt messages, or you might find that your own favorite flower has a traditional meaning that is perfect for your day.

White Roses: Perhaps the most popular choice for traditional wedding bouquets, the white rose carries several different meanings including virtue, innocence, and chastity. White and red roses together symbolize unity. A full bouquet of white roses symbolizes gratitude. A garland or crown of white roses symbolizes victory or reward.

Pink Roses: Pink roses are the most popular of colored bridal flowers, with the delicate

hue adding romance and femininity to a bridal bouquet. Pinks may range from barely there blush to vibrant pink. Dark pink roses symbolize gratitude. Light pink roses symbolize grace, desire, passion, joy, energy, and youth. Pink roses given to mothers symbolize the gratitude and joy of the love and support mothers have always provided.

Yellow Roses: Yellow roses are a favorite for spring and summer weddings, with colors ranging from pale buttercup yellow to bright sunshine yellow. Yellow roses symbolize joy, friendship, and devotion. As with many symbolic items, there's a flip side. Yellow roses have also been branded with some negative meanings, namely jealousy and—yikes!—infidelity. Such is the nature of traditions that have been handed down over time, subject to translation issues from generation to generation.

Red Roses: When brightly colored bridal flowers came on the scene in the late 1990s, red was the number one color chosen by brides for their bouquets. After all, a bright red bouquet stands out in contrast to a pristine white wedding gown and photographs well. It symbolizes true love, passion, desire, deep love, and respect. Red and yellow roses together symbolize excitement. A red rosebud symbolizes purity and loveliness.

Lilies

These bright or white flowers, which come in several different varieties, have become a favorite of brides for their fragrance and because the large dramatic flower is a unique addition to any bouquet or arrangement.

Lilies are also a good way to save on your wedding budget, since one big Stargazer Lily can take the place of several roses or other smaller flowers in a bouquet. Growers have perfected the art of variegating lilies to provide more colors than ever before, and they're also producing enormous blooms that brides often choose to carry in place of a bouquet.

Lilies are not just a spring flower anymore. The lily is now considered a hot summer flower, and the Casa Blanca lily is a top choice for winter weddings. You can also choose from a large variety of lilies: tiger, Asiatic, Turk's cap, Madonna, leopard, Easter, trumpet, Canada, meadow, Carolina, prairie, Sierra tiger, alpine, and Asiatic hybrid. Do an online search or peruse photos from your floral designer to see the beauty and differences of each variety. You'll find solid colors as well as striped or ruffled-edge lilies, and each has its own symbolism.

Those who believe in the language of flowers might also remember an age-old superstition that lilies are the flowers of death. (Pop culture experts say this is the reason behind the naming of Lily in *The Munsters*.) That dark symbolism no longer holds true. Lilies have been depicted as a symbolic flower often associated with images of the Catholic saints, with a meaning of virtue attached. So don't fear using lilies in your wedding day flower plans.

White Lilies: In religious lore the white lily is a symbol of sainthood and great virtue, heroism, and faith. White lilies symbolize purity and virginity and communicate the sentiment, it's heavenly to be with you. The day lily symbolizes motherhood in Chinese symbolism, so consider this flower for your mothers' pieces. The Eucharis lily symbolizes maiden charms, which makes it a popular choice for bridesmaids.

© Drue T. Overby | Shutterstock

© ultimat'rule | Shutterstock

Pink Lilies: Hues of pink add a touch of color to traditional and unique floral pieces for weddings, and brides often like to add some dimension to their bouquets by mixing the colors and meanings of pink and white flowers. Pink lilies symbolize beauty, charm, happiness, fondness, and friendship. The pink perfection lily symbolizes a man's appreciation of a woman as perfect in his eyes, and it can also be used to connote the perfection of marriage.

© ukrphoto | Shutterstock

Stargazer Lilies: The Stargazer Lily is known for its big, bright, open, and sometimes multicolored petals. Stargazers are one of the most fragrant lilies, and some people have strong allergic reactions to their scents. So test these flowers against your sensitivities and consider that guests too may have allergic reactions to the stargazers if they are put in the table centerpieces. Stargazer Lilies symbolize brightness and beauty and the love of astronomy.

Lilies with Negative Meanings

Orange lilies symbolize hatred. You might not like your future mother-in-law, but don't hand her this telltale bloom. Many guests are well-informed of the language of flowers, and they may tell her the symbol within the flowers she is wearing. Tiger lilies symbolize pride. As one of the seven deadly sins, it's not a symbol you should bring into your wedding day. Yellow lilies can symbolize falseness. On your wedding day you want everything to be truth. A dark-meaning flower like this one has no place at a wedding, where symbols are all about love and faithfulness.

Tulips

Tulips are a traditional spring flower, considered one of the bright blooms that give you the most bang for your buck. They're wonderfully inexpensive when you order them in season and are available in a wide range of colors from barely there blush pastels to vivid brights, primarily in solid colors.

Fashion-forward brides looking to pair a bright bloom with their bridesmaids' gown colors look to the tulip for jewel-toned purples and oranges that pop in wedding day photographs.

Tulips cluster extremely well for both bouquets and low-set centerpiece settings. Because they are not as delicate and fragile as gardenias, they hold up well in arrangements, whether you go monochromatic or multihued in a bright grouping such as all red or all pink. As for size, you'll see minitulips and full-size glorious tulips ready for mix-and-match arrangements, as well. Growers have perfected the science of different bell shapes and sizes for mature tulips, as well as ideal narrow bells for flowers just about to bloom. Tulips work best in large groupings of twelve or more as both bouquets and centerpieces. Smaller, more subtle bouquets may be comprised of three to six tulips.

With regard to symbolism, tulips are a sign of spring's return, new growth, and color after a cold, dark season of dormancy. As such, some couples who have gone through tough times, cold and dark seasons, see the tulip—among other spring flowers—as the perfect symbol of the bright new season beginning with their new marriage. Other couples look to the history of the tulip trade, back to when tulips were a symbol of great wealth in ancient Persia. Presenting a tulip meant a promise of an abundant life.

White Tulips: In an all-tulip bouquet, or as a part of a multiflower bouquet, white tulips symbolize fame and a perfect lover. The tulip in

© Shebeko | Shutterstock

general is, of course, the symbol of Holland, so wedding couples with Dutch backgrounds often like to include the tulip as homage to their heritage. Variegated tulips were once given with a meaning of beautiful eyes, making them an ideal choice for the moms' and men's boutonnieres.

Red Tulips: Red or pink tulips communicate a declaration of love or express the sentiment, believe me. Red tulips are also thought to express a message of irresistible love, bringing the passion of red to this springtime flower. Red tulips are often added to clusters of red roses to add some shape dimension to a bouquet or centerpiece, and the meanings of both work together. Red tulips are most often mixed with pink tulips, a mix far superior to red and white.

© Loskutnikov | Shutterstock

Yellow Tulips: Yellow tulips symbolize brightness and warmth, joy, and seasons of sunshine, which in farming eras symbolized a good crop (i.e., abundance). Yellow tulips can also communicate the sentiment, there's sunshine in your smile. Springtime brides and grooms favor the yellow tulip for its bright visual punch—its electric charge—to a multicolored bouquet. Yellow tulips come in a range of colors, from soft buttercup yellow to bright sun yellow, and gold.

© Terrasign/Dreamstime.com

Daisies

When you think of daisies, you probably think of adorable little girls in a garden, picking white or yellow daisy heads and forming them into garlands. These flowers are symbols of happiness, youth, and natural beauty, and as such they are a light and playful flower that can be added to more informal bouquets and centerpieces.

Of course there are several different kinds of daisies. Standard daisies of the white or yellow varieties are extremely plentiful and inexpensive, while bright Gerber daisies in vivid oranges, pinks, and yellows are among the pricier blooms. Each provides a distinctive effect: Traditional daisies provide a casual, traditional look, while Gerbers pop with modern flair.

Additional daisy varieties include blue, prairie, giant, kingfisher, sunshine, gloriosa, butter, painted, Paris, crown, ox-eye, and—the most popular varieties—Shasta and African daisies. Even though these types of daisies are quite different in appearance, the same symbolism has been applied to most if not all of them.

Each variety can be clustered to different effect, with dozens of happy yellow daisies creating nearly the same-size bouquet as a half a dozen Gerbers. These sister blooms couldn't be more different in appearance, but they hold a marvelous heritage in the meaning of flowers: Have you ever done the he-loves-me-he-loves-me-not petal-picking game?

White Daisies: White daisies symbolize innocence, loyalty, loyal love, and purity. Brides often choose a white daisy as a way to pop a touch of white into an all-yellow bouquet. This makes for a natural springtime look. In keeping with the loyalty symbol, more men wear this type of flower as boutonnieres. Also in keeping with loyalty, and also for purity of friendship, white daisies are now used for bridesmaid bouquets, as well as for flowers for the mothers and grandmothers.

© Linnea/Dreamstime.com

Yellow Daisies: Yellow daisies bring in the meanings of joy, natural beauty, happiness, friendship, innocence, and youth. Yellow daisies symbolize the return of springtime, a new season, new abundance, and cheerfulness. They

© Beawolf78/Dreamstime.com

Daisies with Negative Meanings

It's pretty difficult to find a daisy with a negative meaning, so the true danger is in pairing a white and yellow daisy with one of the negative-meaning yellow flowers. You might be tempted to do this when you see a yellow hyacinth and believe this to be the perfect springtime blend. But in fact what you're saying is, jealousy at play! If you're wary of using flowers with potential negative symbolism, or that might put a curse on your day, daisies are among the safest flowers out there.

also symbolize a child's innocent play, because Victorian-era children often used them to make bracelets and necklaces. While many other flowers have negative meanings from their yellow color, the yellow, springtime daisy is free from this stigma.

Gerber Daisies: Gerber daisies, also known as Gerbera daisies, are bright and vivid, but they're also fragile beauties of sorts. With such big, beautiful heads comes a degree of weight, so special sleeves need to be attached beneath their heads. As such, they symbolize brightness, joyfulness, play, and a bright future, and they communicate the sentiment, I'm strong when supported by you. Since Gerber daisies are among the pricier blooms in the daisy family, modern couples have assigned a symbol of wealth and abundance to these flowers.

© Pblscooter/Dreamstime.com

The Color Yellow: A Warning

In the language of flowers, the color yellow often has some dubious meanings. Yellow carnations mean rejection, and they communicate the sentiment, you have disappointed me. Yellow chrysanthemums mean slighted love. Yellow hyacinths mean jealousy. Not all yellow flowers are curses in disguise, but some brides and grooms decide against the bad luck yellow choices, just to be safe.

～

Traditional Bridal Flowers

When you think of bridal flowers, you think of roses, gardenias, lilies of the valley, hyacinths, and orchids. These are considered the traditional flowers of the bridal world, the expected elements of bouquets and centerpieces, often the top choices for men's boutonnieres as well. They are bridal, after all. And since these blooms have a long-standing tradition in the world of marriage, they have the deepest meanings in the language of flowers. They've been around a long time; your mother probably had them in her wedding pieces, as did your grandmother, as did brides back in the Victorian era.

As bridal flowers, they're often more expensive than other nonbridal flowers, even in off-peak wedding seasons. Floral suppliers and floral designers know that these are the flowers with the most emotional impact, and brides with blank checks will pay more to have the flowers of their dreams. So up goes the pricing. Before you decide to scratch these from your shopping list, though, make sure you don't eliminate their beautiful meanings from your wedding day bouquets and centerpieces.

Build your bouquets and centerpieces to include one to three of these top-priced, dramatic bridal flowers surrounded by lovely flowers in the lower price brackets.

© Zhorov Igor Vladimirovich | Shutterstock

Of the pricier bridal flowers, roses are the most moderately priced, and the most flexible in terms of fitting into different formalities of arrangements and bouquets. Gardenias, on the other hand, are definitely formal blooms. Roses also encompass the traditional bridal look, so a piece with three to five roses will suit a wider range of floral styles. Orchids, by contrast, are often more expensive.

Gardenias: This delicate white flower symbolizes secret love. Even though your wedding removes the "secret" aspect of your love for one another, the gardenia is still in demand as a reminder of a couple's earliest dating days, when one may have secretly fallen in love with the other . . . perhaps from day one. Gardenias also communicate the sentiment, you're lovely, which makes this a fantastic choice for the mothers and grandmothers. This is a sweet message to give to your mother-in-law.

Hyacinths: Yellow hyacinths symbolize jealousy, but most of the other colors of this delicate spring bloom are quite beautiful in symbolism. White hyacinths symbolize loveliness. Blue hyacinths symbolize constancy. Red or pink hyacinths symbolize playfulness. In general, hyacinths represent a sense of playfulness. Avoid the purple hyacinth, as it symbolizes sorrow and the sentiment, please forgive me. This is an apology flower from antiquity, so unless you were a total Bridezilla, steer clear of this bloom.

Lilies of the Valley: These tiny, white bell-shaped blooms draping on a delicate stem are a longtime favorite of brides, adding a feminine touch to a bridal bouquet. Men may also wear a sprig of lilies of the valley as a boutonniere. Be careful: Lilies of the valley hold their shape for just a few hours before their lack of a water source causes them to droop, especially in hot weather. Lilies of the valley symbolize sweetness and tell someone, you've made my life complete.

Orchids: It doesn't get more expensive than this exotic flower, and many floral designers say the cost to import orchids will rise dramatically in the coming years. The value of this flower makes it all the more precious to the wearer, which is why many mothers choose orchids as their signature flowers for the day. Orchids symbolize love, beauty, and refinement. Cattleya orchids symbolize mature charm, another indicator of moms' affinity for this bloom.

Flowers Symbolizing Abundance

Wedding flowers traditionally symbolize love and fidelity, affection, loyalty, and friendship, but many brides and grooms also want some luck and prosperity to come their way as they build a future together. Since so many wedding traditions are built on age-old superstitions, even the most modern bride becomes a believer in good luck charms and positive superstitions. A penny in your shoe? That's for good fortune. Wedding toasts? Most will wish you a long and happy future filled with prosperity and a freedom from want. Even the wedding cake started off as a ritual designed to bring the bride and groom a "mountain" of prosperity.

With so many good luck charms built into your big day, you might wish to add some additional symbols of good fortune and financial gain in the form of the flowers you select.

Keep in mind that some cultures consider the greenery of bouquets and arrangements to carry the symbol of abundance, and great care is taken to make sure that greenery is fresh and healthy for a healthy flow of income. The language of feng shui in Eastern traditions holds that a lucky number of flowers, such as seven or nine, also brings good and increased fortune.

Bells of Ireland: These little bell-shaped white flowers symbolize good luck—not just with money, but also for a lovely home. They also symbolize abundance in the form of beauty, and their white color symbolizes purity. Because this is a grouping of tiny flowers, they also symbolize the abundance of loving and helpful souls in your life. Bells of Ireland paired with other flowers that symbolize good fortune and abundance are said to magnify the attraction of wealth.

Buttercups: The buttercup is another yellow flower that doesn't have a negative meaning. It symbolizes riches. In bygone eras, children would hold buttercups under their chins. If the chin turned yellow, the child would be wealthy someday. This tradition evolved into the incorporation of buttercups into springtime weddings. Modern-day children perform the same buttercup-under-the-chin game, but the meaning has become, you like butter. This silly game has brought a symbol of playfulness to the bloom.

Flowering Cabbages: Flowering cabbage symbolizes profit and many returns. As a good luck charm, this flower was often given to those starting new business ventures. Cabbages are fall plants, often bright green (the color of money) tinged with the good luck color of purple at the edges. Purple was considered the color of kings, so flowering cabbages now symbolize a king's riches.

Ivy

One of the best symbols in all of nature is ivy, which represents loyalty, wedded love, affection, friendship, and fidelity. Many invitation designs incorporate green ivy motifs, bringing this traditional bridal symbol into the grand theme of the day. Ivy can be used in print but is considered most powerful when used in bouquets, as boutonnieres, within centerpieces, and as site decor for the ceremony itself.

Cattails: The cattail is a tall, imposing plant, adding a sense of height and architecture to centerpieces. Cattails symbolize prosperity as well as peace. Cattail mixed with ferns sends a combined message of prosperity and good shelter. Since cattails grow near water, the feng shui element of earth and water attracts prosperity and, some say, good health.

SEASONAL FLOWERS

One way to stay within your budget is to pick flowers that are currently in season on your wedding day. Out-of-season and exotic flowers will most certainly result in jacked-up prices to compensate for travel, delivery, and availability. Picking in-season flowers is also ecofriendly, as your florist will be able to find flowers in your local area, rather than having to search far and wide to have them shipped in especially for your big day.

The good news is that seasonal flowers—regardless of the season—tend to come in a variety of color shades and shapes, which means that simply because you're being economical doesn't mean that you're losing quality. This next section provides plenty of information to help you pick the perfect in-season flowers.

Flowers for Every Season

Nothing announces spring like a field of tulips or sets off a fall day like maple trees shining in the sun. Make your wedding date special by showcasing the blossoms and botanicals that are near and dear to you and that highlight the bounty of the season.

Spring: Celebrate the birth of spring by choosing botanicals that are the essence of fresh and new. Use blossoms that are just beginning to open and berries that are still ripening in your bouquets. Display potted centerpieces of miniature daffodils, tulips, and irises. Create favors of bulbs or tree seedlings to be given away as gifts.

© photo by Junebug Weddings

Tulips, grape hyacinths, alliums, peonies, and checkerboard lilies make up the spring arrangement above. Tuberose, freesia, stephanotis, and hyacinth are all deliciously scented additions to your bouquet. Monochromatic pastel color palettes look naturally soft and feminine, and bright color combinations stand out in bouquets and centerpieces. Which flowers do you love and notice first every spring? Incorporate some of your favorites into your bouquet and centerpieces.

Summer: Show off summer's bright personality by choosing intensely saturated colors. Whether you choose just one shade or mix and match, you'll love the way bold colors look in your arrangements and photographs. Bright and vibrant colors look gorgeous at outdoor weddings, while deeper hues look lovely

© photo by Positive Light Photography

© photo by J. Garner Photography

indoors. If you live where temperatures soar, choose flowers that are heat resistant for your bouquets, boutonnieres, and corsages. Return flowers to water occasionally to keep them from wilting, and have a spray bottle on hand to keep blossoms moist. Hawaiian flowers, like orchids, ginger halcyon, and bird of paradise, stand up to summer's high temperatures.

Fall: Showcase your casual fall style by incorporating beautiful seedpods and grasses into your arrangements, or create a more formal, elegant autumn look with tightly constructed floral arrangements of deep orange or yellow roses. Look for dark foliage to add autumn colors to your floral bouquet, as shown in the image on the right above. Chocolate brown, deep red, and burnished gold are obvious choices for a fall wedding color palette. Make your color scheme

unique by choosing just one of these colors and combining it with harvest peach, Tiffany blue, or a creamy shade of white. Late-summer flowers, like sunflowers, black-eyed Susans, delphinium, and Gerbera daisies, still fit right in at autumn weddings.

Winter: In a cold winter climate zone, try incorporating berries still on the bush, shapely branches, or evergreens into your floral design. For mild climates consider using lots of white in your color scheme, then adding candles and twinkling lights. Gardenias smell as divine as they look in the classic white winter bouquet pictured on page 178. Candlelight creates a riveting focal point for winter floral arrangements and beautifully symbolizes the season. Amaryllis, poinsettias, holly, and evergreens are the traditional botanicals for weddings with a

© photo by J. Garner Photography

Christmas theme. Wreaths on doors and those
used as centerpieces make lovely take-home
gifts for your guests.

In-Season Flowers: Timeline

When flowers are in season, they are plentiful
at floral shops and suppliers in your area, and
you'll have a wider range of colors and varieties to choose from. In-season flowers also cost
less, since they won't have to be shipped in at
a high cost. For instance, you could get purple

irises for your winter wedding, but they would have to be shipped from overseas, where the climate is right for their growth. That can double or triple the price.

Seasonal flowers fit naturally into the month of your wedding, such as tulips for a spring wedding or poinsettias for a winter wedding, so it's not very difficult to consider the most appropriate floral choices for your season. If you have more than a year to plan your wedding, it's a wise idea to visit floral shops one calendar year before your wedding, just to see which kinds of blooms are in stock and how plentiful they are, and perhaps discover a unique type of flower you didn't consider before, such as lisianthus or ranunculus, flowers that add a unique touch to your floral arrangements and bouquets.

Spring	Spring flowers are usually in season from February through April, to the beginning of May. Here are the most popular choices among spring blooms: anemone, Bells of Ireland, casa blanca lily, daffodil, delphinium, hyacinth, lilac, narcissus, peony, ranunculus, Stargazer Lily, sweet pea, tulip.
Summer	Summer flowers are usually in bloom from May until August, and sometimes into September. Here are the most popular choices among summer flowers: alstroemeria, Bells of Ireland, chrysanthemum, english lavender, forget-me-not, freesia, Gerber daisy, hydrangea, iris, larkspur, lily, lisianthus, Queen Anne's Lace, snapdragon, stephanotis, stock, sunflower, tuberose, yarrow, zinnia.
Fall	Fall flowers are usually in season from September through November, often in fiery shades of red, orange, and yellow, as well as bridal whites: aster, chrysanthemum, dahlia, flowering cabbage, marigold, zinnia.
Winter	Winter flowers are usually in season from December until February. You can find flowers from other seasons for fitting design use in your winter weddings, but you'd have to order them to be imported from other regions or other countries, at higher prices. In season choices include amaryllis, anemone, Bells of Ireland, camellia, casa blanca lily, cosmos, daffodil, forget-me-not, holly, jasmine, narcissus, poinsettia, ranunculus, Stargazer Lily, Star of Bethlehem, sweet pea, tulip.

Certain flowers are in-season year-round. They are baby's breath, bachelor's button, calla lily, carnations, delphinium, eucalyptus, gardenia, gladiolus, heather, lily of the valley, orchid, rose, and scabiosa.

Visit your local arboretum or garden club to see different types of flowers in season in your region of the country. Get on their mailing list for seasonal displays to expose yourself to a world of interesting blooms, greenery, and flower pairings.

YOUR BOUQUET

All eyes are on you on your wedding day, particularly as you take your walk down the aisle at your ceremony. As a result, your bouquet becomes one of the main attractions of the moment. Since your bouquet is such an important part of your wedding day look, you want to be sure it works for your body, as well as with the style and design of your dress. Floral designers say they won't design a bouquet without seeing a photo of the dress first. After all, it would be a professional embarrassment to them if their creation looked inappropriate, made a super-detailed dress look even busier, lost you behind a bouquet that was too large, or failed to produce a wow factor for a simpler gown. Bouquets can range from small-, medium-, or large-size bouquets to flowing cascades of the same size proportions to single flowers, and more.

If you're looking for what's trendy, you may be doing yourself a major disservice. Forget about those online trend reports that say that wedding bouquets are getting larger. National surveys don't take into account the major bridal rule that you need to choose a bouquet that fits your body size and the style of your dress. You wouldn't go out and buy big shoes if you have size five feet just because an article told you size elevens are all the rage, right?

Here's a quick trick for rounds: To figure out the best size round for you, cut out pieces of paper in small, medium, and large circles and place each one in front of a photo of you in your wedding gown or a gown style you like at this moment. You'll be able to see which size best represents the bouquet size that flatters you and then use the template to design your bouquet.

Small and compact arrangements like posies and nosegays work wonderfully with petite women or sleek simple dresses. Larger round or cascading bouquets pair best with taller women or dresses with full skirts, ruffles, and special detailing. Discuss your dress shape with your florist to find the right balance for your bouquet.

So how big is big? Well, when we say small, we're talking about the size of the bouquet, not the size of a bridal gown. Small bouquets complement simpler, less-adorned wedding gowns such as a column dress, an informal knee-length A-line, or an informal suit dress for a civil wedding. Petite brides can carry small bouquets as a good balance to a tiny frame. Tall brides can carry a small bouquet to show off an intricate dress bodice.

Conversely, a medium-size bouquet allows room for a wide range of colors and flower varieties that add visual punch to a bride of any height or body size. Medium bouquets work well with simpler A-line, column, sheath, and other formal dress styles. Mermaid-shaped dresses with fabric attraction at the bottom of the dress call for a balanced, medium-size bouquet. Floor-length dresses often call for a medium bouquet to accent the long line of fabric in the front of the dress.

Finally, larger, more detailed bridal bouquets are ideal for taller brides, as they create a balancing circle at the center of the body. Plus-size brides should consider a larger bouquet, which provides balance with a wider bouquet at the center of the body. An apple body shape benefits from a round bouquet, which makes the waist appear smaller. A simpler gown style, such as a long satin column dress or sheath, looks beautiful with a larger, more detailed bouquet.

The following pages offer you a variety of bouquets to choose from—from round bouquets to flowering cascades to single stems. There's bound to be something just perfect for you.

Bouquet Style

Next to your wedding dress, your bouquet is perhaps the most iconic symbol of your bridal style, so think of your bouquet as a fashion accessory to help begin your planning. Just like the other fashionable items you wear, your bouquet should complement your height and shape, coordinate with your dress, fit in with your location decor, and accent your personal style.

Your reception location, decor, and theme can also guide your choices. A single bloom or flower color creates bouquets that are refined and elegant, just right for a classic wedding in a glittering ballroom. Creative combinations of colors and flower types make for more casual bouquets with a fresh-from-the-garden feel. You can also add special details, like ribbon-wrapped stems, charms, or brooches, to complete your bouquet design.

Classic: This classic round nosegay above is made from roses, tulips, calla lilies, spray roses, ranunculus, gardenias, and sweet peas. Lilies of the valley, stephanotis, orchids, tulips, and tuberoses also make beautiful classic bouquets. A solid-colored ribbon-wrapped handle gives a bouquet a clean, classic-looking base and a handle that's easy to hold. You can incorporate trailing ribbons or a decorative fabric cuff that frames the bottom of the bouquet for luxurious texture and interest.

© photo by One Thousand Words Photography

Casual: The loose shape below of the hydrangea, Queen Anne's lace, and peony bouquet gives it a casual, fresh, and romantic feel. Poppies, peonies, ranunculus, lilac, sweet peas, freesia, and delphinium are also lovely in casual bouquets. If you or your fiancé have allergies or are sensitive to strong scents, be sure your bouquet won't be overly fragrant for either of you. Tuck your grandmother's embroidered handkerchief around the handle of your bouquet for a special "something old."

© photo by One Thousand Words Photography

Alternative: Wheat and berries make the seasonal bouquet below ideal for a golden fall wedding. Other creative additions that make a big impact in floral arrangements are succulents, fruits, fern curls, herbs, feathers, and seashells. Paper and fabric flowers make alternative bouquets that will stay beautiful long after your wedding day. For an ultramodern and architectural bouquet, concentrate on the shape and construction of the design.

© Melis82/Dreamstime.com

© photo by One Thousand Words Photography

Small Round Bouquets

Many of the gorgeous wedding bouquets you see in magazines are traditional, round bouquets, also known as posy bouquets. The small round, or posy, was the world's introduction to bridal bouquets when Queen Victoria premiered her own small round and set the standard for the bridal design in vogue during her era. The rest of society took her sense of style as the "it" design, and we still look at the posy as a classic, traditional choice. Back in Victorian

days the posy was quite simple and petite, with just a small selection of blooms. Over time it grew in size, with larger clusters of flowers and the addition of ribbons, lace, and bows.

Posies went out of style for a few decades, perhaps owing to the decadent styles of the

Don't add lots of ribbon or crystal accents to a small round. There's not enough room. Let the flowers be the focus, and avoid overkill. A smaller bouquet magnifies the look and meaning of the few flowers that are used in such a small grouping, so choose well when you decide on the content of this bouquet.

1980s, when big was in and everyone seemed to carry dramatic cascades. But now the simplicity and elegance of the posy is back.

A small round is lighter to carry. With the inclusion of so many flowers, filler, stems, and ribbon ties, a bouquet can weigh up to five pounds! A lighter bouquet is also less exhausting to hold during long photo-taking sessions, and a small round allows you and your gown to be the focal point, as you're not hidden behind a big mass of flowers. A small round is also budget friendly, as fewer flowers are needed to create it and it can double as your tossing bouquet if you wish to enact this tradition.

Here is a primer on what comprises a small round bouquet and how to decide if this style is right for you.

The ultratraditional bride often chooses this bridal white, petite round above as the elegant look for her first appearance at the ceremony. She wants all eyes on her, not on her flowers. The small round bouquet is one of the top choices for formal weddings. An all-white small bouquet is budget friendly, because you don't need as many flowers to create a visual impact. All-white round bouquets are ideal choices for brides wearing gowns with color in them, such as a blush pink dress.

Still an elegant bridal look, the addition of pink allows for a gentle contrast against a white or ivory wedding gown. If your wedding colors include pinks in any shade from blush to vivid hot pink, choose a softer pink for your bouquet. You see baby pink rosebuds in most bridal

© Dallaseven/Dreamstime.com

© Alenkasm/Dreamstime.com

advertisements, and the covers of many wedding books include pink hues. Why is pink a traditional bridal color? The bridal industry has crowned pink as the color of femininity.

Today's modern brides love their color! Some look at sample photos of bridal bouquets and yawn at the look of all-white bouquets. The range of pastel colors that brides wish to carry includes yellow, lavender, baby blue, sage green, light coral, and soft orange. For a small round

The medium round is most often selected by brides who consider themselves conservative. They don't want to make a statement with their bouquets, but they do want them to look pretty and serve as an accent to their entire wedding look. That's the job of any bridal bouquet, but the medium round seems to be the saving grace of brides who worry about going too small or too large with their visual statement. A medium round just is, and that may be your definition of the perfect bridal bouquet.

A medium round bouquet allows you to include more types of flowers, giving you more visual punch with your blend of large and small flowers. It can be made lighter to carry by adding more green filler and leaves, instead of packing the round with flower heads. A medium

you're better off choosing one color of pastel flowers for a monochromatic look, as there's not enough room for a collection of colors.

Medium Round Bouquets

If you love the look of a round bouquet, but a small style is just too diminutive for you, take a step up to a slightly larger round—anywhere from eight inches to a foot in diameter. This size gives you enough room to include a larger collection of flowers, mix different colors, and add more greenery and accents, yet still keep the elegant, classic, sophisticated look of a round bouquet. What's more, it's still a comfortable weight for you to hold and carry.

Bridal magazine editors say that medium rounds are what you're most often looking at in their photo spreads and online galleries, as the larger size allows room for more creativity, detail, and color.

© Andre Blais | Shutterstock

round is also the perfect size to show off tiny filler flowers like lilies of the valley, which gives a sense of motion and liquidity to a tightly packed bunch of flowers.

White typifies the classic bridal bouquet both in color and in size. Create a ballerina bouquet featuring tufts of white tulle or netting with just a few white flowers. This style originated during the World War II era, when flowers weren't readily available and volume was added with tulle. Include one to three different flowers, such as roses, ranunculus, and mini white calla lilies, still keeping the round shape but adding an array of blooms.

Red as a color works for a summer, winter, or Valentine's Day wedding, but it is too powerful a color for springtime. Red flowers come in a range of hues, from lipstick red, deeper burgundy, and deep red chocolate cosmos, a mix of which provides greater color dimension than all-red roses. Red rounds are best accessorized with a few touches of pink or yellow, rather than white.

Oranges, purples, corals, yellows, and blues are the perfect bright colors for medium round bouquets. Mixing bright colors adds new dimension, such as vivid yellows mixed with hot oranges for a stylish summer or seasonal fall bouquet. Choosing bright colors allows your

Photo by Rich Penrose

Photo by Rich Penrose

photographer to digitally "paint" a burst of color onto black-and-white images from your day. A medium round also opens the possibility of carrying a cone bouquet, in which the bottom is elongated slightly for a cone effect.

Large Round Bouquets

You're all about the drama, so what better way to inject some wow factor into your wedding day look—which may include a dramatic designer wedding gown—than to make your flowers really stand out? You don't want a tiny bouquet that looks like something your flower girl should be carrying. You want your bouquet to be big and eye-catching. You want guests to drop their jaws when they see the floral masterpiece you've designed to carry. A big round bouquet takes the traditional round and supersizes it, giving you room for dozens of beautiful classic and exotic flowers, lots of texture, and gorgeous fragrance. You can just see the photos of you accented by your cluster of perfect Ecuadorian roses.

A large round bouquet is the essence of opulence when filled with roses, gardenias, birds of paradise, Stargazer Lilies, and enormous calla lilies, but you have to be careful not to go too big. You don't want guests to think, "She's carrying around a centerpiece!" In all things wedding, there is such a thing as going too far—especially if your large round is just too large for your frame. The bouquet has to fit. And a large bouquet fits a bride who has a large personality as well as a larger or taller frame.

© Norman Chan | Shutterstock

Keep in mind that large bouquets are going to cost more, due to the sheer number of flowers and fillers needed to make it look lush and full. And if you are hiring a floral designer, that expert and his or her team will spend a greater amount of time perfecting your oversize piece. So make some room in your wedding budget. If you choose pricier blooms—this piece is going to cost you.

A large round bouquet makes a big bridal statement that perhaps your gown isn't able to make on its own. If you've chosen a simpler gown that's on the lower-budget end—and you feel sad about not having that pricy designer dress you saw at the gown shop—your large round can add the wow factor you feel you are missing.

A big, bright white bouquet makes a grand statement, especially if you have a higher budget for pricier flowers, including gardenias, lilies, and roses. This big arrangement gives you plenty of room to use five to eight different

Photo by Rich Penrose

Photo by Rich Penrose

types of flowers in your bouquet. A white large round bouquet benefits from a mix of large and small white flowers, such as tiny lilies of the valley accenting roses. A popular filler for the white large round bouquet is the softer Queen Anne's lace.

Stick with four or five different types of flowers for a pastel round, since color adds dimension. For a more polished look, stick with a range of pastels in one color family, rather than mix several different pastels. Soft, small fillers are important for pastel large rounds, because they provide a backdrop for larger flowers. Don't limit yourself to matching the color of the bridesmaids' dresses; complement them with a different hue.

When you go big and bright, you display the joy of your wedding day in vivid color. A bright large round bouquet can take too much attention away from your face. So test the size by holding five or six supermarket floral bouquets up to your face and take one away at a time until you reach the perfect size.

Is the Bouquet Toss Outdated?

The bouquet toss has been labeled out-of-date, out, passe, and even dangerous in this litigious society. Indeed, the dangers posed by flying bodies and aggressive maneuvers to grab the bouquet do open up the potential for injuries and lawsuits, and

© Katseyephoto/Dreamstime.com

it's not surprising that some reception halls don't allow the bouquet toss tradition anymore. They've had enough damage to their chandeliers and tables over the years that the tradition is not allowed on their property.

We've all seen enough YouTube videos of drunk bridesmaids and female guests slamming into the sides of tables or falling backward over chairs, steamrolling Grandma, and knocking over a waiter in a frenzied effort to catch the bouquet. Your hesitancy to include the bouquet toss may come from worries about your friends not behaving decently. You might wish to avoid the entire scene, even if single guests boo you for your choice.

Another factor in the disappearance of the bride's bouquet toss is that many single female guests don't want to participate in this ritual. They don't enjoy being led out on the dance floor, looking desperate to be the next to marry. It's not a fun ritual for them, since marriage is not their ultimate goal. They also might dislike the aggressive nature of some of the younger, more inebriated female guests, not wanting to be knocked over by a flailing drunk girl. This ritual is one that many single female guests began to dread, until it faded from the wedding scene. Including it in your wedding now could be considered retro, and many guests may decline to participate, leaving you with a few preteens and Grandma on the dance floor waiting to catch the bouquet.

Small Cascade Bouquets

Cascade bouquets provide a waterfall effect, in which the blooms seem to spill down in front of of the body in an arrangement with length. Also called a shower bouquet, this design provides a draping display of flowers and greenery from a wider top to a narrower bottom.

Cascades have returned from a short hiatus, with many brides again favoring the flowing natural look, especially since this style allows a greater degree of greenery and a variety of flower sizes— bigger on top and smaller on the bottom.

Certain flowers work best in cascades because of their size and sturdiness. Larger flowers to use include roses, Dendrobium orchids, calla lilies, and daylilies. The best small flowers are baby rosebuds, lisianthus, stephanotis, and mini daisies for an informal cascade.

The best cascades have a proper balance of length, with the piece ending at the top of the thigh. True, yesteryear's cascades practically reached the floor, but you don't want to look like a Kentucky Derby winner with a blanket of flowers. Small cascade bouquets are also known as teardrop bouquets or trail bouquets. Keep in mind your body size, knowing that the correct cascade design will play up your features, flatter your shape, and show off your gown perfectly.

A small cascade bouquet gives a gentle flowing effect with its elongated tail, which many petite brides love for its slight elongating of the body. It also has motion when you walk—but not to a pendulum degree. A small cascade is a formal look, adding classic detail to even the simplest dress. While small, it looks larger than it is, so you may include fewer flowers and still produce a lovely bridal effect. A bouquet of this size is surprisingly light to carry.

A petite bride may wish to hold a small white cascade bouquet, as its size is a good

© Tatiana Morozova | Shutterstock © Tatiana Morozova | Shutterstock © Hynek Kalista | Shutterstock

DIY: Sprays

Floral sprays are stems that contain multiple small flowers. For the draping part of sprays in a cascade bouquet, insert a good curtain of blooms in a matching color scheme and in the natural bunches in which they grow. Sprays are a great way to save money, often priced at 40 percent less than single-bloom flower stems. You can make sprays as short as three inches and as long as two feet.

balance to a smaller frame. With a white bouquet you have the option of using one to three different types of flowers for optimal effect. Using a single size of the same type of flower creates a sophisticated, classic look. Even with a small cascade, you can start with larger flowers on top and trail down with smaller flowers at the bottom.

You have your choice in color range with pastels, from barely there blush pastels to more vibrant pastels. Mix blush and vibrant pastels for a lovely "color fading" effect from top to bottom. The most popular pastel cascade bouquets are pink, lavender, yellow, and baby blue. Small white flowers complement the pastel cascade— either as tiny dots of stephanotis or trailing lengths of lily of the valley—to create a bridal look.

Be careful with a small bright cascade, as a too-vibrant piece can look like a costume in this size. You don't want to look like you're carrying a toy bouquet. Fewer bright flowers work best in small cascades, with just a half a dozen or so bright flowers at the top and smaller flowers or sprays at the bottom. Complement a small bright cascade with plenty of greenery to make your colors pop.

Medium Cascade Bouquets

Cascade bouquets came into vogue in the beginning of the 1900s, adding an extra streak of floral length to the previously popular posy bouquet. Brides of that era increased the size of their cascade to show that their families had

© Cindy Hughes | Shutterstock

wealth and elevated standing in society. The trend caught on, and cascade bouquets grew, often formed into not one but two or three different floral "tails" in the front of the bouquet for a wider waterfall effect without the "blanket" look.

The medium cascade is among the most formal of the traditional bouquet styles, good for both indoor and outdoor formal weddings. This style doesn't work for informal weddings, because the draping effect isn't complemented by informal flowers such as daisies and tulips. Roses, ranunculus, lilies, gardenias, orchids, and calla lilies work best with a medium cascade, which might also have more height at the top of the bouquet (such as with standing calla lilies or lilies).

A sister style of the cascade bouquet, the crescent bouquet holds true to its name as a softly arched arrangement. Strong, sturdy flowers such as roses or orchids—blooms that hold

their shape on a strong stem—are wired into a half-moon shape, and this medium-size cascade has only one trailing length in front. This shape adds a bit more modernity to a cascade.

Sturdier blooms have a place to shine with this constructed form of bouquet. Thick stems hold the flower heads upright, adding some architecture to a bouquet that would otherwise point too downward. Medium cascades work with the largest range of body types and heights, elongating the body as they accent (not hide) the dress behind them. Even though this is a more sizeable bouquet, an angled handle allows you to carry its weight quite comfortably.

The medium cascade holds one dozen large flowers or two dozen small flowers, with plenty of greenery trailing as the foundation for smaller flowers in the waterfall front. White cascades fulfill the bridal look, and the cascade gives the bouquet movement and direction. A white medium cascade bouquet accented with tiny white flowers and lots of greenery is the most popular cascade design. For the most formal look, white cascades usually hold roses, calla lilies, and gardenias.

Given the larger size of this cascade, a pastel arrangement can be lush with over three dozen light-hued flowers. Pastel cascades achieve more balance by mixing pastels with white flowers. Pastels should be mixed evenly throughout the cascade. Given the larger size, going from dark on the top to light on the bottom can look unbalanced and come across as a cheesy 1970s look. Use three to four different types of flowers to create depth and dimension.

Because there is so much area to cover, the top colors for bright cascades are red and orange. The medium cascade is the perfect size for flowers of all one shade. For destination weddings coral and turquoise are the top shades for cascade bouquets. Bright colors also encompass dark flowers such as cabernet calla lilies, deep burgundy roses, and deep terra cotta roses either as the sole color or slightly accented with small white or lighter-shade flowers.

Oversize Cascade Bouquets

During the World War II era, cascade bouquets grew in popularity, and in size, almost to excessive levels. Tiny, delicate brides carried walls of flowers in their cascade bouquets, almost hiding behind them. You may have seen this bouquet style in your grandmother's or great-grandmother's black-and-white wedding photos. The gown was enormous; the train was huge; the veil stretched for yards and yards, pooled behind the bride; and the bouquet was a blanket of flowers that you wonder how she held upright.

Cascade bouquets began to shrink over time, until a legendary bride brought them back into vogue. The late Princess Diana carried a large cascade bouquet at her royal wedding, and the trend was back again. Media types renamed this style of bouquet the princess bouquet in Diana's honor, and brides of the 1980s and 1990s flocked to it.

Today the large cascade is chosen more for its balance to the bride's height and body size in an effort to find the perfect complement to the bride's silhouette—not too large nor too small. A tall bride may want a large cascade to bring the eye downward and thus give the illusion of being shorter, and a plus-size bride may utilize the cascade's pointing-downward effect to distract from her body width.

When you carry an oversize cascade, you make a grand statement when you first appear at the ceremony. A lush, oversize cascade symbolizes opulence at your formal wedding. A big, dramatic cascade also presents fabulous photo opportunities, especially solo shots of you holding your once-in-a-lifetime bouquet. If you do choose a larger bridal bouquet, you can balance the look by going much smaller with your bridesmaids' bouquets and also even out your floral budget. Perhaps most important, large cascades are the best friend of the larger bride, who may be self-conscious about how she looks in her gown.

Choose large white flowers such as Ecuadorian roses, gardenias, calla lilies, and daylilies for a large cascade. Larger flowers mean fewer individual flowers will need to be purchased. Two to three dozen white flowers will fill a large cascade well if accented by several dozen smaller flowers in between the blooms. A white large cascade with large flowers benefits from more delicate greenery and filler such as fern.

A light-colored bouquet creates a romantic yet modern look to this traditional style. The most popular colors for pastel cascades in this magnitude are pink, tangerine, and sage green, composed of white flowers with green-tinged edges. A mix of pastel colors in the same color family, such as tangerine, works far better than multihued pastels, which can look too busy.

> ### DIY: Think Light
> Remove some of the heft of a large cascade bouquet by choosing individual flowers that are lighter in weight. A lovely, formal cascade might be composed of gardenias and stephanotis, for instance. Attach a thick, sturdy handle wrapped in ribbon at a forty-five-degree angle from the base of the bouquet for the easiest carrying position.

Pastel flowers can be added to a primarily white cascade for just a hint of color to unify this large bouquet style.

The bride who wants to make a statement by matching her big, bold dramatic wedding

© Coo R | Shutterstock

© Lilia Beck | Shutterstock

© Olga Langerova | Shutterstock

Cascade Handle Details

A cascade bouquet features beautiful florals and greenery on the front, but you have plenty of room for additional features because you will be viewed from all angles as you make your way down the aisle. This means flowing ribbon cascades can add a delicate extra length of visual punch to your bouquet and even a bit of sparkle within your bouquet.

Appropriate accents on the front, sides, and underside of your bouquet add a finishing touch, give you a chance to get creative, and are often an easy and inexpensive way to dress up a simpler cascade bouquet. For instance, your floral designer can make you a roses and greenery cascade bouquet, and then you can add additional blooms and stick-in accents you've found at a wholesaler. This accessorizing of cascade bouquets is a new trend, with brides even pinning a saint medallion or charm to the underside as a way to add extra meaning to the floral piece—as a remembrance of a departed relative or friends or just a token of good luck.

The most important thing to remember when adding accents to your cascade bouquet is that less is more. With such a bountiful arrangement, too much additional ribbon or too much adornment to the front or handle of the bouquet makes it look garish and overdone. So plan for a modest amount of accents, and don't be afraid to cut out any accents or flowers that seem extraneous.

Function is key for a cascade bouquet handle. Since this is a heavier floral piece, you'll need a sturdy handle that won't break off. Many floral designers use heavy-duty duct tape to add extra strength to an angled plastic handle and base, and then they wrap it with ribbon, fabric, or another adornment.

Wrapped Handle: The handle of your bouquet should be fully wrapped from top to bottom. Given the size and weight of a cascade, a three-inch wrap will not hold all the stems together. Common wrapping materials include ribbons made of silk, satin, and velvet, as well as lace. You can also wrap the handle of your bouquet with material left over from altering the bottom of your gown or trains.

Trailing Lace: Lace trails can range from two feet long to floor-length. They can be attached to the underside of the bouquet so as not to obscure your flowers. They can also be attached to pearl- or crystal-headed pushpins so that they seem to stream right out from the middle or sides of the bouquet. If you're doing it yourself, find Chantilly,

Alençon, Battenberg, Venice, organza, chiffon, and beaded or rhinestone-trim laces at craft or fabric stores.

Trailing Ribbon: Lengths of ribbon can extend from the bottom or sides of the bouquet, as well as from the handle itself. For a more romantic look, roll the ribbon up into a spiral coil and attach it with a small rubber band. Let it sit for a while, then remove the band to produce a slightly curled effect. Different types of ribbons to consider are satin, silk, velvet, brocade (for fall or winter weddings), and those fashioned from the cut alterations of your bridesmaids' dresses.

Pushpins and Inserts: The most common pushpin accents to a cascade bouquet, as well as to all bouquet styles, are pearl-headed and crystal-headed pins. These pins may be inserted between the flowers or directly into the flower heads. Accent pushpins should be evenly spaced throughout the bouquet. Check with your floral wholesaler to see the range of seasonal and decorative stick-ins available, including seashells, butterflies, ladybugs, crystal stars, and faux gemstones.

dress with a big, bold dramatic bouquet chooses vibrant reds en masse. Taller brides are best suited to a bold, brightly colored oversize cascade. An oversize cascade doesn't have to be all flowers, either! You can have a dozen or so bright flowers with a mass of greenery for a cascade effect. Don't use too many flowers, or your oversize cascade will look too overdone.

Greenery

Green leaves, ferns, ivy, and grasses have long been touted as bridal budget savers, costing far, far less than hundreds of roses. Money savings aside, greenery adds a bountiful, natural look, especially to cascade bouquets, where the leaves and ferns may be the stars of the arrangement.

With silken flowers and beautiful blooms in your cascade bouquet, the lacy bodies of ferns, the deep green ivy leaves, and the curl of grasses bring additional textures and dimension to your bouquet, as well as to your centerpieces, so be sure to turn back to this chapter when you're designing your table accents.

Some brides decide they love the abundant look of greenery so much that they choose to skip the flowers entirely and build a cascade bouquet entirely of greens, ferns, or ivy—or a mixture of all three. Greenery is also used as decor, such as cascading garlands draping across a mantel or tucked into chandeliers, and as buffet table fillers, set around food platters to make the table seem more lush and full.

Garden weddings are an ideal setting for an all-green cascade bouquet, as it fits in with the natural aspect and still measures up as a formal bouquet. Can't decide on flowers? Can't afford flowers? Perhaps these greenery options are best for you.

Ivy: The most common ivy used in bridal bouquets is English ivy. For a larger leaf to the traditional bridal ivy, choose the six-inch-leaf Algerian ivy. For heart-shaped ivy leaves, choose the ivy with the variety name scutifolia. For curled ivy leaves, check out the Goldilocks variety. For tiny ivy leaves, choose itsy bitsy ivy. For ivy with colored leaves and veins, look at

California gold ivy, which blends gold, yellow, and green.

Ferns: Ferns come in many different frond shapes and sizes, so balance size and style with your bouquet. Maidenhair fern is the most popular for bouquets due to its delicate, tiny leaves. Southern maidenhair fern has the smallest and most delicate fronds. Boston fern stems can reach up to three feet long, making them a good choice for oversize cascade bouquets. Verona fern features fronds with a lacy appearance. For ruffled-edged ferns, consider crispum fern, fluffy duffy, fluffy ruffles, and childsil ferns.

Lily of the Valley: You'll most often see lilies of the valley as tiny, white, bell-shaped cascading flowers with twenty to twenty-five individual blooms per stem. Lily of the valley is also known

as May lily, May bells, our lady's tears, and lily constancy. There are Chinese and Japanese versions of lily of the valley, which have larger bells, as well as a Montana-style version, which has a slightly green tint. Lily of the valley is a poisonous flower, so never use it as cake decor.

Be careful about using greenery in your bouquet if you have allergies. Some ferns and many grasses are known allergens, and it would be awful for you to discover on your wedding day that you are indeed allergic to your own bouquet. Test-drive any grasses or ferns at a garden center or supermarket floral department before you invest in them.

Hand-Tied Bouquets

Hand-tied bouquets allow the flowers to shine in a round, gathered arrangement, but the stems also participate in the traditional bridal look as ribbon-wrapped handles of beauty. The result is a tightly clustered round of flowers with a little something extra underneath, such as satin ribbon wrapping or a handle that trails lengths of ribbon or lace.

The hand-tied bouquet can be either formal or informal, depending on the types of flowers you choose and the combination you create. The most commonly used flowers in hand-tied bouquets are roses, ranunculus, calla lilies, daylilies, tulips, coneflowers, phlox, cosmos, and peonies. These so-called sturdier flowers with thicker or stronger stems will hold the weight of a flower head and keep the shape of the bouquet.

Smaller flowers such as lilies of the valley, Queen Anne's lace, and Bells of Ireland are often added to give a delicate touch to balance out a collection of big, dramatic blooms. Hand-tied bouquets are also referred to as clutch bouquets, and you can design them to have the entire stem wrapped in ribbon or just tie the stems with ribbon directly under the flowers, leaving the natural green stems exposed. This effect gives your bouquet a just-picked-from-the-garden look.

Hand-tied bouquets are often a great choice when you have a small floral budget. If you're working with a floral designer, this type of bouquet is easy to construct, takes less time to put together, and requires less material. The effect of a decorated stem treatment gives an appearance of more length to your bouquet. A hand-tied bouquet can be as small or as large as you want it to be and as light or as heavy as you wish. Hand-tied bouquets are the easiest style to make yourself, if you're considering DIYing the flowers. You just need to gather and wrap the flowers securely.

Pastel flowers stand out in a hand-tied bouquet when you add plenty of greenery. Hand-tied bouquets made of one kind of flower, such

> ## DIY: Stripping Stems
>
> Make sure that all stems have been completely stripped of leaves, thorns, and the rough edges of the stem where the thorns have been cut off. You don't want any sharp edges to your wrapped or unwrapped stems, or else your gown, your veil, or your skin may get snagged. Use a pruning tool to remove all leaves, thorns, and knots. Scissors won't be thorough enough.

as roses, make for a classic, sophisticated look. Mixing flower varieties allows you to change the formality level. Daisies and tulips are less formal, while roses and calla lilies are more formal. A pastel color scheme allows you to complement your bridesmaids' dresses or the wedding decor for a more unified look.

Bright red bouquets are perfectly fine for daytime weddings, so don't eliminate this color choice just because your wedding takes place in the afternoon. Passionate, lipstick red roses are the top choice in this style of bright bouquet. Select a range of reds and add even more depth by selecting flowers in a cranberry color. Reds are almost impossible to match perfectly in hue, so eliminate any clashing tones by purposefully choosing a collection of bright and deep reds.

Orange is a bright, happy color suitable for spring, summer, and fall weddings, which makes it popular for hand-tied bouquets. Orange calla lilies are the perfect curl of sophistication in an orange or orange-based bouquet. Look at vivid yellows and pale oranges as accent colors for your bouquet. Again, greenery brings out the natural look of the hand-tied bouquet's stem and provides the perfect top and bottom color accent to make a tangerine floral cluster pop.

Biedermeier Bouquets

The Biedermeier bouquet is a tight, round cluster of flowers arranged in circular patterns, each consisting of the same flower. You may have a circle of pink roses at the center and then a ring of white roses along the bottom edges of the round. Swiss floral designers first created this unique arrangement of flowers in the late 1800s, naming it after a German style of interior decor. Back in the 1800s the most common style of Biedermeier bouquet included orange and lemon peels for added scent, as these bouquets were often small with fewer flowers.

Today the Biedermeier is back in bigger and fuller glory, sometimes with three or four rings of flowers making up a dramatic round with intricately placed blooms. On the other hand, some are created as dense balls of one kind of flower, such as baby rosebuds, carnations, or stephanotis.

Due to the intensive nature of this bouquet's composition, with so many flowers and so much wiring and pinning required to secure each bloom, this is one of the more expensive bouquets to create or order. It also takes a large amount of skill to craft on your own.

Biedermeier bouquets are ultraformal, ideal for white- or black-tie weddings. They may also be used for daytime formal weddings, in white, pastel, or bright colors. This style of bouquet is ultrainvolved and ultraexpensive to construct, so when a similar, formal look is desired, you might choose a round, tightly packed, hand-tied bouquet. The same round, hand-tied bouquet can be designed for your bridesmaids to match your pricier Biedermeier. Tiny round nosegays carried by your flower girls and the mothers coordinate for a lower price.

A small bouquet consists of one central flower placed at the top of the bouquet, one circle of the same color and type of flower, and then one ring of flowers of a contrasting color. A small Biedermeier might also consist of a central bloom and then two rounds of flowers of the same type and color. Never use more than two colors in a Biedermeier, as you don't want the effect of a striped bouquet. Small bouquets are perfect for monochromatic arrangements.

© Littledesign/Dreamstime.com

A medium-size Biedermeier gives you one extra layer of flowers. Again, avoid alternating layers of colors to prevent the striped look. A medium bouquet is also ideal for a monochromatic arrangement of flowers. Add some contrast with tiny stephanotis or lilies of the valley. Since this is a round bouquet, make sure you have the right body type to carry this shape and size of bouquet. If you're short and round, this is not the style for you.

Use two bright colors for smaller bouquets and no more than three for larger ones to avoid

© Jupiter Images

the striped look. The most common bright Biedermeiers include reds, oranges, and purples. If multiple colors are used in a Biedermeier, they are usually close in color family, such as reds and pinks, rather than contrasting colors like reds and yellows. The bouquet's size is enough of a statement. Going too big with bright colors turns this style into a garish display.

> ### DIY: Thinking Light... Again
> If you'd like to remove some of the weight from your Biedermeier bouquet, or make your DIY approach easier, start with a small Styrofoam ball and use long, crystal-studded pins from the craft store to easily attach each flower in concentric circles. Hot glue guns are often ineffective, as the glue might not take to the Styrofoam.

Single-Stem Bouquets

Sometimes a single flower is all that's needed to make the bridal statement you have in mind. A bride who loves simple elegance might choose to carry one perfect white rose as she makes her approach down the aisle, finding that a single bloom says it all. A single flower symbolizes the unity ritual taking place—with that one flower denoting the one, shared life about to begin—and it also satisfies the bride who wants herself and her gown to be the focal point during that big moment.

Obviously, carrying one single flower is going to save you a lot of money, since you're purchasing one-thirtieth of the materials that would be needed for a round bouquet. And there are almost no labor costs involved. If you're going the DIY route, you couldn't ask for a simpler project to take on, to lovely effect.

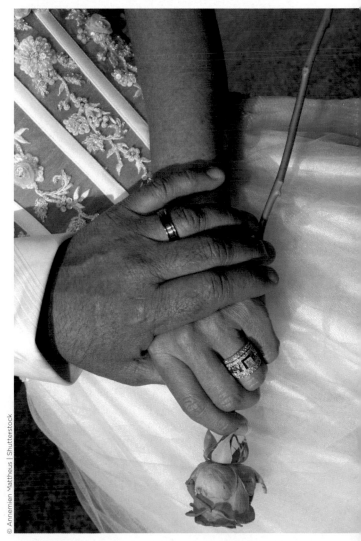

© Annemien Mattheus | Shutterstock

Be careful of nerves! A single-flower will show if your hand is shaking, so if you do have some anxiety with a shaking hand, just lean the top of the single-stem flower back a little bit so that the bloom is resting on your bodice. This will take the quiver out of the carry.

Since this single bloom is the entirety of your floral accent, you'll need to make sure that the flower itself is in spectacular condition, smooth and blemish free with healthy petals and in just slightly bud formation so that it has room to open up a bit throughout the day. A fully bloomed flower at the end of its bloom cycle may begin to drop petals during your big day.

Single-Stem Rose: A single-stem white rose symbolizes purity, an apt symbol for a bouquet symbolizing a pure love. The most popular colors for single-stem rose bouquets are white, red, light pink, and bright pink. A peace rose comes in hues of pink, ivory, and light orange. Use a one- to two-inch-thick ribbon to tie a bow halfway down the stem, rather than wrap the whole stem.

Single-Stem Calla Lily: Calla lilies are heralded as regal flowers and are best suited for formal weddings. Calla lilies are ideal for outdoor weddings, both formal and less formal. Calla lilies come in shades of white, pink, light green, orange, and cranberry or merlot. If you carry a single calla lily as your accent flower, your bridesmaids can carry smaller calla lilies as single flowers or as bunches to offset your dramatic, larger flower.

Single-Stem Gerber Daisy: A Gerber daisy head is large enough to make a visual impact. Gerber daisy heads are extremely heavy for their relatively delicate stems, so many suppliers attach a plastic support cone to the base of each flower head. Keep that support cone on the flower until just before you walk down the aisle. The most popular Gerber daisy single-stem colors are bright pinks, oranges, yellows, and reds.

DIY: Timing

Ideally you'll acquire four or five single flowers, store the cut stems in a water-filled vase, and then choose the one best and prettiest bloom to carry during your ceremony. Make your selection two to three hours before the wedding and have the stem wrapped according to your wished-for design. The leftover flowers can be wrapped for the bridesmaids or mothers to carry.

Flower Bunches

If a single flower is too small, and a round is too formal and expected, consider a floral bunch for your bouquet. This grouping is not as organized and symmetrical as a round or Biedermeier bouquet. Flowers are not organized in circles or definite patterns. Instead, the bouquet has that just-picked look and as such is far more appropriate for a less-formal wedding.

One of the trends in bunches is the presentation bouquet. Think about the long-stemmed bouquet presented to the newly crowned Miss America. She holds the lush collection of flowers across her lower arm as she takes her first walk down the aisle with her new title. That's the same look you're afforded with the presentation, or arm, bouquet.

Many brides love the arm bouquet design, as it allows the bride to comfortably take her father's arm as he escorts her down the aisle, and then the arm of her husband as he escorts her back up the aisle.

Because you will use this bouquet for your wedding and not a pageant, you will want to fill the bunch bouquet—in a long style or as an eight-inch-stemmed, less dramatic bunch that's not so Miss America—with flowers and greenery according to your wedding's formality, location, and theme.

Bunch of Roses: Long-stemmed roses are the most popular choice for presentation bouquets and for smaller-stemmed bunch bouquets. Roses make this type of bouquet more formal

and may be mixed with other formal flowers such as gardenias and calla lilies. The most popular colors for rose bunch bouquets are white, red, and pink. A simpler bunch might contain a dozen roses, while a larger, more dramatic bunch might contain three dozen roses.

Bunch of Calla Lilies: A grouping of six to twenty-four calla lilies creates an elegant, formal effect for your bouquet. Calla lilies may be used for both daytime and evening formal weddings, both indoors and outdoors. The most popular color for the calla lily bunch bouquet is, of course, white. Monochromatic calla bunches are the most formal; mixed-color callas work for less-formal weddings. Sage green calla lily bunches are a top choice for outdoor and green or organic weddings.

Bunch of Gerber Daisies: Brightly colored Gerbers look best in a bunch of twelve flowers or more. A bunch containing fewer than six daisies can look wimpy, especially if a hot day causes them to droop. The most popular colors for Gerber bunch bouquets are bright pink, bright red, bright orange, and bright yellow. Add a few stems of greenery to a bunch of Gerber daisies because their relatively flat heads and thick green stems need some accenting in a bunch.

Bunch of Wildflowers: Smaller is better for a bunch of wildflowers, as the mix of different colors and shapes of wildflowers offers more than enough dimension without looking overpowering. Always get wildflowers from a floral center or wholesaler; flowers picked from a field or the side of the road may be poisonous. For a different wildflower effect, try bunches of heather or lavender. Wildflowers work best with a partially wrapped stem rather than a fully wrapped stem.

Wildflower Bouquets

Bouquets of wildflowers add a lovely, natural look to an outdoor wedding in a garden, backyard, rustic setting, state park, or other informal setting that's all about natural beauty. The Mother Nature element of the wildflower bouquet creates a gathering of coordinating blooms and stems, instead of a mass of nearly identical, round, silky roses. The wildflower bouquet has texture and individuality, as well as that often-desired just-picked look.

© Kristajean/Dreamstime.com

A wildflower bouquet is not for every bride. Some brides feel the non-rose design looks too "old" or too much like dried flowers, "something my grandmother would have on her kitchen table." And other brides have longtime fond memories of picking wildflowers during family vacations to the mountains, scent memories about fields of lavender, or a tradition of creating wildflower bouquets with a younger sister and now with a niece. The inclusion of wildflowers takes on a very personal meaning when you have a history with wildflowers. Including them in your floral design pays homage to a very important part of your background and upbringing. Or perhaps you just love the natural look, the less-constructed effect, the mix of flower types and soft colors.

Many wildflowers don't have long stems, so prepare to have a slightly shorter bouquet. Wildflower stems may be more delicate than thick rosebush stems or wide and reedy tulip stems, so if you choose to wrap the length of your stems, choose simpler, solid-color fabric rather than lace, which can look too "busy" with the different textures of wildflowers. For multihued bouquets, solid-color ribbon is a better choice.

Wildflower bouquets based on herbs include rosemary, sage, and thyme, which have some scent but not the overpowering aromas from plants like chives. Wildflower bouquets based on flowers include lavenders, delphiniums, veronicas, larkspurs, cornflowers, poppies, asters, bellflowers, and forget-me-nots, among

Be Careful with Do-It-Yourself Wildflower Plans

Wildflowers offer the opportunity for you to pick or grow your own flowers, but be careful not to choose poisonous flowers. Watch out for wildflower allergies! Test bunches before your big day. Bugs, mites, bees, and worms tend to live in wildflower patches, so be sure you don't have a stowaway on your just-picked wedding flowers. Acquaint yourself with local poison ivies and oaks so you don't mistakenly pick a troublesome, dangerous plant. Your state parks department website should have a list of plants to be wary of.

others. For smaller filler flowers, use lilies of the valley, Queen Anne's lace, columbines, sweet peas, and any small star- or bell-shaped flower.

The average wildflower bouquet is twelve inches long. A wildflower bouquet longer than fourteen inches looks too much like a presentation bouquet and would look like a messy bunch of weeds in your arm. Hand tying is the best format for wildflowers. A longer, thinner bouquet complements a wider silhouette of gown, while a thicker (eight- to ten-inch) wildflower bouquet looks better with a sleeker silhouette.

Stems should be wrapped either three-quarters of the way or all the way to add strength to the stems and provide a uniform look. For slightly more formal bouquets, use satin ribbon to wrap the stems. For more informal bouquets,

While cascade bouquets most often call for fully wrapped stems as a functional aspect of a heftier bouquet that has to keep its shape and be easy to carry, you have far more design options for the stems of floral bunches. You can have a fully wrapped six inches of stem, or you can tie a length of ribbon in a neat bow at the center mark of the stems, allowing the clean-cut green ends to poke out of the bottom.

A thicker width of ribbon, such as one to two inches, looks best for a taller bunch of wildflowers, while a half-inch ribbon is perfectly balanced on a shorter stem-cut bunch. Your decision about stem treatment for a bunch bouquet has much to do with balance and color, as you want a pretty ribbon bow to serve as an accent and not overpower smaller, more delicate flowers.

Your chosen stem treatment will determine the length of stem you will leave at the base of your bunch flowers, as some wrap designs look best with shorter stems and others benefit from lengths of stem that are longer and more eye-catching. Once you discover the proper stem treatment for this less-formal bouquet style, you can then think about how to dress it up with decorative fasteners, pins, and other devices.

The key to finding your stem-length balance is trial and error. Take some inexpensive tulips, daisies, or other flowers you find in the grocery store floral department and bunch them. Then beginning at their original length (perhaps nine inches), cut them down a few inches at a time and wrap and rewrap the stems to find the style and length that suits you best.

© Sean Azul

Partial Ribbon Wrap: The most common partial ribbon wrap is created from two- to three-inch-wide ribbon wrapped one-third to halfway down the stem and then fastened with a bow. Use a length of floral tape to spiral wrap an inch of the stems, then cover that tape wrapping with fabric ribbon. A one- to two-inch-wide ribbon wrap is ideal for a cluster of six to twelve individual flowers. Match the color of the ribbon to one of the flower hues in your bouquet.

Full Ribbon Wrap: For a full ribbon wrap, start wrapping at the base of your flower heads and wrap all the way down to the bottom of the stems. Leave the very bottoms of

© Sean Azul

© Michellepi/Dreamstime.com

the stems exposed, or wrap them with ribbon to cover the entire stem. The most popular types of ribbon for a full ribbon wrap are satin, silk, and lace. A full ribbon wrap looks best when you match the fabric to a color in your flowers.

Lace Wrap: The delicate nature of floral bunches lends itself well to the lace-wrapped handle. The top types of lace for stem wrap are Battenberg, Chantilly, and Alençon. Consider laces embedded with silver thread for a bit of shimmer. Look at laces that feature tiny hand-sewn bugle beading for an authentic Victorian look. Antique lace is a lovely way to insert "something old" into your day. Antiques stores are a terrific source for a range of lace styles.

Stem Adornments: Use pearl-headed floral pushpins spaced two to three inches apart along one side of the wrapped stem. Use crystal-headed pushpins as an alternative to

give your bouquet body some extra sparkle. As a new trend, attach tiny silver charms to your wrapped stem handle. You can find charms in craft or card stores. Find a circular charm or silver monogram plate to hot glue to the flat bottom of the ribbon-wrapped stems.

© Sean Azul

use a wheat- or pastel-color raffia to either wrap the stems or provide an accent bow. Lace stem wrap may be used if you have chosen all one type of wildflower, such as lavender.

Alternative Bouquets

Everything old is new again in the world of wedding flowers, with styles once popular back in the 1920s and 1940s making a resurgence in the twenty-first century. We call back to the bouquets of our grandmothers and great-grandmothers as a way to carry on a small touch of family lineage and connect with the matri-archs of our family trees. And yet we still seek individuality and personalization in bouquet styles. In short, we want the best of the past, present, and future.

The bouquets shown in this section are similar to round and hand-tied bouquets, but they have names, identities, and rules all their own. They also tell guests a lot about the bride's personality. What kind of bride departs from a traditional round and carries, for instance, a tussy mussy? One who romanticizes past days of decorum, or perhaps a Jane Austen fan.

Perhaps you'd like to depart from the usual shape of a bridal bouquet, and you'd like to extend that Biedermeier shape into a completely round bouquet? Thus, a pomander is for you. It's your ornament of floral beauty. There are no rules about alternative bouquets, and the etiquette of first, second, or destination weddings do not apply. The choice is truly yours to make.

Nosegay Bouquets: A nosegay is a densely packed bouquet very similar to a traditional round but smaller in size. A small nosegay is ideal for a petite bride, while a larger nosegay flatters a taller or larger bride. Use tighter round flowers such as roses, ranunculus, and peonies to best fill a nosegay. Nosegay bouquets were originally quite small, just under four inches in diameter, but they have grown in modern times to a width of six inches or so.

Photo by Rich Penrose

Pomanders: A pomander is a small cluster of flowers formed in a ball shape and suspended by a length of ribbon. Pomanders are most often four to six inches in diameter. The most common flowers included in pomanders are the smaller blooms of roses, dendrobium orchids, delphiniums, ranunculus, lisianthus, pansies, and grape hyacinths, with stephanotis pinned in. Pomanders are also a top choice for junior bridesmaids, flower girls, mothers, and grandmothers.

Photo by Kristen Jensen

Make sure that your chosen bouquet style, if an alternative design, either matches or complements the styles of your bridesmaids' bouquets. It would look odd if you carried a Victorian pomander while your bridesmaids carried very modern presentation bouquets or rounds. It's always better to match the styles and differentiate with the bouquet sizes and/or types of blooms within them.

Tussy Mussies: A tussy mussy bouquet is a small nosegay bouquet inserted into a small metal vase. The tussy mussy design allows you to carry a smaller cluster of flowers yet still make an elegant, formal statement. Tussy mussies, an import from France, originated in the eighteenth century. The tussy mussy cone or holder may be made from silver, gold, pewter, porcelain, or cobalt glass and adorned with beaded designs stamped into silver metals.

© Yuki/Dreamstime.com

BOUQUET COLORS

Here's where it really gets fun: Bouquets can come in a wide range of colors. Really, there are no rules here. Sure, some colors go better with other colors, but more and more brides are becoming quite adventurous with their color schemes. Of course, if you'd prefer a traditional classic white bouquet, that's completely fine. Or, if you're into making a big statement with bright reds or pinks, go for it! You want to be sure your bouquet fits with the color scheme of your dresses, as you don't want to clash, and you don't want to detract too much from the overall big picture. This next section will give you all the guidance you need to make these big—and fun—decisions.

The Color Spectrum

The inspiration gallery on the facing page will help you pick out which colors you like and which ones you can do without. Once you select the color family, then you can make informed decisions on the kinds of flowers you'd like to fill out your bouquets—all the information of flower names that you need is listed below.

All-White Bouquets

Many brides know the color of their bouquets before they even decide on a shape, style, size, or the flowers that will be included. They have always had the dream of an all-white bridal bouquet, just bursting with silky white flower petals, round white rose heads, tiny dots of lily of the valley, and exotic stars of stephanotis. Just the thought of it takes their breath away.

If you're locked on the idea of the all-white bridal bouquet, you might consider yourself a traditional bride, but you can also be a very modern bride, filling that all-white palette with some unexpected flowers—going beyond the classic bridal flowers of roses and gardenias.

Many brides say they started off with an all-white bouquet as a way to pay homage to mothers and grandmothers who also carried all-white bouquets on their wedding days, but then

being modern brides, they took that palette and elevated it to a new level with some quirky or creative style decisions.

It is not true that an all-white bouquet will automatically cost you more money. The price you pay depends on many factors: the types of flowers you select, whether or not they're in-season or imported, the design and style of your bouquet, and the size of your bouquet. True, you may need more white flowers to make a visual impact in any floral piece, but that doesn't always add up to a bigger drain on your wallet.

Another aspect of the all-white bouquet is that it might allow you to use the white version of your birth-month flower, or the birth-month flower of your wedding day, in order to convey a particular message from the language of flowers through your bouquet.

Here are the pros and cons of this bouquet: It's a very traditional look, and white flowers work in every season and with every formality. A range of white flowers also allows you to get creative and still have a bouquet that looks bridal, as a wide variety of flowers come in white. However, there often is not enough contrast between the white of your wedding gown and the white of your bouquet flowers. The blooms don't show up dramatically in front-angle photos, and smaller white flowers such as lilies of the valley tend to wilt a few hours into the day.

Soft, Pastel Bouquets

Adding pastels to a bridal bouquet, or building a bridal bouquet out of all pastels, allows you

The Color Spectrum

© Andreblais/Dreamstime.com

Shades of white vary, with some flowers appearing crisp white and others looking more beige. Try stephanotis, calla lilies, dendrobium orchids, roses, ranunculus, peonies, tulips, Bells of Ireland, and lilies of the valley, among others.

Photo by Rich Penrose

Pastels range from pinks to coral, lavenders to mixes. Try lisianthus, larkspur, dogwoods, geraniums, tulips, peonies, carnations, begonias, crocuses, asters, pansies, sweet peas, lilacs, and lavenders, among others.

© Andreblais/Dreamstime.com

Mixing light and dark lavenders gives the impression of a much fuller bouquet. Ask about the unique imported hibiscus "Blue Bird," which adds an exotic touch to pastel bouquets.

© Mrorange002/Dreamstime.com

All-red bouquets convey passion for your partner. The most popular flowers include roses, calla lilies, Gerber daisies, ranunculus, and berries.

© AD | Shutterstock

Blue is the top color choice for brides marrying by an ocean. The most popular flowers include dark blue hybrid delphiniums, monkshoods, larkspurs, and lisianthus.

© Alexandrza/Dreamstime.com

Bright green bouquets are a top choice for garden and ecofriendly "green" weddings. Try Bells of Ireland, viburnums, hydrangeas, ladies mantles, spidermums, and calla lilies.

> ## Do Your Research
>
> Look at floral websites to see the many different types of pastel-color flowers available. Floral clubs and organizations, such as an orchid club, will be your best sources of information about blooms you never even knew came in the colors you desire. Flip through flower and garden catalogs as well to discover new varieties of flowers such as roses, tulips, and begonias.
>
> ∾

to bring color and personality into the flowers you'll carry on your wedding day. As trends continue to evolve, different shades of pastels are "in" during different seasons, often following the fashion trends set by the apparel industry. When sage green gowns are the new hot color, pastel bouquets serve as accessories by bringing that hot color to the forefront.

Pastel bouquets are also a top way for a bride to coordinate her look with her bridesmaids' dresses and also with the floral decor she'll use throughout her wedding site. Always with a mind toward what will look best in styled photographs, a bride wants color contrast in her floral pieces that will allow them to fit into the surroundings of her dream wedding day. An all-white bouquet denotes the absence of color, while a blush pastel bouquet provides a signature look.

Consider the bride whose favorite color is lavender. She may dress in lavender, own a favorite purple sweater, wear purple earrings, and now gets to carry her signature hue on her wedding day.

Bright, Vibrant Bouquets

A bright bouquet creates a dramatic effect when you appear for the ceremony and everyone sees you for the first time. It also adds an element of "wow" to your photographs. Imagine the beauty of an elegant black-and-white wedding portrait, with only your bouquet in full, glorious color. As the experts say, the color pops, and professional photographers love to get creative in spotlighting the bride's symbolic bouquet. The color contrast between a pristine white wedding gown and a fiery orange or lipstick red bouquet turns photos into art.

The hue you choose depends on your personality—the bride who chooses bright colors loves to make a statement and wants to depart from bridal white or baby pink roses to be modern and original—as well as the season and location of your wedding. Bright oranges, for instance, are ideal for both spring and autumn, while greens may work for any season. Jewel-toned, bright bouquets appear at outdoor, daytime weddings, at beach weddings, and in lavishly decorated ballrooms as a testament to this color palette's popularity in any locale. Worried about a bright bouquet being "too much" as the color indicator for the entire wedding setting? You don't have to have matching, bright, jewel-toned centerpieces, altar and pew decor, and bridesmaids' bouquets. Those can be softened with a mix of brights in complementary shades, pastels, and whites, while yours is the only bouquet to pop with monochromatic or mixed bright color. You'll get the best of both worlds.

Single-Color Sensations

A monochromatic bouquet depends on the uniformity of the blooms in the piece, and special care needs to be taken—especially with round bouquets—to evenly space the flowers when the bouquet is packed with roses, for instance. With a singular color scheme, there's no room for error, and balance is achieved with the perfect choices in matching hues, flower size, and spacing.

Texture is achieved with greenery and filler, and some flowers with ruffled edges may provide all the accent needed in a bouquet of this design.

Monochromatic bouquets are ideal for both formal and informal weddings, both indoor and outdoor, and the personalization comes in the color chosen for this floral spotlight.

Many different flowers are ideal for the monochromatic bouquet, including roses, ranunculus, gardenias, and stephanotis on the formal end, and Gerber daisies, tulips, hydrangeas, and peonies on the lighter, less-formal end.

Single-color bouquets may be white, pastel, or bright. Red and pink are the top choices after classic bridal white, and bright orange and cranberry top the list for fall weddings. In spring, lavender and light orange are the front-runners. For destination or beach weddings, bright corals lead the way.

Monochromatic bouquets often need a greater number of flowers, as the uniformity of hue doesn't give the depth and illusion of lushness afforded by a bouquet of multicolored

© Truyen Vu | Shutterstock

© Duktil/Dreamstime.com

© Ksurrr/Dreamstime.com

blooms. So expect to order up to two dozen more flowers to pack your bouquet well. The colors don't have to match exactly. Mixing shades that are close, such as red and cranberry, still creates a monochromatic look.

Monochromatic White Bouquets: For a small bouquet, two dozen white flowers are ideal. In a smaller-size bouquet, a single type of flower, such as roses, is ideal. For a medium-size bouquet, choose three dozen white flowers. A medium to large monochromatic bouquet has room for multiple varieties of flowers such as roses, calla lilies, lilies, gardenias, and stephanotis. Add a touch of color to an all-white bouquet with a pastel or bright ribbon. This adds a pretty color contrast in person and in photos.

Monochromatic Pink Bouquets: For a formal bouquet, choose several dozen pink roses in a tightly clustered gathering of identical blooms. For an informal bouquet, consider a hand-wrapped bunch of pink tulips or an array of pink tulips and wildflowers. Another informal monochromatic bouquet is one made with a dozen hot pink Gerber daisies or bright pink zinnias. Even if shades of pink range from pale to brighter, this still counts as a monochromatic bouquet.

Monochromatic Red Bouquets: With vivid red shades, just a dozen blooms is sufficient to make a visual impact. Choose your shade of red based on the season. Brights are perfect for summer, and crimsons or burgundies are perfect for fall and winter. Your skin tone determines the tone of red that works for you. Paler brides are complemented by lipstick red, and darker or olive-skinned brides carry cranberry red best. Add dimension with smaller and larger red flowers.

Monochromatic Purple Bouquets: Pale lilac bouquets are ideal for spring and summer. Darker jewel-toned purple bouquets come to us from the hot colors of fashion runways. So when *Vogue* says purple is in, it's also in for weddings. Paler lilac bouquets benefit from the placement

of a contrast color, such as tiny darker purple flowers or tiny white flowers. In larger monochromatic purple bouquets, add dimension with subtle color contrasts of ruffled-edge flowers for texture and petals with a thin petal edge hue.

Color-Mixed Bouquets

For some brides, one color is not enough—nor is one color family. Why limit yourself to pink, when there are so many glorious colors of the season that mix together so well?

If you were torn over your selection of the one color for the bridesmaids' dresses—not able to choose between reds, pinks, oranges, and yellows—you can bring in all your favorite colors in your bridal bouquet. No cuts necessary!

The key is to choose the right mix of colors for a bouquet that looks formal and professional. After all, you don't want it to look like a mass of mix-and-match primary colors, similar to those bouquets sold at gas stations on the Fourth of July. As a rule, primary colors of red, yellow, and blue should work alone, with their own complementary colors bringing out their beauty.

You'll find several different "classes" of color-mixed bouquets, from a white and pastel pairing to a husbandry of brights and deeper jewel tones. The palette is up to you to design.

Go to your local home improvement store and head right for the paint department. Grab a bunch of paint color strips in your chosen shades of colors and hold them against each other so you can see how well that hunter green works with persimmon orange, or the white

with the pale blue or the aqua with chocolate brown. When you find the color mixes you love, you can use these shades to guide your shopping spree or inform your floral designer or wholesale assistant.

Pastels work in any season, with any formality, and in any setting and have become a top choice for brides who want a traditional bridal look without everything being pure white.

A primarily white bouquet can be "punched up" with the addition of a dozen pastel flowers. White and pink are the traditional and most popular bridal-mix flowers. White and lavender provide the perfect bridal bouquet accents to all-lavender bridesmaids' bouquets, while white and sage green allow you to coordinate with your bridesmaids' all-sage bouquets. Mix white with a variety of pastel colors for a one-to-three ratio of whites to pastels.

Avoid equal numbers of white and bright flowers, or the bouquet will look too contrasted. Keep the ratio at one to three, with either one-third whites to two-thirds brights, or vice versa. For a dramatic mix, choose white flowers and up to three different bright flowers, such as reds, oranges, and hot pinks. Fill your bouquet with brights and use the white flowers as pinpoint accents, either as the color theme for just your bouquet or for all the ladies' bouquets.

Leave the white to your wedding dress and fill your bouquet with a mix of pastel tones and brights in the same color family. Pastels and brights allow you to capture a wide range of hues in the same color family, such as pinks and oranges. For a less-formal mix, blend pastel and bright tulips or Gerber daisies, with wildflowers as filler. For a beach or destination wedding, copy the colors of the ocean—baby blues, aquas, and more vivid blues with sand-color tans or light corals.

For fall or winter weddings, mix bright reds with deeper burgundy or cranberry colors; add chocolate cosmos for a richer bouquet. Bright purple irises will pop against deeper purple geraniums, asters, and tulips. Brights electrify a deeper-colored bouquet, whereas pastels soften the arrangement. Bright yellows mixed with gold-toned flowers and fillers lend an air of opulence to an evening wedding, or a sense of brightness to a daytime wedding.

BRIDESMAIDS' BOUQUETS

Bridesmaids' bouquets can match your bouquet, or they can be completely different—both from each other and from you. It's really a matter of what you're drawn to. You want to be sure to consider the color of your bridesmaids' dresses when selecting their bouquet colors. You might also consider doing slightly smaller bouquets for your girls, as a cost-saving measure.

Traditional Bouquets

When choosing your bridesmaids' bouquets, you have a choice: They can look exactly like

© photo by La Vie Photography

yours, or you can design a little something different for them to carry. In this section you'll explore the traditional choice of having your bridesmaids' bouquets look similar to yours as a way to tie your wedding look together, remain bridal in the effect, and create a unified look in person and in pictures.

Except on rare occasions when a bride wants her bridesmaids to have exactly the same style and size bouquet as her own, the overwhelming trend is to go a little bit smaller in size yet still include the exact same flowers as those in her bouquet.

Another way to set apart your bridesmaids' bouquets is to choose one of the flowers from your bouquet, such as roses, and build the bridesmaids' bouquets with only that type of bloom, while yours includes an array of different, lovely blooms as well.

You could achieve this by simply designing identical rose, calla lily, and gardenia bouquets for you and your bridesmaids, but adding lilies of the valley to yours. Just a small detail like this can set yours apart without making the bouquets look too different.

Traditional, romantic bouquets include soft-petal flowers such as roses, calla lilies, gardenias, and other classic bridal flowers. A softer bouquet is designed with plenty of curl to floral petals, such as with calla lilies and lilies. To add romance to a traditional bouquet, include flowers with ruffled edges, such as peonies. The most common traditional bouquets for bridesmaids are rounds and hand-tied clusters just a little bit smaller than the bride's bouquet.

A dramatic bridesmaid bouquet almost always includes a bright burst of color. The most common bright colors for dramatic bridesmaid bouquets are red, orange, vivid pink, and purple. Size does not equal drama, so even a smaller bouquet (four to six inches across) can pack a punch when the colors pop. If your bouquet is all pastel, add a few brightly colored blooms to your bridesmaids' bouquets to add that burst of energy.

If your wedding style is partly romantic and classic, but you still want an artsy pop to your bridesmaids' bouquets, add crystal or gemstone push-ins to blooms. Decorate with feathers, which give a soft yet artistic texture to the bridesmaid bouquet when used in smaller quantities (fewer than ten feathers per bouquet). Bright, colorful ribbon within the bouquet or trailing from the handle gives an artsy effect.

© Olga Langerova | Shutterstock

The copycat bouquet is identical to the bride's bouquet in size, shape, and color. Many brides find that since their dresses differ, especially when bridesmaids choose their own styles of gowns, the unified look can be achieved through flowers. If you're carrying a smaller, hand-tied bouquet, it's often easier and less expensive if your bridesmaids' bouquets are identical. A copycat bouquet may still include a slightly softer shade of color from the brighter one in your own bouquet.

Cascade Bouquets

The flowing look of a cascade bouquet is a top choice for outdoor weddings, as it adds another dimension of greenery and the same flowing

© Shanliangd/Dreamstime.com

direction as many trees and flowering plants found in nature. For bridesmaids, this bouquet style can tie them into the scenery, and it can also be a gorgeous way to dress up simpler, unadorned bridesmaids' dresses. With the absence of a lot of bodice beadwork or the sleek silhouette of a silky A-line dress, a cascade gives shape and design to the front of the dress.

For the most part, bridesmaids' cascade bouquets are smaller in size, reaching perhaps just a foot in length, and usually have fewer flowers than the bride's bouquet. They might require up to two dozen flowers rather than the three dozen found in the bride's collection. The size, of course, depends on the bridesmaids' heights and body shapes, as a floral piece needs to accent a woman's appearance, not overshadow nor overwhelm her.

When a bride carries a cascade in keeping with the shape that works best with her figure, it's a mistake to give the same size bouquet to all the bridesmaids in an effort to have a matching set. This is the number one mistake made by brides who favor cascades: They hide their bridesmaids because they believe the bouquets need to match. Not so. Smaller is often better, and you can add an extra few inches to a taller bridesmaid's bouquet to balance out her frame.

And don't forget that bridesmaids' cascade bouquets can consist of all greenery, such as ivy, fern, and grasses, while only yours contains flowers in addition to the same mix of greenery.

A small cascade bouquet for a bridesmaid can be half the size of the bride's cascade bouquet and still look perfect. A small cascade might have six to twelve small to medium-size flowers, or twelve to sixteen small flowers. A small cascade can feature flowers at the top in an arch shape and then greenery reaching downward. A small cascade looks lovely as mostly greenery, with tiny white flowers added to the cascade.

A medium cascade bouquet for a bridesmaid can be three to six inches smaller than the bride's. A medium cascade might have twelve to eighteen flowers. This bouquet looks best with flowers clustered at the top and smaller flowers placed evenly in the bottom trail of the cascade. A medium cascade offers the opportunity for not just one trailing length, but two made from greenery and spots of flowers.

For informal weddings, bridesmaids' cascades might be placed with bright Gerber daisy heads, while the bride's bouquet is bridal white. For informal or outdoor weddings, cascades can be filled with wildflowers. A cascade can be created from 100 percent Queen Anne's lace, for an ultraromantic and ultra-inexpensive look. A cascade can be created from ivy, with tiny white or colored flowers, while the bride's bouquet has just touches of ivy throughout.

Taller bridesmaids benefit from longer cascades that reach to the top of the thigh. Shorter bridesmaids benefit from shorter cascades that reach to the top of the thigh. Heavier bridesmaids benefit from wider, rounder cascade tops with longer trails at the bottom. Thin bridesmaids look lovely when their cascades match the width of heavier bridesmaids, as you don't want to call attention to the differing body shapes by having bouquets of varying widths.

Single-Stem & Bunch

Giving bridesmaids single-stem flowers or less formal bunches is a top budget-saving strategy. At the same time, it provides a lovely, delicate look. Because fewer blooms are needed, supply costs go way down and labor efforts are also reduced. This can turn into a savings of 60 to 80 percent on your bridesmaids' bouquet expenses!

Some brides decide that they will be the only one to carry a full bouquet, as a way to stand out in person and in pictures. They coordinate their bridesmaids' single or bunch flowers by choosing one to three of the flower types included in their own bouquet, which ties together the look of their entire group.

When it comes to formality, a single-stem bouquet can be every bit as formal as a round bouquet when you choose a "formal" flower such as a rose or graceful calla lily and tie it with a thick satin bow. Single-stem bouquets work for both formal and informal weddings, as do hand-tied bunches. It's all about the composition you choose for these elegant but simple flower pieces.

Single-stem flowers look best with longer stems, no less than six inches, with ribbon ties at the midsection. It is this ribbon accent that can bring gorgeous effect to the bouquet.

Single-Stem Roses: A single-stem rose is the number one choice for the simple elegance bouquet. The maid of honor might be given two or three single-stem roses, while the rest of the bridesmaids carry one apiece. For a coordinated look, match the color of the ribbon tie to the color of the rose, such as white satin for a white rose. Single-stem roses look best when you wrap them to include their green leaves as color contrast.

As with all single-stem bouquets or groupings of less than six flowers, you run the risk of having a nervous bridesmaid's quivering hands shake the bouquet. Advise your ladies to hold the single or bunch against the front of the body to give it some grounding and support. The upright carrying method also looks more uniform than the arm's natural propensity to hold the flower pointing outward.

Single-Stem Calla Lilies: A single calla lily is also a top choice for bridesmaid floral pieces, with white being the top selection. Look at different hues of calla lilies, from variegated light green or pink, to deep cabernet. Like roses, calla lilies look best when a bit of greenery is wrapped to the stem then tied with color-coordinating ribbon. The maid or matron of honor might carry two or three calla lilies to set herself apart from the bridesmaids.

Single-Stem Daisies: Daisies embody a less formal, playful look and are perfect for outdoor or afternoon weddings. Since it's just one daisy in the hand, choose a big, bloomed Gerber daisy in a bright color such as pink, red, orange, or yellow. White or light yellow daisies look best in bunches, not as a single-stem bouquet. Match the ribbon tie to the color of the daisy, and add a more playful look by wrapping the stem in a wide spiral the green of the stem length.

Bunch Bouquets: A hand-tied cluster of flowers creates a slightly larger look for your bridesmaids to carry, yet still remains smaller in size and budget than a full bouquet. Bunches may be created with formal flowers or informal flowers such as wildflowers. Consider giving each bridesmaid a bunch that contains different flowers, such as the roses, calla lilies, and day lilies that comprise your own bouquet. Coordinate the ribbon wrap to the color of one flower in the bunch.

© Dole/Dreamstime.com

Color Schemes

If you've chosen your bridesmaids' dresses, you already have the color from which to base your floral decisions. If you don't have the dresses chosen yet, then you should wait until you do decide on a color before you order any brides-maids' bouquets. The hues need to coordinate, not clash, since the bouquet really is an accessory to your bridesmaids' outfits.

You have several options when it comes to the color or colors of the bridesmaids' bouquets, and one of the most important factors to consider is the season of your wedding. Certain colors, such as pink and yellow, work better in spring and summer, and certain colors, such as cranberry and brighter purples, are perfect for fall and winter. The season of your wedding is going to dictate your overall wedding floral design, so the bridesmaids' bouquets will need to coordinate with the overall theme. Many brides choose the colors of the bridesmaids' bouquets first and then choose the dress design and hue. See the chart about flower colors on page 211.

Your bridesmaids' bouquets don't have to match the color of their dresses exactly. A complementary color makes the bouquet stand out, and a vivid color will really make it pop in person and in photos. And while you can insert a little bit of difference in each bouquet, such as a bridesmaid's favorite lily in one and a favorite calla lily in another bouquet, the bridesmaids' bouquets shouldn't vary too much. You don't want them to be so different in shape and color that they look like they were all designed for five different wedding parties. Instead, give bridesmaids their choice between two flower varieties.

Pastels: Pastels work with both light- and dark-colored bridesmaids' dresses. When your bridesmaids' dresses are a dark color, the most popular flower color choice is a lighter shade of that same color. Pastels look best in color mixes, rather than in monochromatic clusters. Punch up pastel bouquets with a few darker flowers in darker shades, or pastel flowers with darker petal edges. Pink and orange pastels are most popular.

© Cindy Hughes | Shutterstock

Brights: Bright-color bouquets work best with pastel-color bridesmaids' dresses, such as a light pink dress with a vibrant pink bouquet. The most popular bright bouquet colors for brides-maids are red and orange. In fall and winter, brights take on more jewel tones, such as deeper purples, navy blues, or emerald greens. Many brides choose the color of their bright birthstones as the foundation color for their brides-maids' dresses and bouquets.

© Jay Hocking | Shutterstock

© Eric Limon | Shutterstock

For a pink dress, consider light to darker pinks, or light to darker greens. Avoid peach tones. For a red dress, consider pinks and reds. For a lavender dress, consider purples, pinks, blues, light greens, and yellows. For a black dress, consider richer reds, deeper purples, and jewel-toned greens as well as all white. For a coral dress, consider deeper corals, whites, and yellows. Avoid peach and pink. You also can bring in an ocean theme of blue.

Mixes: Rather than choose one color to complement your bridesmaids' dresses, you get to choose five or six colors for a lush bouquet. Mix light and darker shades to give a bouquet more dimension. A common cost-cutting tactic is to include four or five pricier flowers and then fill in the rest of the bouquet with filler such as stock or larkspur for inexpensive color "dotting." When mixing vibrant colors such as red, be sure to add several different lighter shades for dimension.

Bouquets Similar to Yours

Perhaps you want all the bouquets to match. You figure you'll be set apart by the fact that you're wearing a wedding gown and that it would unify the look of your group if you all carried matching or similar bouquets. Some brides don't need or want an all-white bouquet for themselves and colorful bouquets for their bridesmaids—they feel it's just too pedestrian.

Brides who choose identical bridesmaids' bouquets to their own style say, "We are a group that's so close, we should carry equally gorgeous bouquets," and "It may be my day, but I belong to this group of equals, so it will be identical flowers in our bouquets." Others simply love the look of all-matching bouquets they've seen in photos. By contrast, they think the one white bouquet surrounded by little pink bouquets looks too cliché. Identical bouquets also make it easier for DIY bouquet making, because you don't have to keep track of which flowers to set aside for your bouquet or which bouquet needs to be made larger than the others. When you're creating one bouquet style and size, the task may go much faster and easier. Brides who choose similar bouquets prefer a slight bit of difference between themselves and their bridesmaids (even with the wedding gown!), but they too dream about a more uniform look.

Note that your maid of honor can carry a bouquet identical to yours, just a bit smaller so that yours is still evident as the Bride's Bouquet and hers is slightly different from the bridesmaids' bouquets.

Size: Choose an identical style, but design it as two-thirds the size of your bouquet. The bridesmaids' bouquets might match the design of your bouquet but be a much smaller posy bouquet. Brides who carry a dozen single-stem flowers as a bouquet can give their bridesmaids one to three identical flowers to carry. In cascades, your bouquet might be longer and more dramatic, while your bridesmaids' bouquets might be a small-scale arch or one-third-size cascade.

Flower Choice: Choose a similar shape of flower to make your bridesmaids' bouquets like yours, such as tight ranunculus to coordinate with your roses. If your bouquet has a

Photo by Rich Perrose

Photo by Rich Perrose

large collection of calla lilies, choose mid- to large-size single-stem callas for your bridesmaids. Build your bridesmaids' bouquets from one variety of flower in your bouquet. To keep your budget in mind, use pricier, more exotic flowers such as gardenias in your bouquet and more inexpensive flowers such as peonies in your bridesmaids' bouquets.

Colors: If your bouquet is all white, allow your bridesmaids to carry colored bouquets in pastels or brights, or a mix of colors and white. If your bouquet is pastels, have your bridesmaids carry all-white bouquets for a unique twist. If your bouquet contains a mix of pastels and brights, build your bridesmaids' bouquets out of all pastels. If your bouquet is all brights, mix one shade of pastels into your bridesmaids' matching bouquets.

Accents: Eliminate the trailing ribbons found in your bouquet so that the bridesmaids' bouquets are less adorned. Add pearl stickpins to give your bridesmaids' bouquets a matte effect to pair with the crystal stickpins in your bouquet. If you'll have crystals pushed into your flower heads, eliminate that accent for your bridesmaids' bouquets. Consider greenery as an accent; give your bridesmaids' bouquets more greenery than flowers for a lush, natural, organic look.

© Andreblais/Dreamstime.com

© Elenathew/Dreamstime.com

Maid of Honor Bouquet

Your maid or matron of honor is the VIP of your bridal party, and after all she will do for you—help you prepare for the wedding, throw you a shower, and organize the bridesmaids' dress order—just being your support system—you may want to set her apart from the bridesmaids with a little something special in her bouquet design.

Most brides design slightly larger, more lush bouquets for their maids of honor, or they create a focal point through their choices of flowers. Some brides design a bouquet that's nearly identical to their own and then reduce the size or content of the bridesmaids' bouquets as a way to elevate the maid of honor's piece.

Some brides have their maids of honor carry bouquets in a different color than the rest of the bridesmaids as a way to set them apart or as a color complement to the different dress style or color they will wear.

Regardless of your design choices, you can flex your creative muscles and perhaps use some floral elements you thought about using in your own bouquet. Or, you can get a few exotic and expensive flowers for your maid of honor, while your bridesmaids' bouquets are made of more moderate yet pretty blooms.

Photo by Rich Penrose

Some brides have more than one maid of honor, resulting in two or three specialty bouquets. If you have two maids of honor and one bridesmaid, make all their bouquets of equal size and composition for a unified look. A maid of honor's bouquet can match your bouquet with an accent of different-colored ribbon on the handle or as trails. The most common scenario is designing a maid of honor bouquet that's slightly smaller than your bouquet.

The decision on color for a maid of honor's bouquet is purely a matter of personal style. A monochromatic bouquet may be the perfect accent when bridesmaids have two-color or mixed bouquets. A maid of honor may carry a monochromatic bouquet, while the rest of the bridesmaids carry mixed bouquets. Set the maid or matron of honor apart with three or four colors in her bouquet, while bridesmaids have only one or two colors.

The maid of honor's bouquet might be two-thirds the size of your bouquet. For a dramatic size difference, choose a smaller posy style for the maid of honor, as well as for the bridesmaids, while your bouquet is grand and lush. If your bouquet will be small, honor attendants' bouquets need to be even smaller. If bridesmaids will carry single-stem bouquets, the maid of honor can carry either three blooms or a bunch of six to nine.

Different-colored flowers—such as bright orange lilies—can be the accent in the maid of honor's bouquet, while the bridesmaids carry paler orange bouquets. If crystal or pearl stick-ins will accent your bouquet, add a half a dozen of the same stick-in design to your maid of honor's bouquet. Your maid of honor can be the only one carrying a bouquet with a stick-in accent. For an informal wedding, consider adding a tiny silk butterfly stick-in.

Photo by Rich Penrose

Photo by Rich Penrose

BOUTONNIERES

Boutonnieres may seem like nothing but a blip in your overall floral vision for your wedding. But they should not be overlooked, nor decided upon hastily. You want to be sure the boutonnieres you choose coordinate with your bridesmaids' bouquets, and that your groom's boutonniere coordinates with your bouquet. It's also nice to distinguish between groom, groomsmen, and fathers, so be sure to take this all into consideration.

Groom's & Men's Boutonnieres

That little floral accent on the groom's lapel, as well as on the lapels of groomsmen, fathers, grandfathers, godfathers, and ring bearers, often takes a cue from the flowers in your bouquet. You might choose one signature bloom from your collection, such as a rose, and design a stylish boutonniere that all the men wear in a uniform look, or you can follow the trend of having each man wear a different, yet coordinating lapel flower, such as a dendrobium orchid for the groom, a sprig of stephanotis for the best man, a rose for a groomsman, a delphinium for another groomsman, and so on.

What matters most, as with all design elements of your wedding, is that the boutonnieres work with the formality, season, and style of your wedding and that the flower or flowers you choose are fresh, beautiful, and perfectly crafted to keep their shape while worn all day.

Note that the size of the boutonniere is very important, because a tall man wouldn't look right wearing a supersmall boutonniere, while a shorter man would look comical wearing a larger, rounder boutonniere. Be sure to consider your men's heights and relative sizes (lean, stocky, etc.) so that the perfect dimension of boutonniere can be chosen to flatter them all. Lapel width is also a factor for floral dimension.

Traditional Roses: The most common boutonniere is a single rose, with or without a sprig of baby's breath and greenery. While white is the most popular color, red and sweetheart pink are popular to coordinate with the bridal theme. Spray roses allow you to have multiple small roses in one boutonniere. Consider the leonidas rose, which is a blend of red and orange, or a peace rose with darker shading at the edges of the petals.

© photo by La Vie Photography

Traditional Dendrobium Orchids: The dendrobium orchid allows the men to add a bit of unexpected flair to their boutonnieres with an exotic bloom. The dendrobium orchid looks best when not accented with baby's breath or other filler flowers. Several dendrobiums may be wired together for a slightly larger, more dramatic boutonniere. A white dendrobium orchid paired with seeded eucalyptus and eucalyptus leaves provides an unexpected mix of flower and greenery.

© Fderib/Dreamstime.com

Traditional Mini Calla Lilies: If you have calla lilies in your bouquet, the natural decision may be to create your groom's or the men's boutonnieres with single or triple mini calla lilies. Callas come in white, light green, yellow, even darker cabernet colors. Mini calla lily boutonnieres do not need filler flowers, as their unique shape and curl of the petals provide the perfect amount of visual effect. Calla lilies suit formal wedding style requirements just as well as roses and orchids.

© Andre Blais | Shutterstock

© photo by John and Joseph Photography

Casual Boutonnieres: The chartreuse orchid below sets off the groom's tie and has its own special twist that makes it look fun and casual. If your florist isn't staying to pin on boutonnieres and corsages, designate someone to do it as guests arrive. Mini calla lilies offer beautiful choices for boutonnieres, while hypericum berries, coffee berries, and ferns make stylish alternatives for a casual affair. Lavender, stephanotis, and gardenias are fragrant choices for boutonnieres and corsages.

The Top Trends in Traditional Men's Flowers

Most boutonnieres consist of a single, fully bloomed flower, which often costs under $5. Use sprays for multiple flowers per pin. A new trend to achieve color coordination is to use bright and striped ribbon. You'll now find fasteners made with strong magnets that attach the boutonniere from the front to the back of the jacket. Just be aware that anyone wearing a pacemaker will not be able to use magnetic fasteners. Ask all your men ahead of time if they're clear for this option.

Alternative Boutonnieres

For some wedding couples, the traditional rose boutonniere is not what they have in mind. They want something unique, fun, and outside the usual realm of bridal flowers—maybe a floral from their love story, such as the tuberose that was in their engagement bouquet or the lisianthus that graces the garden outside their vacation home.

Besides visual appeal, nontraditional flowers are often less expensive than those bridal roses, orchids, gardenias, and callas that have always been in such demand for weddings and so are priced higher during peak wedding season. Compared to these bridal blooms, nontraditional flowers might cost half as much!

When you open your mind to alternative flowers, you find yourself researching and learning about a world of gorgeous flowers that are still masculine enough for the men to wear, and you may also find a bloom to add to your bridal bouquet. Who says the men's flowers have to come from your collection? It could work the other way around! Floral designers say they love it when wedding couples ask to see nonbridal blooms, because they can show off their talents in unique ways and share photos in their portfolios from other types of special events.

Seasonal Flowers: For spring weddings, consider a mini tulip, daffodil, or peony. For outdoor summer weddings, use a bright Gerber daisy, zinnia, ranunculus, mini calla lily, or rose. For fall weddings, leonidas roses with their orange hue are ideal, as are orange, red, or yellow mums or zinnias. For winter, a red rose fits the seasonal theme, and some couples have fun by adding mini jingle bells to the boutonniere.

Unexpected Flowers: Lisianthus creates an ideal, colorful boutonniere with or without filler flowers. Freesia presents the chance to incorporate

a blush color, such as two narrow pink blooms in a single boutonniere. Tuberose allows you to include a bridal white flower, but it's not the expected rose or stephanotis. Kalanchoes provide the same tiny flower effect as baby's breath, just in colorful star shapes.

Cone of Florals: A stiff fabric cone can be fashioned to hold a single flower or sprig of flowers.

© Andreblais/Dreamstime.com

© Andreblais/Dreamstime.com

DIY: Internet Research

The Internet is full of videos with step-by-step instructions for making your own boutonnieres and corsages. If you're looking for a DIY project that's easy and fun, look no further! This is the perfect project for you to take on.

Keep the "hug factor" in mind. You don't want to choose an alternative flower that bleeds color onto fabric or a prickly flower or leaf that pinches during a hug. Whenever an alternative flower is in question, either test it or ask the floral designer or wholesaler about its feasibility for the hug factor. Be aware that pins and other fasteners may pose a pinch factor for your groom or the men when they are hugged as well.

A small laser-cut metal cone can also hold florals when pinned to a lapel. Most metal cones are made of filigree silver, and they may be solid or of latticework construction. Small blooms or bunches of filler flowers such as lilies of the valley are ideal for cone boutonnieres.

Nonflorals: Construct a fabric leaf to take the place of a floral boutonniere. Cut a leaf shape from a swatch of leather, wool, or stiff cotton

© Digitalphoto/Dreamstime.com

and decorate as needed. For a beach wedding, a starfish-shaped pin can take the place of a floral boutonniere. For an autumn wedding, fashion a boutonniere from a small, glued-together arrangement of pinecones with acorn accents. If the men are going to wear suits, give them colorful pocket squares to wear, rather than floral boutonnieres.

Flower & Berry Boutonnieres

In any season, and in any formality of wedding, a top trend for boutonnieres is to add a tiny sprig of berries to a single flower or cluster of flowers to add a natural touch to the piece. In light of the trend for "green" weddings, berries are becoming more popular because they bring an organic effect, extra pop of color, and unexpected texture to the men's lapels.

When we say berries, we don't mean blueberries or strawberries of the edible variety. That would just be silly and would obviously wreck a pricy suit or tuxedo. The berries for use in boutonnieres are natural, hard berries that are often used as filler in bouquets and centerpieces.

Grooms who choose berry accents for the guys' boutonnieres like the mix of shapes in their small lapel pieces. Round berries can accent a cone-shaped mini calla lily or the curl of rose petals or the dramatic shape of an orchid. The circle effect might also coordinate with the design of the vest and tie, if they haven't chosen a solid color. Think of berry accents paired with flowers as a way to customize the groom's or groomsmen's look, an artistic touch to replace the ho-hum baby's breath.

Make sure that berries are hard and solid before adding them to any boutonniere. Again, hugs are frequent during weddings, as is slow dancing, and you don't want a crushed boutonniere to leave what looks like a bloody stain right over the groom's heart. Ask your floral designer, wholesaler, or supplier to show you the hardest berries in stock, and consider berries in whites and oranges.

Tiny white stephanotises provide an ideal basis for an artistic boutonniere, with either white or colored berries accenting the piece. The star shape of stephanotises pairs nicely with the round shape of berries, so you can even

choose slightly larger berries. It can be difficult to match white tones, so be sure to see examples of any white berries to be paired with stephanotises. You can also use faux berries in a boutonniere. This is a subtle look when paired with fresh flowers.

A sprig of ivy can add dimension to a traditional white flower boutonniere—whether it be roses, orchids, callas, or stephanotises.

Ivy symbolizes fidelity in marriage. The hand shape of ivy brings the different shapes of the flowers and the dots of berries together as a well-designed floral piece. Match the color of the berry to the veins or streaks of color in the ivy, such as a light green or pink, to keep from having more than three colors in a boutonniere.

Use just a sprig of berries—fresh or faux—as the boutonniere. A three-inch-wide sprig of

berries is the ideal proportion to the standard lapel. Stick with one type of berry for this boutonniere. You don't want a grouping of two or more berries to look like a fruit salad! A large, dramatic leaf such as coleus, or a single fern, can be a great backing to a sprig of berries.

Setting the Groom Apart

In the vast majority of weddings, the groom's boutonniere is designed to stand apart from the groomsmen's, fathers', and ring bearer's boutonnieres. It may be that the groom is the only man to wear a white flower, or that he is the only man to wear a rose, while the rest wear sprigs of stephanotis. Your options are endless, and you'll explore your design choices here.

Again, keep in mind the size that best flatters the groom, as you don't want to go too small or too large for his frame or lapel. Also keep in mind the season of the wedding, since that may inspire a design idea such as his wearing a white tulip and his men wearing orange for a spring wedding.

Your final style consideration is of course the formality of the wedding, as this will determine if he wears a classic rose or if a tuft of wildflowers to match your casual bouquet would be the perfect fit.

Grooms enjoy having their say in the design of the floral piece they'll wear, so be sure to show your groom the options shown here as well as photos from bridal magazines and websites. He needs to know the great many choices he has . . . including that he can add an unexpected accent to his floral piece.

Choose a flower type from your bouquet, such as a rose, and use that as the only rose in any boutonniere. The groom can wear the most formal type of flower from your bouquet, and the groomsmen can wear less formal or filler-type flowers from your or your bridesmaids' bouquets. For a beach or destination wedding, the groom can wear an exotic flower such as a hibiscus or bird of paradise. Your groom can wear the same type of flower that was in the bouquet he presented to you when you got engaged.

If the groom wants to wear a white flower, his men may wear pastels or brights. Since many grooms like to add color to their own

© Olivia Marone | Shutterstock

daisies are your theme, the groom can wear a large Gerber daisy, while the other men wear smaller stock daisies in white or yellow. Size can be built into a boutonniere by designing a three-flower piece for the groom, while the other men get single flowers. Give the groom several flowers, while the groomsmen's pieces consist of just a single flower with ivy.

SUPPORTING CAST'S FLOWERS

Just like your bridesmaids and groomsmen, your flower girl, ring bearer, parents, and grandparents will need some floral recognition. The following section gets into some serious detail about the kinds of flowers that will work just perfectly for your supporting cast.

Flower Girl's Basket

It's the traditional accessory of the flower girl, a pretty basket filled with flower petals that she sprinkles ahead of the bride's path. In today's modern times, the petal basket has gotten a makeover. You'll still see the classic white basket, perhaps covered with white satin and tied with little white or pink bows, but you may also see wooden or bamboo baskets to reflect a more natural look at "green" or organic weddings. In some ultrachic weddings, the basket is covered with red satin, and the petals are white, carried by a flower girl in a white dress with a red sash.

The basket itself might also have more style, departing from the traditional little round with the hoop handle. Now you may see heart-shaped baskets, ovals, squares, butterfly shapes

looks, the new trend is for the groom to wear a bright color, while the other men wear softer shades of the same color. If a groom wants to wear pastel, his men can wear brights.

The groom can wear a full-size white rose, while the other men wear baby rosebuds. If

---

Designing Your Boutonniere

Visit www.fiftyflowers.com as well as the websites of both local and distant floral designers to see their galleries of boutonniere styles. With just a few clicks, you may discover the perfect design to help you create the groom's ideal custom boutonniere. The more graphics you can show your groom, the better. Men say they prefer to be exposed to a range of unique designs, whether in print or online.

〜

---

for garden weddings, and fabric braid handles instead of flimsy balsa wood handles seen on the classic woven basket. Not all brides are shopping at a dollar store for their baskets, and many are going the DIY route, if they're not paying over $50 for a basket in a bridal designer's line.

This flower girl accessory has certainly become a stylish carrying piece, and the petals inside—if there are any—serve to play up the natural beauty of the basket itself. A new trend in flower girls' baskets is to use florals to decorate the baskets and then fill them with something other than rose petals, such as a theme-appropriate collection of seashells for a beach wedding, colorful ornaments at a holiday wedding, or bright oversize confetti that the flower girl tosses into the air as she walks down the aisle.

petal color, such as all-pink petals. Most brides choose a colored petal so that the handfuls the flower girls scatter will show up against a white aisle runner. Choosing a monochromatic basket avoids the "too much" effect of having too many colors, which may be the case if your and your bridesmaids' bouquets contain a mix of more than four colors each.

Perfect Petals for Baskets: The traditional petal has long been rose petals for their larger size and curl, as well as their coordination with the flowers in bouquets. For a romantic, frilly look, other petals with unique shapes and curl include those from ranunculus and peonies. As a callback to the "he loves me, he loves me not" romantic notion, your flower girls could scatter daisy petals. As a budget choice, your flower

Traditional Petal Baskets: The traditional petal basket is a white, round basket with a round or oval handle made from the same material as the basket. Baskets may be left in their natural material, such as wood, or covered with material. The most common basket material is satin in white, pink, yellow, or other hue that coordinates with the bridal party. It's best to fill baskets with petals only halfway, which is just enough for visual effect and saves you money on your petals purchase. A new trend in basket decor is to match the fabric color, such as a pink satin, to the

© Tracyhornb/Dreamstime.com

© April Turner | Shutterstock

girls could scatter carnation petals, which often cost half as much as rose petals.

Flower Girl's Nosegay

Why choose a nosegay, or a smaller bouquet, for your flower girl to carry? You might like that image of the Mini-Me version of you, or you saw it in a magazine and thought it was sweet, or your site doesn't allow the scattering of flower petals . . . so it would be pointless for your flower girl to carry a basket of petals. Some brides also choose to avoid the cliché look of a flower girl carrying a petal basket, and others don't want to slide on slippery rose petals while walking down the aisle. There are tons of reasons why a flower girl might be given a small bouquet to carry, not the least of which is that the little ones love hearing, "Your bouquet looks just like mine!" from the bride she's looking at in awe on wedding day. Having her own bouquet makes the flower girl feel special.

Nosegays are ideal for any formality of wedding, from ultraformal right down to casual, and your styling of flowers and fillers determines how well they fit into the theme of the day. When it comes to color for the flower girl, you can match this bouquet's hue to the bridesmaids' bouquets, or you can allow the little one to carry an all-white nosegay like your bouquet. The flower girl's flowers can also match the flowers worn on the men's lapels, such as a nosegay made of all pink roses.

White nosegays can be designed as a smaller-size match to your all-white bouquet.

If the flower girl is wearing a white dress, an all-white nosegay can get lost in the monochromatic look, so consider pastels or greenery to add dimension. Just four or five flowers are all that's needed for a flower girl's nosegay. At a less formal wedding, the all-white nosegay can be made of baby's breath or your white bouquet filler as a way to save money and still provide a bridal look.

The flower girl's nosegay can be a smaller-size match to the bridesmaids' bouquets. If you've set apart your maid or matron of honor's bouquet as a monochromatic pastel bouquet, with bridesmaids carrying mixes, the flower

Photo by Rich Penrose

girl's bouquet can match the maid of honor's style. Generally, a flower girl looks best carrying a lighter-colored nosegay, because darker hues like burgundies create a more adult effect.

Choose two or three varieties of flowers from your own bouquet, and then create the coordinating mix from those. Choose smaller flowers or sprays for nosegays to add the effect of extra blooms without adding too much size or weight. One fun trend is to include the flower girl's birth-month flower in her nosegay bouquet.

For your outdoor, garden, or informal wedding, the flower girl can carry the same type of wildflower bouquets that your bridesmaids carry. You can choose one kind of wildflower in a single color scheme, or you can mix it up with different types in different colors. Ask if your flower girl has allergies or sensitivities to wildflowers before buying or designing such pieces. Choose a wildflower color that matches the flower girl's sash.

Bunches provide texture and color impact. Stems should be left long and stems fully or partially wrapped with ribbon. Bunches of roses, daisies, lilies, or other blooms do not need greenery or filler flowers to make a visual impact. Keep proportion in mind for the littlest of girls; if your bridesmaids are carrying six long-stemmed roses along one arm, choose three flowers for the flower girl.

Flower Girl's Wreath

While you're certainly the center of attention on your wedding day, a true beauty in every sense of the word, your flower girl receives a different type of attention: Aren't they just adorable?

While a pretty party dress helps to create the adorable flower girl image, it's the flowers that make the impression all the sweeter. Over the following pages, you'll design your flower

girl's wreaths, nosegay, and other floral accents. Your first focus is on wreaths. At first thought, you might think flower girls' wreaths are always worn on the head as a delightful crown of flowers, but that is not the only use for this pretty style. Today's flower girls might also carry their wreath hoops in place of petal baskets, and more than one flower girl has held her floral wreath in front of her as if driving a car! The effect, no matter how the girl wears or carries her floral wreath, is always a crowd-pleaser.

Again, your flower and style choices should adhere to the formality and season of your wedding, as well as to the uniformity of your entire bridal look. One popular trend to consider is to have your flower girl wear a floral wreath headpiece if you will wear a floral wreath headpiece or flowers in your hair.

Even when a flower girl wears a white party dress to match the bride, the most common floral head wreath is made of pastel flowers. A pastel floral wreath looks marvelous when coordinated with pastel flower petals in a carried basket or with a colored sash worn around the waist. The most common tones for a flower girl's wreath are pinks, yellows, and lavenders. Use small

flowers, such as baby rosebuds, instead of full, round bloomed roses.

Another option is to style the Mini-Me wreath to include the same types of flowers as those in your bouquet, all in white. An all-white wreath can be accented with a few pastel or bright flowers. If you're on a tight budget, add plenty of white by including just a few white roses and using baby's breath. A floral wreath can be made purely of baby's breath—without roses. This keeps it light to wear and inexpensive to make.

Rather than have a dozen and a half flowers attached all the way around a wreath, affix

© photo by Positive Light Photography

just three big roses or flowers to the crown of the wreath and wrap the rest of the circle with ribbon. Space these three flowers a few inches apart and separate them with baby's breath or other filler. Re-create the look of your three-stone ring by placing one large flower in the center and one smaller flower on each side, then wrapping the rest with satin ribbon.

Flower Girl Sashes

This accessory has become an essential for color-coordination purposes, and brides love how adorable the little ones look with a big bow tied in the back. A simple fabric sash tied around the flower girl's waist adds a pop of color to her dress. If she's wearing a white dress, the sash can coordinate her with the color of the bridesmaids' dresses—and might even be made from a remnant of a bridesmaid's dress after it's been cut for hemming. If she's wearing a colored or floral dress, the sash can tie her hue to that of the bridal party or the overall floral and color scheme of the wedding.

Before you choose sash flowers, you'll need to decide on the color and width of the sash, as these factors directly affect your floral piece design. The width of the sash, for instance, determines the size of the floral piece pinned to it. You don't want a floral piece that is so small that it looks like an afterthought, and you don't want one that's too large so that it is too cumbersome for the girls.

An important factor is the weight of the floral piece to be attached to the back, front, or side of the sash. Smaller flowers are of course less weighty and may even escape the attention of the flower girl over the course of the day, far more so than a big, heavy floral piece.

Design the florals so they are easy to pin onto the sash so that the floral piece can be removed after the ceremony. Kids with flowers on their sashes have complained that they can't sit in their chairs, and some have even reached back and ripped the florals from the dress, ripping the dress as well. So arrange for quick removal.

Roses: A cluster of three roses is the most popular choice for a flower girl's sash accents. If the flower girl is wearing a white dress and colored sash, use white roses. If she is wearing a colored dress with a white sash, use either colored roses or a mix of colored and white roses. There's no need to add filler or greenery to this pin-on piece, although a tiny sprig of white flowers like kalanchoe or stephanotis works well with roses.

Daisies: Accent the sash with a cluster of daisies measuring three to four inches across. The most common floral placement is on the back of the sash, incorporated into the bow. Individual

daisies can be attached along the entire front of the sash. For example, you can glue or pin daisy heads to the fabric in three- to four-inch intervals. A top look is to alternate white and colored (such as yellow) daisies along the front of the sash.

Pastels: Daisies, zinnias, and other flat-headed flowers work best for the flower girl's sash. Even if you're not using the same types of flowers as in your bouquets, you can match the flower colors. For the floral to show up nicely against a fabric sash, choose a brighter color of flower (such as hot pink) to stand against a lighter-hued sash (such as baby pink). Pastels work beautifully if all of your girls wear black dresses.

Bright Single Flowers: A single rose head can be accented with a sprig of tiny flowers and placed anywhere on the sash. A single, big Gerber daisy head makes a subtle statement when glued to the front center of a sash. The most popular colors of single Gerber daisy heads for sashes are hot pink, orange, red, and yellow. Flank a single flower with sprigs of delicate white or pastel flowers such as inexpensive baby's breath, kalanchoes, or lilies of the valley.

Fathers' & Ring Bearer's Flowers

At most weddings, the fathers and ring bearer also wear boutonnieres, regardless of whether they're wearing a tuxedo or a suit. Some couples also choose to honor their grandfathers, godfathers, stepfathers, and male ceremony participants with boutonnieres of their own.

These boutonnieres are custom created to the right size and formality for the wedding, as well as at widths designed to suit each man's or boy's size. To personalize, you might wish to style one type of boutonniere for grandfathers—such as a single white rose—and then have a different type of flower for the godfathers, and so on. Some couples design one type of boutonniere for all the men, including the fathers, setting no one apart.

For the boys, boutonnieres are best kept very small, to keep the youngest of ring bearers from becoming annoyed at a bulky boutonniere on the jacket they're already annoyed to be wearing!

Your style choices can be inspired by the season, your wedding colors, and even the location, such as an island flower at a destination wedding. The formality also opens the options for informal weddings to include daisies or wildflowers like the ones in your bouquet.

The white flowers of formal or informal boutonnieres can be the same as those in your bouquet. The white flowers can also be the same as those used in the groomsmen's boutonnieres. The most common white flowers for fathers and grandfathers are roses, mini calla lilies, and stephanotises, with traditional white fillers such as baby's breath or kalanchoe. Orchids and gardenias are considered too feminine for men.

Dads and other men can wear boutonnieres that match the groomsmen's shades in pastels, or they can be a shade darker. If the groomsmen are wearing pastel roses, these men can perhaps

© Nickvango/Dreamstime.com

© Mrorange002/Dreamstime.com

© Andreblais/Dreamstime.com

wear smaller pastel roses or multiples of smaller roses. The most popular pastel colors for dads and other men are greens, blues, pinks, oranges, lavenders, and yellows. Mix pastels to match the mix of pastel colors in your or the bridesmaids' bouquets, staying within two or three shades of hue.

If the groom or groomsmen will have bright boutonnieres, these men can as well. The most popular bright colors for men are red, purple, and orange. If you're considering bright colors for these men, be sure to let them know ahead of time that you have chosen, say, a red flower so that they can choose an outfit that will not clash, such as a blue striped shirt. With bright colors, it's always better to design smaller boutonnieres.

The top trend is for the ring bearers' flowers to match the groom's flowers in color and style. The ring bearers' boutonnieres can be designed to match the best man's, which can be set apart from the groomsmen in shade and floral type. The ring bearers' flowers should be half the size of the men's. The ring bearers' boutonnieres can consist of one flower, while the other men's contain several. Be sure the boys do not have floral allergies.

Ring Bearer Pillow: A ring bearer's pillow made from flowers is a superfun and creative alternative to the traditional. Be sure it's sturdy, and don't let little ring bearer or flower girl hands handle it too much before the ceremony begins. Decorate your fabric ring pillow with fresh

© Jeffwillia/Dreamstime.com

© photo by John and Joseph Photography

flowers that coordinate with the rest of your floral decor.

Mothers' Corsages

The most traditional mother prefers the classic corsage, affixed to either a dress strap or the jacket she wears over her dress.

For the past few years, the collarbone-level corsage has been a mainstay only for traditional-minded moms as some moms and brides find the look to be too reminiscent of prom corsages from yesteryear. Those who choose to stick with

the look say they are of two camps: They either want the most traditional rose-and-gardenia or orchid corsage, or they want a little something more dramatic, oversize, and artistic.

Here you'll explore the different twists you can take with a classic corsage, including adding unexpected flowers and greenery for a mom's ultimate personalized flower accent. This too needs to work with the formality of the event, as well as with the style of her dress, so color, shape, and dimension become important factors to share with your floral designer or to keep in mind if you will create the corsage on your own.

Simpler corsages work with both simpler and more detailed dresses and gowns, while oversize and multiflowered corsages do not work with a dress that has a lot of design elements, such as a beaded bodice.

Roses: A simple, classic corsage may be made with a single giant Ecuadorian rose in full bloom. Triad corsages are created with three roses, plus coordinating flowers such as stephanotises, for a corsage that reaches four to five inches. A more dramatic look extends to over six inches, with five to six roses used in a slight S shape. The corsage may be monochromatic, such as with all white roses, or it may include pastels, seasonal colors, or brights.

Orchids: Orchids provide dramatic shapes to the mothers' corsages. Ask mothers to show you the size corsage they would like to wear. Petite moms look best with smaller corsages, especially with the shape and drama of orchids. Dendrobium or cattleya orchids are top choices for mothers' pieces. Cattleya orchids, originating from Costa Rica to tropical South America, are a favorite at cultural weddings.

Gardenias: Make sure mothers' gardenia corsages are freshly made so the flowers are in ideal shade and shape to wear. Gardenias are so visually stunning that they do not need additional flowers as accenting. Gardenias are quite fragrant, so be sure the mothers are aware of the strong aroma. For a larger, more dramatic corsage, use two or three gardenias per piece, with or without accenting flowers of other varieties.

Mothers' Wristlets

Moms want to look modern, sophisticated, and fashionable at your wedding, and to them, a

> ### Coordinating the Look
> If you prefer an entirely coordinated floral look for all of the bouquets and personal flowers carried or worn by your bridal party and moms, choose one or two of the same types and colors of flowers from your bouquet and bring those into the moms' corsage design. For variety, give the moms larger roses than the ones in your bouquet, which will still match your theme.

traditional pin-on corsage is too old a look, too cliché, and again too promlike.

With so much care put into choosing the perfect gown to wear as the mother of the bride or groom, many moms do not want to puncture the beautiful fabric with a pin-on, nor alter the look of their gowns in any way, such as with a corsage. For these style-conscious moms, the wristlet corsage is the perfect answer. It allows them the honor of a floral piece, identifying them as a mother at the wedding, and it doesn't detract from their fashion statement.

Again, the formality of the wristlet is determined by its style and the flowers and filler or ribbon accent you and your moms choose, and a wristlet is acceptable for any formality, style, and location. What's more, the wristlet is one area in which the moms get to make their own decisions, guided by you, of course. They can decide if they want a more demure, smaller floral piece in traditional roses, or a larger, more dramatic, artsy statement such as with an orchid or unexpected colors.

Roses: The traditional mom often chooses full rose heads for her wristlet. The roses may be of any coordinating color, including all white, if she so chooses. Be sure the rose heads are bloomed at the time of wearing, since a tightly budded rose does not give the proper textural effect. The average wristlet has two or three roses without greenery or filler flowers that can make the piece too large.

Orchids: A wristlet is best designed as a petite piece, but one dramatic, large orchid may be the ideal balance to the mother's wrist. Work with the colors of the orchid, such as including tiny purple filler flowers to work with an orchid's purple streak. Be sure the orchid chosen works in balance with the mother's body size, such as a thinner, more elongated wristlet for a more petite mother. A plus-size mom can balance her look with a longer wristlet with one or two narrower flowers.

Let the beauty of the wristlet be in the beauty of the flower itself, not in a collection of multiple blooms. Choose smaller roses, gardenias, orchids, or other flowers to add multiple blooms and still keep a smaller silhouette. An alternative to the wristlet is a floral bracelet. Mothers can determine their best sizes by going to a floral shop to hold different flowers against their wrists.

A large, dramatic wristlet can add visual punch to a mom's simpler, more conservative and less adorned dress. A mom may be able to purchase a less expensive, simpler dress,

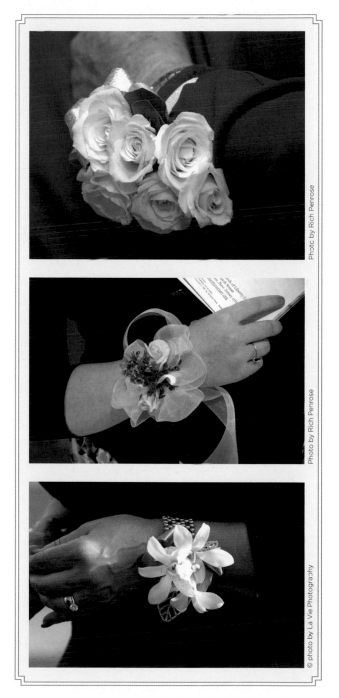

Photo by Rich Penrose

Photo by Rich Penrose

© photo by La Vie Photography

knowing that her dramatic orchid wristlet is going to impress. Larger wristlets are often made of two or three dramatic flowers plus a small amount of greenery or filler, or four to six smaller flowers. Larger wristlets are most often longer, extending halfway up the forearm.

Mothers' Nosegay Bouquets

In the past, moms had two choices for their personal flowers on wedding day: corsages or wristlets. No one seemed to venture from these traditional forms of floral tribute. Now moms are considered a part of the bridal party, and as such are given their own nosegay bouquets to carry.

The key is that moms' nosegays are styled to be smaller than the bride's and bridesmaids' bouquets, tightly packed clusters of gorgeous flowers, often in styles that don't need to match anyone else's. This means moms get the fun and joy of designing their own small nosegays with the colors that work best for their gowns and the flowers that work best with the formality and season of the wedding.

For the moms' nosegays, use much of the planning wisdom already shared in this book and add some delightful personalization that adds a message of love and honor to the most important women in your life.

Remember: Nosegays are also the perfect tribute florals for grandmothers, godmothers, stepmothers, favorite aunts, and other special women in your life. What's to be gained by keeping the moms' bouquets small? It saves money, often costing one-third the price of a bride's bouquet, and it still looks elegant and sophisticated.

Formal: If your wedding will be a formal, traditional one, the mothers' nosegays will often be

© Crysrob/Dreamstime.com

smaller versions of your own bouquet. Keep the formality with the flower choices, such as roses and ranunculus, but add depth and originality with different filler. Nosegays made without filler, with just flowers, impart a more formal look. Add something special to the nosegay handle wrap, such as a charm attached to lovely ribbon.

Outdoor: Incorporate the same types of flowers that will be featured at your outdoor wedding site, such as the apricot-colored roses found en masse in the gardens. For an informal outdoor wedding, the mothers' daisies might be yellow while yours are white. A tight cluster of tulips makes for a lovely spring nosegay for the moms. The moms might carry paler shades of the bridesmaids' richer-tone Gerber daisies or roses.

Subtle: As with your gown, the mothers' gowns may be visual masterpieces, not needing floral accents to make an impact. Some moms design very understated nosegays with all one shade of roses, as a concerted effort not to compete with the bridesmaids' or bride's bouquet. The key to subtlety is a single shape of nosegay, such as a round with no trailing ribbons. Subtle nosegays are most often pastel in tone, including traditional bridal flowers rather than exotics.

Bright: Brights create a visual pop that works perfectly only when the rest of the bridal party carries bright colors too. Moms can bring in brights when mixed with pastels or deeper jewel tones, according to the color theme of the

© Gordon Ball LRPS | Shutterstock

wedding. Keep bright nosegays on the smaller side as just a touch of color that coordinates with the dress color. Never try to match a bright bouquet color to a bright dress color, as it's almost impossible to match tones.

Grandmothers' & Other Mothers' Flowers

A wedding is a joining together of two people in love, and the people around the bride and groom also share the spotlight as VIPs of the wedding day. The entire family descended from these people; some play important roles in guiding your lives, and others are responsible for having placed you in the right place at the right time to meet the love of your life. That deserves a corsage or nosegay, right? Without these women, you might not exist, or you might be living on a different continent, enmeshed in a different world and life altogether.

In any capacity, the special women in your life are partially responsible for how you turned

> ### Presenting Floral Pieces to Grandmothers and Others
>
> If these honored women will be present at the site where you will be getting dressed and receiving your own bouquet for prewedding photos, take a moment to present each woman with her floral piece. As you present the corsage, nosegay, or wristlet, say a few words of thanks and tell each woman what she means to you. Prepare a printed love letter to each woman on your VIP list, sharing your sentiments, thanking them for their lifetime of love and support, as the perfect wedding day keepsake.

flowers if you are not sure of the recipient's dress color. Use the grandmother's, godmother's, or other VIP woman's birth-month flower in her corsage.

Wristlets: Create identical wristlets for each of these honored women, such as classic white rose wristlets, which will often work with any style or color of dress. Keep wristlets on the smaller side, no larger than four inches, to work with every woman's body size. Add a meaningful charm to each wristlet and tell the recipient the charm's meaning, such as gratitude, luck, or good health. Limit the ribbon bows, which are not very modern looking and may clash with the color the women are wearing.

out, and they certainly played a role in creating the warm and welcoming family atmosphere that may have sold your fiancé on wanting you in his life forever. He is marrying into your family, after all. He may love these women, too.

So, given their special place in your life—or in the lives of your fathers, if you're not particularly close to a stepmother—it's time to design special floral pieces for these ladies of your lineage.

Corsages: Grandmothers and other traditionalists might hold a fondness for the pin-on corsage, so be sure to ask if they'd like this style. Create smaller corsages to prevent competing or clashing with the recipient's dress accents such as sequins or bugle beading. Stick with white

Nosegays and Pomanders: Grandmothers and others will be delighted to resemble the mothers and bridesmaids with their own nosegay bouquets. Again, these should be smaller than the bridesmaids' and bride's bouquet. Filler and

Photo by Rich Penrose

stock allow for budget-friendly nosegays that contain just a few pricier flowers. Pomanders, small balls of flowers connected to a wrist-worn ribbon, are a lovely choice for mothers and grandmothers.

CENTERPIECES

The centerpiece is the crown jewel of the reception decor. It continues your floral theme from your ceremony to the reception, and allows you to infuse some personality and personal touches into the party. Since centerpieces—and centerpiece accents and table "extras"—are fun for DIY projects, we've included lots of DIY sidebars throughout to help you in your DIY journey.

When considering centerpiece styles for guests' reception tables, you'll probably think about the centerpieces you've seen (and maybe even won) at other weddings you've attended. Some may have been breathtaking with their oversize cascade of soft blooms, and some may have been subtle and romantic. Others may have looked like the bridal party took obvious steps to save money, such as a single flower in a bud vase looking lonely and forlorn at the center of an enormous table for twelve guests. You know when a centerpiece just doesn't fit with the table style, so here's where you'll begin designing your own traditional floral pieces for guests' tables.

Low-Set Centerpieces

We'll start with small, low-set centerpieces. These are the classic choice, both friendly to

the budget by virtue of needing almost 50 percent fewer flowers than elevated styles and functional for guests whose views of you and each other are not blocked by eye-level florals. Low-set centerpieces rise no more than one foot above the tabletop, with some styles no more than six inches.

© Stbosse/Dreamstime.com

Formality is conveyed, again, in color and the individual floral choices you make. When you're designing a small, low-set centerpiece, each flower carries a significantly larger amount of "style stamp," meaning that every wide-open rose connotes an elegance and exorbitance, more so than if grouped in clusters of dozens of roses.

Don't forget that a set table has color, style and formality accents in the form of decorative china (perhaps with a floral flair in the pattern design), stemware, flatware, colorful plate chargers, and the linens on the tables themselves. It could be that your best choice is a simple, low-set floral meant to bring out the beauty in the place settings, not stand alone as the sole focus on the table.

The traditional all-white bridal arrangement of low-set flower centerpieces often includes the most traditional blooms: roses, stephanotises, calla lilies, ranunculus, and gardenias. If you'd like to step away from traditional, expected white blooms, consider white tuberoses, coneflowers, and lisianthus. When you design an all-white centerpiece, you usually have to use a greater number of flowers to make a visual impression.

The most common low-set arrangements contain pastel mixes of roses, lilies, calla lilies, and filler flowers such as stephanotises or lilies of the valley. Blending two or three shades of pastels in a low-set centerpiece allows you to make an impact with fewer individual flowers.

For a traditional look that's halfway between all-bridal and seasonal stylish, choose one pastel color from your theme and mix it with white florals and greenery.

For a springtime wedding, create centerpieces from low-cut, tightly wrapped bunches of tulips, such as pinks, yellows, whites, and reds with three-inch stems. In summer use bright roses and daisies. In autumn choose low-set (three-inch stems, tops) clusters of mums in rich fall shades of burgundy, gold, persimmon, and merlot. In winter choose low-cut red roses for a festive holiday look, as well as deeper jewel colors of purple and emerald green.

© Mrorange002/Dreamstime.com

© Mrorange002/Dreamstime.com

There's no rule that says you have to stick with just one circular centerpiece for each guest table. Choose two to four pretty low-set vases (two to four inches high) and add two to four flowers in each for a gathering of centerpieces. For oval or rectangular tables, line up three to six (or more) small vases that contain two to four flowers each as a linear group centerpiece. Add visual dimension by using vases of different sizes.

Elevated Centerpieces

The placement of your centerpieces could make all the difference, and elevating them above the table extends your floral design upward to create a grander, more visually stunning effect when guests first walk into the room. It's a misconception that elevated centerpieces have to be enormous, containing dozens and dozens of

flowers each. Today's candelabras and wrought iron centerpiece holders allow you to elevate more moderately sized centerpieces, as the holders themselves are so beautifully decorated in their own entwined or Tuscan-inspired designs or even offer several levels for the placement of two to four nosegay-size floral pieces. The advent of decorative centerpiece holders allows you to create the impression of a more elaborate centerpiece just by virtue of lifting them up with decor below.

There is one big factor to keep in mind when considering elevated centerpieces: the existing decor of the reception room. When a room has color-contrast moldings, elaborate cathedral ceilings, fireplaces, and other room accents, elevated centerpieces are often used to "point" to the architectural elements above, creating a more unified look and thereby often requiring more modest floral arrangements. If the room is basic, elevated pieces add accents.

Formal: Design formal elevated centerpieces as larger, more elaborate versions of your bridesmaids' bouquets, with 30 to 50 percent more of the same types and colors of flowers. Use the top bridal flowers such as roses, gardenias, and calla lilies. Include just two or three gardenias or other pricy blooms in these centerpieces and fill liberally with stock to add volume. For formal

weddings, elevated centerpieces usually come in the same color scheme as your or your bridesmaids' bouquets.

Informal: At less formal weddings, either indoors or outdoors, you do not have to design elaborate, enormous bridal-flower-filled centerpieces. Not all elevated centerpiece holders require round bouquet-type florals; consider tall, thinner candelabras and their vase-type tops designed to hold a bunch or nosegay. Use informal, inexpensive flowers such as tulips, Shasta daisies, begonias, peonies, and zinnias. Use more greenery in informal centerpieces, such as masses of ivy.

Bring the eye upward with flowers with sturdier stems to stand tall above the centerpiece, such as sunflowers, birds of paradise, and roses. Consider flowering branches such as apple blossoms, cherry blossoms, and dogwoods that can stand more than a foot above the holder. Use nonflowering branches such as white birch to give height and dimension. Use straight or curly topped bamboo for any style or formality of wedding. Bamboo is a symbol of good luck.

The new brand of centerpiece holders features unique ways to lift florals upward, including tri-tiered designs for multiple floral groupings and pillar candles. Use a vase on each level to hold small groupings of flowers and cascading greenery. Lay nosegay bouquets, which you have measured to fit the diameters of each layer, on each tier. Alternate nosegays

Ecofriendly Tip

Here's a "green" secret to make medium-size centerpieces look larger, fuller, and more elaborate on their elevated holders: Include longer, trailing flowering branches to hang down in a cascading effect from the bottom of the arrangement. Forget about using lace or ribbon trails. These are too obviously a step taken to add dimension, and they can catch on fire if you have candles on your tabletop.

or vase-set bunches with pillar candles so that you need only one-half to two-thirds the floral pieces.

Round Centerpieces

Considered the most traditional of bridal centerpieces, the round design is what most people immediately think of when considering centerpieces. It's also the style that most floral designers feature on their websites or show you during consultations.

Most couples don't even know that they have additional options, such as elongated centerpieces to suit an oval or rectangular table. Since we are looking at traditional centerpieces on these pages, we'll start with the classic round centerpiece and then explore additional shapes and sizes so that you can design your dream floral accents for all your festive and elegantly appointed tables.

Now you might be questioning whether or not your planned round centerpieces will work for oval-shaped tables, and the answer is yes. Rounds will work for any shape table, but it's nice to know that you can style centerpieces in different shapes if you want to.

The hallmark of the round centerpiece is its fullness, whether you pack it densely with all blooms and few greenery pieces or flip the proportion to include more greenery than flowers. The choice is yours, but what you're after is a full, round shape and the perfect vase or holder as its foundation.

Create the effect of multitype white floral centerpieces by packing each with both large and small rose heads as well as rose sprays. Use one to three pricy blooms, such as gardenias, and fill the rest of the centerpiece with less expensive white florals, such as stock and lilies of the valley. Fill a round, white centerpiece just with stock, lilies of the valley, lisianthus, Bells of Ireland, Queen Anne's lace, and other small blooms.

The concept of color ranges from all pastel, to a mix of pastel and brights, to all brights. The most common trend for colored round centerpieces is to combine the two brightest colors in your or your bridesmaids' bouquets. Dual-toned centerpieces look more styled and elegant than mixes of four to six different colors. Pastels mix better than brights when paired with white flowers, as a bright and white arrangement can be too stark.

These creative holders, vases, and bowls make great settings for your round centerpieces: glass round cylinder vases, low-set round vases, tin-footed pedestal bowls, and mint julep cups. For a really creative twist, use top hats with waterproof bowls set inside, or set waterproof bowls inside garden baskets. Centerpiece containers also make great take-home gifts for guests.

Make round centerpieces look even larger by placing round mirrors beneath them, and add votive candles on top for the reflection of the flames. Set the centerpieces atop round sprinklings of flower petals. Create pedestals for the centerpieces by painting craft-store-bought rounds of one-inch-high wood platters in a color that coordinates with your wedding hues. Set a silver platter beneath a glass or silver centerpiece holder.

Elongated Centerpieces

When your reception tables are oval or rectangular, designed to seat over ten guests apiece,

© Bedo/Dreamstime.com

you can style your centerpieces to complement the shape of the table. Since the table is elongated, so too is the centerpiece. This means you may have an oval-shaped centerpiece for an oval table, or a rectangular centerpiece to fully center a longer rectangular table.

Many couples are choosing to have their reception site set with tables of different sizes and shapes. The mix of table styles allows couples to suit their guest list groups more effectively than awkwardly dividing natural circles of family or friends into the prescribed eight to ten slots at a standard round table. That family of twelve can sit together at one long table, while a group of fourteen colleagues get their own oval table, and that group of six friends gets a spacious round table nearby. The freedom to choose tables in all shapes gives you the freedom to custom design centerpieces that complement each table style.

Elongated centerpieces work with all formality levels and seasons—it's always up to the types of flowers you choose, your color scheme, and the smallest details within the floral arrangements.

Find oval silver or glass centerpiece bowls at a craft store. Use a good mix of different-size flowers so that a single-bloom design doesn't come out looking like a big pink football. Go for height at the center of the oval and taper down with smaller flowers at the edges. Oval centerpieces may mean you have more space to fill, so do it with more greenery rather than pricy flowers.

© Debstheleo/Dreamstime.com

Visit a craft store to purchase rectangular glass vases or wood containers to paint in a color that matches your theme. Create painted rectangular box centerpieces and fill them with colorful fruits and flowers. For long tables, create multiple rectangular centerpieces and set two to three of them along the length of the table. Measure the width of the tables to be sure you're not creating centerpieces that are too large for guests' dining space.

For long, narrow tables, design thin, narrow centerpieces. Design long, narrow flowerboxes and set two to three to a table. Give the impression of long, narrow centerpieces by placing small square glass vases with single flowers in them in a line down the center of the table. Use an S-shaped flowerbox; fill it with flowers and greens. Check gardening websites and catalogs for unique flowerboxes to use for centerpieces.

A traditional centerpiece for a beach wedding is a round or elongated container filled with sand and seashells. Place starfish and seahorses, found at craft stores, in each sand-filled centerpiece. While fruits are used in some nonfloral centerpieces, so too are vegetables with great color, such as red bell peppers or gourds and pumpkins at fall weddings. For a winter wedding, create a centerpiece made from glass ornaments dotted with tiny white or colored flowers.

Floating-Flower Centerpieces

Water is an essential element in all of nature, the essence of life, and a must for vitality, which is why water has quickly become one of the most popular, symbolic decor choices for weddings.

A single flower floating in a beautiful water-filled glass or crystal bowl is the picture of traditional elegance, a look that fits all wedding styles and formality levels. There are more creative decisions than you might expect with this style of centerpiece, which makes it a natural choice for the wedding couple who wants a gorgeous look regardless of the fact that this is one of the most budget-friendly decor choices possible. One flower. One bowl. One generous helping of water. This can cost less than one-tenth of the average bountiful centerpiece expense, but it makes twice the impression.

For formal weddings the most popular floating flower is the gardenia, even though its weight might mean that it's not actually floating. It could be resting on the bottom of the bowl with the water level reaching just the start of the petals.

For informal weddings daisies and lilies are the top floating-flower choices, and floating

flower petals work for all wedding formality levels, styles, and locations.

Single Floating Flowers: In a standard glass bowl or vase, at least six inches across, float a single flower for a classic, elegant effect. The flower should take up no less than a quarter of the space in the bowl. To give the flower more flotation, allow it to sit on two to three of its own leaves. Add colored glass stones to the bottom of the vase or bowl to add a complementary hue.

Dual Floating Flowers: In a larger bowl or vase, float two matching flowers to symbolize the union of your two lives. Again to symbolize your union, float a flower matching those in your bouquet with the same type of flower the groom wears in his lapel. Large flowers such as gardenias look terrific nestled together in a medium-size bowl. For the best effect, choose the same color for both flowers.

Flowers En Masse: Use enough flowers to fill the entire surface of the bowl, with blooms floating on top of the water and colored stones at the bottom. Fill the vase with enough flowers to submerge all or many of them. This effect is now most commonly done with rose heads. Fill your vase two-thirds full with flower heads and then fill the rest with water for a floating and surface effect.

Floating Flower Petals: For the ultimate budget choice that still provides a festive and pretty look, float rose petals in the bowl or vase. For a larger, more formal petal, use calla lily petals. For petals with color, consider tiger lilies, peace roses with darker pinks on the edges of the petals, or striped petals. Just a few flower petals are needed for best effect for a medium-size vase or bowl.

© Magicfanfa/Dreamstime.com

© Richar Robinson | Shutterstock

And More Centerpiece Ideas

© Stbosse/Dreamstime.com

© Eric Limon | Shutterstock

© Andretblais/Dreamstime.com

© Dallaseven/Dreamstime.com

© Gingy25/Dreamstime.com

© Dallas Events Inc. | Shutterstock

© Mrorange002/Dreamstime.com

© Carrollmt/Dreamstime.com

Photo by Kristen Jensen

© Carrollmt/Dreamstime.com

Themed Centerpieces

Whether it's cultural, outdoor garden–themed, season-related, or color-based, themed centerpieces are a fun way to pay homage to, or simply play up, certain well-loved aspects of your wedding or life. A top trend in personalizing weddings is to use the colors, themes, symbols, and foods from your heritage in your centerpieces and decor. Since you are blending your lives together, you might be in a position to creatively mix and match yours and your groom's heritage items.

You can also create garden-themed centerpieces that are perfect for outdoor locations, such as a botanical garden, estate home, or even your own backyard. Some sites are so well bloomed and magnificently planted that you might think you have very little to do when it comes to decor. But your one vital task is to design centerpieces that tie into both your surroundings and the colors of your bridesmaids' dresses, bouquets, and other accessories.

Playing up the seasons in your centerpieces is also a popular trend. Remember: You're not limited to pumpkins and mums for your autumn wedding, nor are you stuck with snow and wrapped gifts for your winter wedding. Play up seasonal fruits in your centerpieces as accents, such as incorporating bright red or green apples, or go big with an ice sculpture.

Introducing color in your centerpieces is important, as it ties in with the rest of your color accents: bouquets, dresses, etc. Try playing up reds and pinks, blues and purples, yellows and oranges, blacks and whites, or your own combinations. And remember: You don't have to limit yourself to two simple colors. Instead, have some fun mixing and matching within similar color families.

Chapter 6

THE PAPER TRAIL

$\sim$

So you've gotten engaged, set the date, and set up some of the preliminaries of your wedding, but now here comes the fun part: You get to announce your wedding to the world! With the busy schedules we all keep these days, save-the-dates have come into fashion as popular additions to the traditional wedding invitation. The save-the-date is typically sent out around nine months before the wedding, and it sets the tone for the style and look of your wedding, be it casual and fun, or formal and black-tie. Following the save-the-date, about six to eight weeks out from the wedding date, the invitation is sent out. It, too, follows in the same style and creative flair as the save-the-date, and the theme continues.

The paper trail winds up after the wedding, with the sending of your thank-you notes, which are often fashioned to model the look of the invitation and the save-the-date before it. This part of the planning is where you get a chance to be very creative and really infuse personality or set the tone for the night. Have fun with it, and don't feel limited by the options available in this book. We encourage you to do some extensive Internet and window-shopping research (even places like Target now sell wedding invitation kits). Don't be afraid to DIY, either. This part of the wedding planning can be a great cost saver if you take on the DIY initiation.

Regardless, we encourage you to use this chapter as inspiration, to help you identify your

© photo by Junebug Weddings

creative style, and to properly inform you of the correct invitation wording so that you can properly inform others of your big day.

INVITATION BASICS

When it comes to sending your wedding invitations, what you say and how you say it are important. An invitation acts as an informative guide for your guests, providing them with their first impression of your unique wedding style. You want to be sure that everyone receives basic information, including your names; the names of your hosts (traditionally your parents); the dates, times, and locations of both your ceremony and your reception; and an easy way to RSVP. Once those things are covered, there is no limit to the stylish options available for wedding invitations full of personality.

© photo by Junebug Weddings

Order your invitations four to six months before your wedding and be ready to send them out six to eight weeks before the event. For holiday weddings or weddings at the peak of the busy wedding season, consider ordering them even sooner. Order plenty of extra invitations and envelopes to ensure that you're ready for inevitable mistakes and changes, and save a few for yourself and your family to use in albums and scrapbooks.

Choose papers, inks, fonts, specific wording, and design elements that show off your style and provide important clues as to the level of formality and type of attire expected.

Invitation Style: Choose colors that complement your wedding color palette and designs that fit your style. Refer to your budget to determine if you'll be working with a custom-invitation designer or ordering ready-made invitations. Both can be absolutely beautiful. Be sure you have confirmed your date and time with your ceremony and reception venues before you have your invitations printed. Send an invitation to yourself first to see how well it travels through the mail.

RSVP: Include an RSVP card and a self-addressed stamped envelope to make it easy for your guests to respond. Strict rules of etiquette require guests to promptly respond in writing to wedding invitations. Many people are not aware of this. Ask guests to respond by a certain date so there's no confusion. If you don't mind a

© photo by Junebug Weddings

© photo by Junebug Weddings

phone call or e-mail response, add your phone number or e-mail address to your response card.

Addressing Your Guests: Begin your invitation wording with the names of your hosts or your own names if you are hosting your wedding yourselves. Use wording that matches the formality of your event, but always adhere to basic rules of etiquette no matter how informal your wedding. Choose heavy papers, fine tissue liners, and formal fonts to announce an elegant black-tie affair and fun design elements like polka dots and bright colors to announce a wedding with a casual, informal feel.

Ecofriendly Options: There's no need to sacrifice color with environmentally friendly soy-based inks. The clear, clean oil they're made from actually makes colors look brighter. Select tree-free papers made from cotton, linen, or bamboo for

invitations that feel fantastic to the touch and are completely recyclable. Embrace the green movement by choosing a company dedicated to reducing its carbon footprint. Look for companies that recycle, cut down on waste, and belong to a carbon offsetting program. Reduce your carbon footprint and work with your invitation designer to cut down on the quantity of paper used in each invitation. The traditional layers of tissue and the multiple envelopes that used to be standard can easily be forgone in order to "go green" with your wedding invitations.

MATCHING YOUR STYLE

The invitation design sets the tone for your wedding. If you're having a black-tie affair, your invitation should give off that sense of formality, both in look and in wording. Or, if it's a more casual beach affair, creatively insert some fun beach accents, like shell prints or some sand.

Let this next section be your inspiration, and follow it up by letting your creative flag fly.

Classic Designs

Throughout most of the twentieth century, etiquette dictated that every couple's wedding invitations be designed essentially the same way. Printed on white paper with black ink or gold embossing powder, formal invitations included an inner and outer envelope, a reception card, an RSVP card, and traditional wording.

Preferred printing methods included the letterpress, with its old-fashioned movable type that furthers the handcrafted look, and the time-honored method of engraving, which still produces the most precise, elegant script available. Blind embossing (engraving without the ink) was often used to create lovely monograms, borders, and return addresses, and calligraphy ruled the day as the popular way to address envelopes and create the handwritten look used by engravers.

Today's classic, formal invitations still incorporate these processes and follow the rules of etiquette in regard to proper wording, but choices of papers, inks, fonts, and embellishments are now personalized to offer you invitation options that are much more than what's commonly expected. By incorporating traditional designs with modern details, you're free to create a uniquely sophisticated statement.

The bride's parents are the traditional hosts of the wedding, and their names are spelled out first in the invitation. "Mr. and Mrs. Parents of

© photo by Junebug Weddings

the Bride request the honour of your presence" is the expected wording for church ceremonies. *Favour* and *honour* are the old English spellings used in traditional invitations. Addresses should be spelled out in full and there are no abbreviations used except for "Mr." and "Mrs."

Today's letterpress invitations, like the one below, are often printed on cotton (tree-free) papers. Since the first printing of the Gutenberg Bible, the fine art of letterpress has been used to

© photo by Junebug Weddings

create one-of-a-kind invitations. Thermography has begun to replace engraving as the most popular method for printing classic invitations. Use fine tissues and vellum to add refinement and to act as a covering for engraved invitations to keep them from smudging.

Black-and-white is still the color combination most associated with the invitations of chic, formal affairs. Strong colors like red, bronze, and gold accentuate classic black-and-white designs. Mounting your invitation on a bifold or trifold mat so it can be easily displayed highlights the important nature of your event. Artistic embellishments like your choice of modern fonts or decorative motifs and borders help you show off your sophisticated style.

Soft colors like powder pink, apricot, taupe, and dove blue look lovely and add a delicate touch to creamy off-white papers. Vintage-inspired fonts and embellishments are timeless additions that add a feeling of quality and easy elegance.

Casual Designs

Casually designed invitations give you the freedom to veer off the ultratraditional track to get creative and express more of your personal wedding style. Formal wording can be softened, papers and colors can come from a broader artistic palette, graphics and patterns can add fun and excitement, and natural accents can be used to show off the theme of your event.

Even when using casual wording for your invitations, it's always smart to stay respectful and gracious. Be sure you're acknowledging those hosting your event and warmly welcoming those being invited. Whether your invitations say something simple like, "Together with their parents, Kimberly Elizabeth Loewen and

Classic swirls, floral details, and other organic and nature-inspired embellishments lend romance to your invitation design. Feminine, handwritten typefaces and calligraphy take the romance even further and will never look dated.

Adam Curtis Bamberg invite you to share in the joy of their wedding day," or "Joyously, gleefully, giddily, and ecstatically, we invite you to celebrate as Kim and Adam tie the knot," choose your words carefully and with reverence for those helping you.

Instead of the classic wording like "request the honour of your presence," you can say something more casual sounding, like "invite you to share in the joy of their wedding day." You can include your parents' names in the host line, whether or not they are the event's main financial contributors, or simply say "together with their families." Get even more playful with your wording if it matches the tone and theme of your event.

Handmade papers, with their slightly irregular surfaces, are pretty and feminine with a homemade feel. Modern-style invitations can benefit from papers with ribbing, strong angular textures, or lush metallic finishes. Casual invitations can use color combinations not traditionally considered bridal. Bold colors and detailed paper textures can add depth and personality that classic white card stock simply can't touch.

Go bold with intensely colored papers, inks, and strong contrasts. Look at samples, visit stationery stores, and find examples of designs you love for the best and most useful inspiration. Have fun experimenting with color; you may be surprised at the combinations you love most!

Patterns and graphics offer an even further addition of creative expression, and there are unending possibilities to choose from. Do you and your partner gravitate toward abstract patterns or realistic imagery, feminine flourishes, or angular geometry? Narrow it down to your favorite themes and work with your designer to come up with the perfect look, or play with unusual combinations that creatively represent you both.

Use graphics that represent your specific wedding details. Choose flowers you'll be using in your wedding decor, a pattern that will carry through to your table settings, or decorative accents present in the architecture of your venue. Find inspiration for invitation graphics in your wedding dress or other wedding day fashions. Balance the masculine and feminine in your invitation graphics so that you'll both love the look. Try one's chosen pattern in the other's favorite color, or vice versa.

Organic accents inspired by the natural world work wonders to communicate your wedding theme. You can incorporate colors or imagery inspired by Mother Nature, eco-friendly materials, or an authentic bit of nature itself to convey the style of your event.

Tie a beautifully pressed golden leaf to the front cover of your fall wedding invitation, or use a small twig as a closure to radiate the fresh new feeling of spring. Actual organic details incorporated into your invitation design can be powerful and unique design elements. Organic graphics and patterns can evoke the season you're getting married in: tulips for spring, poppies for summer, leaves for fall, and holly for winter.

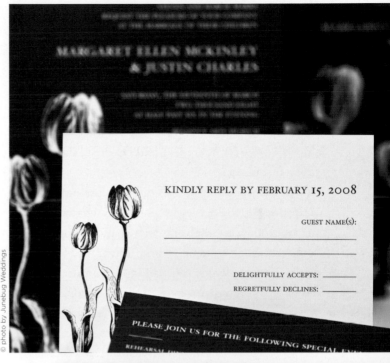

© photo by Junebug Weddings

© photo by Junebug Weddings

Playful Designs

Nothing announces a fun, lighthearted wedding like a playful invitation. Creatively communicate the location, season, or theme of your wedding, or something unique and personal about you as a couple. When and where you met, your individual hobbies, and your shared life passions all make for interesting and heartfelt invitation inspirations.

By incorporating whimsical elements into your design, you let your guests know that the upcoming event is one with a fun-loving approach. Look to your favorite things in life or the history of your courtship for whimsical design possibilities. Your guests are the people you know and love the most, so they will appreciate the personal detail these invitations convey.

Old-fashioned candy buffs? Create sweets-themed invitations and other paper items. Did you meet way back in elementary school? Your invitations could be reminiscent of a classroom

blackboard or red and blue striped penmanship paper, or it could include folding instructions to make it into a paper airplane. Have you traveled together to interesting places? Incorporate graphics of the rich colors that surrounded you in India, the palace guards you loved in London, or the elephants you saw in Africa.

Color is key in invitation design, and it can easily be the main focus of any beautiful paper

creation. Using two shades of the same color, like rich fuchsia and petal pink or grass green with light chartreuse, can look amazingly complementary while not overloading the senses. Contrasting colors like red and purple or navy blue and yellow create dramatic impact and vibrant style.

Bright colors, like bold pink, look great against crisp white paper, and black accents help them to really pop. Use a rich color for your paper stock and print the text and graphics in white for a negative space design approach. Fun and playful patterns like polka dots and stripes are at their most vibrant in strong, bright colors. Exaggerate the natural colors of the graphics on your invitation to make your theme seem celebratory and larger than life.

If your wedding has a strong theme already in place, or if you have an idea for something truly unique, make the most of it in your invitations and start tying it in early. This is a great chance to really think outside the box and come up with a suite of designs that all originate from one central concept. Invitations can come in all kinds of alternative formats, from rock concert posters and library cards to old-fashioned train schedules and recipe cards. You are limited only by your imagination, so have fun creating ideas together.

Beach-themed wedding invitations can incorporate seashells or whimsically drawn waves, starfish, crabs, seahorses, sea anemones, or coral to get guests excited for the laid-back

feeling of the event. Vintage-themed weddings can incorporate old-fashioned fonts, cameo-like silhouettes, art deco designs, or antique fashions into their invitation designs. Vineyard weddings can incorporate wine labels or a stamp inspired by a winery logo into the invitations and other paper products.

Invitations don't have to be made only of paper. Ribbons, creative closures, glassine envelopes, and other materials can be included in their designs. Fabric can be printed on and combined with paper for wonderfully tactile invitations. Visit your local stationery store to see the different sizes of envelopes available. Large or odd-size invitations will require additional postage to make it successfully through the mail.

Alternative Designs

If great design is a true love of yours, then go all the way with your invitations and choose

© photo by Junebug Weddings

star-style envelopments have a base that holds your invitation card and flaps on each edge that fold closed toward the center. Paper invitations can be mailed nestled inside flat gift boxes and surrounded with decorative papers or treats. Take a look at your local paper store or online to see the variety of options and DIY kits available.

If you or your fiancé work in the tech industry or are right at home with your computer and electronic gadgets, consider using CDs, DVDs, digital images, or websites to add fun to your wedding invitations. This CD of love songs in the photo below was sent to guests to get everyone caught up in the romance before arriving at the wedding. Invitations in the form of a DVD can match a cinematic-themed wedding or act like a high-tech website, informing guests of your favorite restaurants, clubs, and places to

an alternative size, unusual structure, or high-tech format to make them truly one of a kind. The tiniest details can add up to create a truly unique invitation design. Once you get your basic design ideas down, think about ways to expand the concept to every piece of your wedding paper ensemble.

Paper can be ordered in numerous shapes and sizes of ready-made pocket folders and enclosures. Pocket folders allow for extra pages to be included inside and can open either horizontally like a book, vertically like an envelope, or from the center outward in all directions.

Gatefold invitations, like the one shown above, have three panels, while single folios have just two. A booklet-style invitation is like a mini album, with multiple pages available to communicate lots of useful information. Blossom- or

© photo by Junebug Weddings

visit to help travelers feel more at home. Include a DVD slide show of images of you, your partner, and your family and friends.

You can create postage stamps with your own photo or graphic for an ultrapersonalized touch. Every piece of your invitation suite can have unique design elements. The envelope, RSVP card, return envelope, and reception card can all have different but complementary details printed on them. Many invitation designers can adapt one of their existing designs with personalized elements just for you.

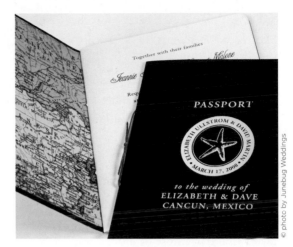

Destination-themed weddings offer the perfect inspiration for creative invitations. Pull graphics, colors, and cultural details from the travel industry or the country to which you're headed to create invitations with a spirit of adventure. For international travel, create a booklet invitation that looks like a realistic passport. Airline boarding passes make for fun and familiar designs for destination save-the-dates, wedding invitations, or seating cards. Include an elegant map in your invitation for destination weddings or for out-of-town guests. Have one custom illustrated with your wedding venues and other points of interest highlighted, or find a charming old-fashioned reproduction that will lend an air of history to the trip.

ALL THE DETAILS

The invitation itself is just one small part of the actual invitation package. Also included is information on attire (sometimes), hotels, and more. But in addition to these "extras," there

---

Weighing Your Invitations

If your wedding invitation is an odd size, rigid, or heavy, or if you would like to avoid automated printing on your envelope, take your finished invitations to your local post office, have them weighed for exact postage, and ask about having them hand cancelled (processed by hand).

are also other paper extras for the wedding, like reception menus, table seating cards, and sometimes even creative paper favors. Again, as a cost-saving initiative, you might find it's more budget friendly to tackle some of these paper "extras" yourself, but that's completely your call.

Informative Extras

Tying together your invitation wardrobe has never been easier. From one-of-a-kind save-the-dates to matching programs, gifts, menus, and favors, there is a host of unique ways to finish your statement and keep your guests informed.

If you're planning on inviting guests who will need to travel to your wedding and make arrangements months in advance, then a stylish save-the-date card sent six to nine months before your wedding is a thoughtful way to let them know how much their presence will mean to you.

Once your big day dawns, those attending your wedding will appreciate a detailed program that helps them prepare for the specifics of your ceremony. When you've tied the knot and it's time to enjoy your reception, seating cards act to direct guests to their places, where they're likely to find people they will connect with. Simple tabletop accents like creative wedding favors, trivia questions about the two of you, or stories about your courtship will entertain your guests and break the ice with friends and family who are still getting to know one another.

For an easy way to communicate with guests from across the globe, consider building a personal wedding website. Include directions, RSVP options, lodging information, and local attractions for out-of-town guests.

Save-the-Dates: Whether they're custom designed or DIY, designing a save-the-date is a fun way to start planning your wedding together. Choose colors and styles that complement your main invitation. This will set a cohesive tone right from the beginning. Keep in mind the time of year and location when sending your save-the-date cards. Remember that traveling on holidays to popular destinations can be problematic. Include lodging and travel information if you have special tips to share.

© photo by Junebug Weddings

Ceremony Extras: Besides letting guests know how your ceremony will unfold, programs give them something to read while they wait for you to come down the aisle. Include the names of your wedding party and how they are affiliated with you to help familiarize guests from

approved foods. Table cards typically identify tables by name or number; try using place names like London or Paris for a chic urban event or names of artists for a reception held at a museum or art gallery. Recipe cards given as favors that offer dishes or drinks from your family or favorite restaurant will be used again and passed on.

Your Wedding Website: It's considered improper to include registry information on your wedding invitation, but listing it on your wedding website is perfectly acceptable. Many sites allow you to have photo galleries, which can be great for introducing your family members and members of your wedding party to your guests who may not know everyone. If you've designed a simple ecofriendly wedding invitation, you can direct guests to view your wedding website to get all the additional information they will need.

different parts of your life. Sweet extras like the story of how you first met or when you first knew you were in love let your guests in on what makes your relationship unique.

Reception Extras: Printed menus let guests know what to look forward to and alert them to anything that may not be on their list of

The wording on each piece of your wedding stationery ensemble should match the overall style of your wedding, whether formal or casual, to set the tone and let guests know what kind of event it will be. If you jump around in your level of formality it may cause confusion.

Thank-You Notes

To celebrate your marriage, your friends and family will shower you with their good intentions. They'll give you presents, throw parties in your honor, and share their time and talents with you. To show your gratitude, you'll want to share your thanks with them in ways that will touch their hearts.

Start by sending a handwritten thank-you note to each and every person who gives you something of value. Mention the giver's gift or contribution and why you appreciate it. While handwritten notes may be rare these days, they are still a necessary part of wedding etiquette, and sending them is something you shouldn't overlook. Try to send them out within three weeks of receiving gifts, and don't procrastinate.

For people who go the extra mile to show their support, look for thoughtful gifts and creative ways to say thanks. Did your favorite cousin give you the china pattern that you wanted? Then have him over for dinner to enjoy it. Did your sister walk the aisles of every local wedding show with you without complaining?

Then treat her to a day at the spa to give her a chance to put her feet up. However you choose to express your appreciation, be thoughtful and authentic.

Printed Notes: Order your thank-you notes with your invitations and other printed items; you may get a price break from your printer. Every gift giver puts careful thought into his or her gift. Be just as thoughtful with your reply. Thank-you notes are the last impression that guests will have of your wedding. Their importance cannot be overemphasized. Don't listen to people who say you have up to a year to reply; three months is the maximum time allowed.

© photo by Junebug Weddings

Handwritten Notes: Don't worry if your handwriting is less than perfect. As long as it's legible, it's the effort that counts. Hand address your envelopes and your cards. Preprinted labels and messages are an etiquette no-no. Should you receive a gift that's not quite your cup of tea, don't rave on about how much you love it.

Just say "Thank you for the (fill in the blank). I'll think of you whenever I use it."

Thoughtful Gifts: Bake some cookies or make a cake for a person who gave you nice things for your kitchen. Send perennial flower bulbs to a gardening enthusiast for a lovely gift that will be appreciated year after year. Start an annual "girl's night out," and celebrate with your bridal party every year the night before your anniversary. Send a wedding photo that includes the recipient as a follow-up to your thank-you card.

© photo by La Vie Photography

Your Gratitude List: Make it a habit to celebrate the reasons that you're grateful for each other. It's a sweet and touching way to connect and a great habit to begin together now. Don't forget to make a record of all the gifts you receive and who gave them. With all that's going on it's easy to forget which gift came from which person. Resist any temptation to take your thank-you notes with you on your honeymoon. There will be time to send them when you get back.

Keep an ongoing gratitude list and schedule time at least twice a month to write and send out your thank-you notes together. Have fun with this important obligation by setting up special cocktails, drinks, or snacks or listening to your favorite music.

Speaking of Gifts & Thank-Yous . . .

Registering for all those wonderful wedding gifts is a perk of being soon-to-be marrieds and is a helpful guide to your family and friends who want to congratulate you on your new life together.

Work together to choose items in every price range that you are confident you'll love to own, and register soon after you announce your engagement for all of those prewedding events. Stay focused on the kinds of things that will really fit in with your lifestyle, and try not to get tempted or overwhelmed by all the options.

That said, you should try to have fun with it, too. These days all kinds of stores have wedding registries, and there are numerous gift registry websites that allow you to choose items from any online shop. You can even register for help with your honeymoon or fun activities like dinner out on the town, French lessons, or couple's cooking classes.

Etiquette states that you should never include your registry information in your wedding invitation. Have your parents, maid of honor, and best man spread the word, include it in invitations to other events like wedding showers and engagement parties, or list it on your wedding website.

Monogrammed towels and sheets are classic wedding gifts that never go out of style and can be made with old-fashioned or modern lettering. Picture frames come in handy after a wedding for all your beautiful wedding photos. New luggage in different sizes makes a great gift, and you'll use it and appreciate it for years to come. Balance big-ticket items for your home

© photo by Junebug Weddings

with less-expensive options like basic linens, decor accessories, or small electronics.

If you love to cook, register for fun and useful kitchen tools and utensils as well as various cookbooks. Mixers, blenders, and other small appliances can be handy yet affordable gifts. Registering for a formal china pattern is the most classic registry item and makes a wonderful family heirloom. Check each store's return policy before you begin your registry so you will know what to do if you don't receive full sets of things like china, silverware, or glassware.

Specialty foods and wines are perfect gifts for food aficionados and couples building their wine collection. Register for a food or wine of the month club. Let your hobbies guide your unorthodox registry items. Register for activities on your honeymoon like spa treatments, romantic dinners, or helicopter rides. Outdoor gear and athletic stores offer registries to help you on your next hiking, hunting, or camping trip. Build your music library by registering for new CDs or music downloads.

If you already own enough essentials for your home, choose a charity that's close to your heart and ask guests to make a donation in lieu of wedding gifts. Register with stores that partner with charitable organizations so that part of the proceeds from your gift sales will benefit those in need. Give guests the option of a traditional gift or a charitable gift, as some people will be excited to buy something special just for you.

Chapter 7

FOOD & DRINK

࿇

Depending on the time of your wedding and the type of reception that follows, you might find yourself hosting a dinner party for 150 people. That is, food is expected and should be included in your wedding day celebration. If your wedding is being held at a catering hall, country club, hotel ballroom, or other established venue, chances are you'll work with the in-house catering/kitchen staff to create your dining menu. This will involve you going to a tasting prior to your big day to finalize the menu. It's a fun—and yummy—part of the wedding planning.

But while the food—appetizers, buffets, and sit-down meals included—is wonderful, we consider the food highlight of the night to be your wedding cake. Consider it to be like the star on the top of the tree—the cake just completes the night. Cake cutting has become a fun part of the evening's celebrations, with your guests huddling around you both as you daintily (well, okay, sometimes daintily) feed each other your first bite of the delicious dessert. It's a highlight that truly says, "How sweet it is to be loved by you!"

And if cake isn't your thing—that's fine, it isn't everyone's thing!—there are plenty of other types of desserts to serve that are fun, whimsical, and simply delicious. Ice cream buffets, candy bars, and Venetian tables have all received top billing by modern brides in recent years. Remember, it's your party, your rules. Eat what you like.

We can't enter into a discussion about food without mentioning the lots of yummy cocktails that go with it. We're particularly excited to provide you with several inspiration galleries showcasing some of our favorite and most festive cocktails that may just be perfect for your occasion—complete with full recipes, too!

Just writing this has made us hungry—and we hope that the next few pages of text and photos make you hungry, too. We hope you enjoy every morsel that follows.

THE MENU
Depending on whether you're having your reception in an established venue with an in-house kitchen or you're bringing in your own caterer, how you go about deciding your night's

© photo by GH Kim Photography

© photo by Positive Light Photography

© photo by GH Kim photography

menu will differ. This next section points out general bits of information that will be important when you decide on food, regardless. Chances are this is one of the first big parties you've thrown, so you want to be sure you're doing it right.

Catering Menu

When it comes to your wedding, food can be the largest cost of your event, and the difference in price between a classic plated dinner and an hors d'oeuvres reception is quite large. Look at all your options creatively, interview different caterers, and consider your budget in order to choose the best option for you.

A seated dinner, which is the most formal choice, can consist of simply an appetizer, entree, and dessert, or be a more elaborate meal with five full courses or more, including palate cleansers and wine pairings. Buffets tend to lend a more casual feel and allow you to offer your guests more food options on a more flexible schedule. Alternative menus like picnics, culturally themed meals, or dessert-only receptions add fun to an event and incorporate your personal wedding style.

When hiring a caterer, look over your contract carefully and be very specific with what you are asking for. A typical contract should include the complete menu, the number of guests and courses, tableware rental if provided, the date your final guest count is due, the number of servers and kitchen staff the caterer guarantees, gratuity, tax, deposit, and payment requirements, as well as policies about leftovers, overtime, cancellations, and liability.

Classic: A plated dinner allows your guests to relax and have more time to visit with other people at their table. You can serve a single entree to everyone or offer guests entree options. This can be organized in advance through your wedding invitations, or guests can order from their server at the reception itself. Even if you don't offer guests choices for their main course, be sure to have some vegetarian options on hand for guests who don't eat meat.

Casual: Be sure your buffet has space on either side to walk easily and plenty of serving platters

© photo by La Vie Photography

so guests can move through quickly. Smaller buffet stations can be spread throughout the reception hall to encourage mingling and create an interactive food experience. Specialty buffets that have a themed focus can support your larger wedding vision. Choose a regional focus like Italian, French, or Japanese foods, or highlight the local specialties from your own area.

Alternative: A reception of heavy hors d'oeuvres can be a lower-cost alternative to a sit-down dinner or buffet while still offering guests a delicious light meal. Be sure to specify this kind of food service on your invitation. Draw food inspiration from the seasons. Have a summer barbecue, a spring garden picnic, a fall harvest—themed feast, or a winter champagne dessert reception. Morning weddings and elegant brunch receptions allow for creative breakfast-inspired menus and cocktails.

Playful Additions: Late-night events need extra nourishment to fuel the dance party; miniburgers and fries are always a hit. Send guests home with tasty midnight snacks like donuts and chocolate milk, or give them a delicious morning after with locally made pastries, homemade granola, and specialty coffees and teas. At a small, intimate hors d'oeuvres reception, make great food a main focus. Have an open kitchen

© photo by Junebug Weddings

© photo by Positive Light Photography

© photo by Junebug Weddings

Vendors working at your reception will need dinner as well as your guests. Communicate with your caterer and be sure they have a plate of nourishing food or a special vendor meal reserved and ready to serve each professional at a time that doesn't conflict with the services they're performing. Remember: You should start determining the type of meal you'll be serving based on the time and style of your reception about four months before your wedding date. See our handy timeline chart on page 348 to stay on target.

area so guests can watch the chef and skilled kitchen staff in action.

Cake Alternatives

If a classic tiered wedding cake doesn't ring your bell, then by all means serve your guests a mouthwatering sweet alternative that does. (If, however, you want the cake, see our complete cake section on page 288.)

Cupcakes have become a wildly popular wedding cake alternative, and for good reason. Who can resist them? They are small, adorable, and delicious, and you don't have to worry about coordinating the cake cutting and serving. Each guest can simply take the cupcake he or she wants to enjoy during your party.

Choose a selection of cupcake flavors and a single way to decorate them to keep your look cohesive. A tower of cupcakes on a multilayered cake stand looks impressive and echoes the traditional shape of a tiered wedding cake. When it comes time to cut the cake, a small cake set on top of your cupcake tower allows you to have the traditional cake cutting and a fun topper for your cupcake display.

If pies and tarts are your favorite desserts, why not serve them at your wedding? A table loaded with a selection of fresh berry, fruit, nut, or cream pies is sure to be a big hit. To sweeten the deal, have whipped cream, vanilla ice cream, and candied nuts available to top each slice. Find pretty cake stands and platters to display your pies and tarts in a beautiful way. If you have numerous treats available, label the flavors of pies offered so guests know what their choices are and can avoid any they may have allergies to. Serve pies made from a family recipe and hand out pretty recipe cards as wedding favors. Include the story of where the recipe came from and why it's so special.

Minicakes are a fun way to serve wedding cake in a whole new way. Minicakes make a

© photo by Junebug Weddings

big impact, and each guest will feel honored to receive a special, personal confection. Serve them to each person at the end of a seated dinner, or create an impressive display of all the minicakes together so guests can choose their favorite. Choose a design that plays up your wedding color scheme like the baby blue and white minicakes shown on page 280, bottom. Minicakes should be miniature versions of a traditional tiered wedding cake. Cut and feed each other the mini version, just as you would a large cake. Minicakes make great take-home wedding favors so guests are left with a sweet treat from your celebration.

To add a little whimsy to your event, ice-cream sundae bars, snow-cone machines, cotton candy, and dessert buffets are wonderful alternatives to wedding cake that will get your guests involved in the fun. Pass trays full of delectable little sweets during cocktail hour that are a preview of the dessert to come later in the evening. A dessert buffet full of petit fours, tartlets, cookies, brownies, and chocolates is delightful at the end of any wedding reception, whether it's in addition to a wedding cake or as an alternative. Old-fashioned frozen treats, like Popsicles, ice-cream sandwiches, and ice-cream cones, will make your guests feel like kids again.

Novelties

In addition to the traditional dessert—cake—there are plenty of novelties you can add to your already delectable menu. Chocolate-covered strawberries are classic and elegant wedding

© photo by Junebug Weddings

Photo by Kristen Jensen

desserts. Pass them on trays, include them in a dessert buffet, or serve them alongside wedding cake slices for extra sweetness. Chocolate fondue also is a warm, yummy dessert option. Rent a chocolate fountain from a local company, but be sure someone on-site knows how to maintain it so the chocolate doesn't run low or get clogged. Delectable chocolate truffles are perfect wedding favors that are sure to delight most every guest.

Custom wedding cookies are a fun surprise and can be made in any shape, size, or personality. The darling cookies shown above represent the bridal party and would look great creatively displayed at a reception. Photo images can be printed on cookies in edible sugar ink. Serve your favorite cookies at your wedding reception, and then send guests home with a charming jar filled with extras or with dry mix, instructions, and the original recipe.

Candy buffets are as much decorations as they are yummy favors, so you'll want to have enough candy to create an abundant presentation. Choose five to ten varieties of candy and purchase several pounds of each depending on the size of your wedding and the look you're going for. Don't go under one-quarter to one-half a pound of candy per person, or you many run too low. Hard or wrapped candies work well in warmer climates, but the best choices are candies that you personally love and think your guests will appreciate. Include a small metal scoop in each candy jar for easy use. Small Chinese food–style takeout containers, vellum or clear plastic envelopes tied with ribbon, or pretty tins make excellent take-home containers for your candy buffet. Label each kind of candy, especially those containing nuts, so your guests can choose wisely in case of health concerns. A varying selection of large and small glass vases, bowls, and platters makes a charming candy buffet presentation and consider adding accents to match your wedding colors.

THE DRINKS

Regardless of whether or not you're providing your guests with an open bar at your reception, you should take the beverage menu into consideration. Some couples choose to have a limited open bar, with only select beers, wines, and liquors made available to guests, while others go carte blanche. This next section offers a wide variety of choices for you to consider. And, well, if you're having a dry wedding, you can skip over this section.

Cocktails & Beverages

Celebrating with delicious drinks and toasting to your marriage goes hand in hand with wedding tradition, but the bar tab at your wedding can easily become the second-largest cost next to the food. Having an open bar with unlimited drink options is wonderful if your budget allows for it, but if not, don't fear; there are many other options available.

A cash bar, where guests buy their own drinks, could reduce your costs but is generally considered an etiquette faux pas. Your best bet for saving money is to cut down on the alcoholic drinks available and offer guests a simple selection of beer, wine, and soft drinks. If you love the idea of cocktails, choose a specialty drink designed just for the occasion or a limited number of liquors and mixers so you won't be surprised by the bar tab at the end of the night.

Depending on your event venue and the state you live in, there may be extra considerations regarding liquor licenses. Many locations already own one, but those that don't host a lot of events may not. Ask your venue about this early in the process so you have ample time to apply for the proper permits or come up with creative alternatives.

If wine is a passion of yours, play up its presence and showcase the special options your guests can choose from. If not, simply having one good white and one good red is perfectly acceptable. Delicious sparkling wines from the United States and Prosecco from Italy make perfect alternatives to expensive French champagnes. Microbreweries are popping up all over the country, so great handcrafted beer is everywhere. Choose a local beer or two for your guests to enjoy.

Ask your caterer to create a custom cocktail for each of you, and let guests choose which flavor they enjoy best. Serve a signature cocktail from your favorite restaurant, the place where you got engaged, or your upcoming honeymoon location. To save time and cut down the bar line, your bartender may want to mix up some ingredients in advance. Name your custom cocktail

© photo by La Vie Photography

© photo by Barbie Hull Photography

creatively, then leave a menu card at the bar highlighting its ingredients and story.

Set up an attractive, self-serve area for water and nonalcoholic drinks so guests can help themselves instead of waiting in line for the bar. Lemonade is a classic nonalcoholic drink and can be infused with strawberry, mint, or lavender. Label alcoholic and nonalcoholic drinks carefully so guests and parents will know which drinks to choose. Fun drinks for kids like Shirley Temples, root beer floats, and

Italian sodas will make them feel special, like the adults. When it comes time for the toasts, be sure there is a nonalcoholic option like sparkling cider easily accessible for kids and guests who don't drink. Your waitstaff can give guests the option if they're passing out glasses, or guests can choose either from the bar.

Specialty glassware will make the drinks at your reception feel more elegant. Be sure you have enough appropriate glasses for champagne, wine, beer, cocktails, and nonalcoholic drinks. Soda and wine bottles can be custom ordered with labels that feature your wedding date, wedding logo, or a photo of the two of you; these make great wedding favors. A special set of champagne flutes for the two of you can make your toasts even more special and become lovely family heirlooms.

Signature Drink Ideas

Just like with flowers, you can add a theme to the cocktails that you serve at your reception. On the following pages are some cool drink recipes for you to try and perhaps make as your signature drink.

Take Charge of the Bar

Order your own signature wine from a local vineyard. Have a label made up from an engagement photo or motif from your wedding invitation. Remember the kids. Have grenadine on hand for Shirley Temples or serve ice-cream floats. Buy crazy straws to make them smile. Remember: Bar tabs can really add up. If your budget doesn't allow for an open bar with cocktails, stick to beer and wine or other beverages. No-host bars and weddings don't mix well.

Cocktail Ideas

Signature cocktails can also match a more formal occasion through the use of champagne:

The Champagne Cocktail

1 sugar cube
5 dashes Angostura bitters
6 ounces brut champagne
Lemon twist garnish

1. Soak the sugar cube in the bitters.
2. Drop the cube into a champagne glass.
3. Pour in the champagne. Add garnish.

Kir Royale

½ ounce crème de cassis
6 ounces brut champagne
Lemon twist garnish

1. Pour the crème de cassis into a champagne glass.
2. Pour in the champagne. Add garnish.

Hibiscus

2 ounces cranberry juice
4 ounces champagne

1. Pour the juice into a champagne glass.
2. Pour in the champagne.

Bellini

2 ounces white peach puree
4 ounces Prosecco

1. Pour the puree into a champagne glass.
2. Pour in the Prosecco.

Summer Drink Ideas

Planning your big day around a holiday, like a low-key outdoor wedding around the Fourth of July? These drinks will cool off your guests and make a big festive splash:

Independence Colada

½ ounce grenadine
Ice
1 ½ ounces light rum
4 ounces piña colada mix
½ ounce blue curaçao

1. Pour the grenadine into the bottom of a tropical glass.
2. Blend the rum and piña colada mix with a cup of ice.
3. Pour rum mixture into the glass.
4. Float the blue curaçao on top.

Watermelon Kiwi Cooler

Ice
4 ounces dry white wine
1 ounce lemon juice
4 ounces lemon-lime soda
Watermelon balls and kiwi slices garnish

1. Fill a wine glass half with ice.
2. Add all the ingredients and stir. Add garnish.
3. You can substitute sugar-free lemon-lime soda for the lemon-lime soda.

Strawberry Pom Lemonade

Ice
1 ½ ounces strawberry vodka
1 ounce pomegranate juice
½ ounce homemade lemonade
Lemon and strawberry garnish

1. Fill a tall glass with ice.
2. Shake all the ingredients with ice.
3. Strain drink into the glass. Add garnish.

Blue Coconut Margarita

Ice
2 ounces coconut Tequila
1 ounce blue Curacao
1/10 ounce fresh lime juice
1 ounce simple syrup
Shredded coconut rim for glass

1. Rim a glass with shredded coconut.
2. Blend ingredients with a half cup of ice. Add additional ice if needed.
3. Pour into the margarita glass.

Winter Drink Ideas

Perhaps you're having a winter white wedding. If so, these festive drinks might help warm your guests:

Winter Wonderland

Ice
2 ounces coconut rum
1 ounce white crème de cacao
Dash blue curaçao
Coconut vanilla ice cream ball garnish

1. Chill a cocktail glass with ice.
2. Shake all the ingredients with ice.
3. Strain drink into the glass. Add garnish.

Molasses Eggnog

Ice
1 ½ ounces chilled dark rum
5 ounces chilled eggnog
Nutmeg garnish

1. Chill a mug with ice.
2. Pour in the chilled ingredients. Add garnish.

Candy Cane

Crushed candy cane to rim glass
Ice
2 ounces vanilla vodka
1 ounce peppermint schnapps or white crème de menthe

1. Rim a cocktail glass with crushed candy canes.
2. Shake remaining ingredients with ice.
3. Strain drink into the glass.

Mr. Grinch Juice

Red sugar to rim glass
Ice
1 ounce sour apple vodka
1 ounce sour apple schnapps
2 ounces lime juice

1. Rim a cocktail glass with red sugar.
2. Shake remaining ingredients with ice.
3. Strain drink into the glass.

THE CAKE

Wedding cakes are a traditional part of the celebration, but that doesn't mean they have to look traditional. These days, in a modern twist on an old tradition, wedding cakes come in all shapes, sizes, colors, and even themes. Like with centerpieces, they can be decorated to continue your color theme into the reception and food. Or, they can play up certain aspects of your personality. And there is a whole other world of flavors, fillings, and toppings. Delectable, yes—the creative choices of flavors, fillings, and decorations are the secret to a delicious dessert.

© photo by La Vie Photography

Cake Shapes & Styles

Wedding cakes and breads have been a part of marriage celebrations for as far back as Ancient Greece, representing happiness, fertility, and good fortune. Today's beautiful wedding cakes are a far cry from the simple breads used centuries ago and have become iconic symbols of the sweetness and romance of a modern marriage. They are not only delicious desserts but fabulous showpieces that highlight your personal wedding style.

Wedding cake designers range from commercial bakers to highly trained culinary artists and everything in between. Whichever type of service you choose, you'll want to meet with potential cake designers four to six months before your wedding to see photos of their work and to taste samples of their cake flavors and fillings. The more complex the ingredients in your chosen cake, the more expensive it will be. Wedding cakes are usually priced per slice or

serving, and cakes can be made to serve groups from fifty to five hundred, depending on your event. Additional decorations like elaborate piping, marzipan fruits, or crystallized-sugar flowers are dramatic and will be priced in addition to the basic cake. One way to keep things simple is to order a smaller wedding cake than you need and have a matching sheet cake discreetly sliced and served to additional guests.

Don't forget the extra cake accessories you may need, like a cake stand, cake topper, and knife and serving set. Your cake designer should have cake stands and service pieces available to rent, or you may want to find ones you love that you can save as keepsakes. If you choose to have a cake topper, get creative with it! Consider having one custom made, or use a family heirloom topper for a sentimental vintage look.

An all-white wedding cake in a classic round shape is the most traditional option for a

Cake Gallery

Photo by Rich Penrose

© photo by John and Joseph Photography

Photo by Jackie Alpers

Photo by Mary-Anne Conner

© photo by John and Joseph Photography

modern wedding. Layers can be stacked directly on top of each other with decorative frosting hiding the seams, or separated with pillars, columns, or other decorative supports for a taller and more regal effect. Wooden or plastic dowels must be inserted inside the cake to help support the layers and keep them from collapsing.

The cake in the photo shown on the right uses delicate white-on-white frosting decoration to wonderful effect. The couple's monogram, the floral motif, and the smooth ribbons of frosting perfectly offset the strong square lines of the cake's shape. Square cake layers are a modern and dramatic alternative to the traditional round shape, yet still remain elegant and refined. Square cake layers can be low and wide or narrow and tall—or a creative combination of the two.

Fresh flowers piled high make even the most classic cakes look more organic and casual, no matter what the shape. Order extra flowers from your florist for your cake designer to use. The *croquembouche*, the traditional French wedding cake, is made of round cream-filled puff pastries piled high and decorated with spun sugar. Give a nod to your family by choosing a cake that's a regional specialty traditional to your heritage.

Unusual geometric shapes and unexpected proportions give this wedding cake an alternative twist. Consider three or four single-layer cakes arranged together, instead of one traditional tiered cake. Wedding cakes can be made in the shape of nearly anything you love, be it person, place, or thing. If you're interested in

a truly unusual cake, designers who specialize in these works of art can sometimes ship them across the country, if necessary.

Traditional White Cake

The traditional white wedding cake graces the covers of the top bridal magazines. Ultrafamous cake bakers spotlight them on the home pages of their websites, capturing all the majesty and high-style class of a traditional, formal wedding and its other vision in white.

If you're considering a traditional wedding cake, you now get to choose between all-white, or if—like so many brides and grooms—you'd prefer, a little color on your cake, even if it's just the hues of the flowers that decorate it. But here we're starting with the classic, all-white cake, pristine white from top to bottom and every accent in between.

At formal, semiformal, and informal weddings, the traditional white wedding cake is often made from three tiers of cake. The tiers may be stacked directly on top of one another—the most modern look—or may be separated by a series of pedestals set on each cake layer for a raised, architectural effect. For best effect choose a shade of white for the frosting to match the shade of white of your gown, since you will be standing next to the cake in important photos and must match it. Three-tiered cakes allow plenty of room for traditional white flowers, pearl piping, draping icing effects, and the modern fondant-formed white ribbons and bows.

A five-layer cake is most often chosen for a larger, opulent wedding with a big guest list, formal to ultraformal. The layers may be concentric, with each slightly smaller than the one below it, or you can choose a pedestal-separated cake of five same-in-size layers with decor between each layer. Five-tier cakes are often secured with a dowel inserted through the center and cut to invisibility on top and fastened to the cake base. The extra decor space invites accenting with a greater number of frosting roses, piping, pearls, hand-iced replicas of the bride's gown lace, or a dramatic cascade of fresh flowers down all five layers.

Not everything about the wedding has to be simple and minimalist in order to have a simply accented cake. You may just love the look of a big, beautiful cake that's not too "busy" with

© Jacqui Martin | Shutterstock

all kinds of piped designs, swirls, bows, and the like. A simply frosted cake may feature a pattern of piped icing pearls adorning the sides of the cake layers, or just a few frosting flowers on each cake layer. A simply accented cake can have frosting, fondant, or real flowers just in a tuft on top with none cascading down.

The most common style of lavish cake decor is the large, lush cascade of flowers—fresh or fondant-made—draping down the side of the cake or spiraling around it. An elegant all-white cake may be intricately iced with a very detailed pattern of iced pearls on the sides of the cake layers, or piped to look like strings of pearls draping along the sides. Using phenomenally detailed stencils, your baker can ice on intricate decorative patterns in white icing to give a non-contrasting yet still stunning patterned accent on the sides of the cake layers. Fondant allows the cake artist to make virtually anything, so the cake may be created to resemble the tiers, ruffles, or satiny draping of the bride's lavish gown.

Modern & Colorful Cakes

Wedding cakes may also depart from the traditional all-white variety to stand out as brightly colored, modern, and immensely detailed masterpiece cakes. You'll see light pink cakes, vibrant spring-colored cakes with a range of pastel flowers and accents, sweet purple cakes covered with icing-made lilacs, and other colorful creations.

As with the white cake, it might be an all-blue cake in monochromatic style, or again it might be a departure from that classic design

Photo by Jackie Alpers

and "pop" with a range of brights such as candy-colored bright reds and pinks for a summer wedding or deep jewel-tone blues and purples for a winter wedding.

Pastel cakes work for both formal and informal weddings. A pastel cake may be accented with icing with either slightly brighter frosting or—as a nod to the traditional bridal cake—with white frosting flowers and icing effects. Some of the most popular choices for pastel wedding cakes are pink, lavender, sage green, baby blue, butter yellow, tangerine, and light coral.

Bright cakes stand out in spring and summer in seasonal hues; in rich reds and burnt sienna in fall; and in ruby, emerald, and sapphire in winter. Bright cakes may be frosted in a bright color—such as orange or coral—and accented with piping and fondant effects in lighter shades of the same color family. Or, the cake may be frosted in a bright color and accented with coordinating brights, such as a bright pink cake accented with fucshias, yellows, and oranges. If you love the look of a bright cake, you can "go bridal" by accenting with large fondant white ribbons and bows or a wrap of fondant white around the base of each cake layer.

The color might be a black-and-white motif to match the color theme of the wedding, with a white cake iced in ultra-intricate black fondant swirls and laser-cut fondant layers set over the white iced cake.

The color may also be swirls, such as four or five hues of blue swirled to make the cake look like the ocean or a clear blue sky. Or the swirls may take on a tie-dyed effect for an informal outdoor summertime wedding.

With frosting effects or cutout fondant layers, you can create a pastel and white wedding cake. With frosting effects or cutout fondant layers, you can increase the contrast of a white cake with a brightly hued fondant overlay. Create subtler contrast with two shades of

Photo by Jackie Alpers

pastels, such as orange and yellow, pink and sage green, ocean blue and blush blue, or ivory and soft gold. The contrast of a simpler, classic cake may be just a few accent flowers in subtle pastels or the bright "pops" of purple pearl icing dots only around the sides of the cake's bottom layer.

Color creations are perfect for all formalities of weddings—from casual, backyard gatherings to lavish, five-star ultraformal weddings at the country club. And destination wedding sites love to turn out vibrant cakes in the colors of their native flowers.

If as a team you and your groom can't decide between an all-white cake and one with color effects, compromise with a mostly white cake with a few subtle pastel or bright icing effects. On colorful cakes add even more colorful stick-ins—such as multihued artsy circles standing straight up out of the top layer of the cake. Use single-hued flowers, or have your baker add the streaks and lines of floral varieties that have three to four shades in each petal. Stick-in faux butterflies made of silk are the number one cake accent, made with either pastel or bright butterfly colors, and number two cake accent are colorful ribbons wrapped around the base of each layer.

Resist the urge to have too much going on with your colorful, modern cake. Just like with fashion, it's possible to over-accessorize, so choose just three or four colors to create that wow factor a wedding cake calls for, and place them well.

© photo by La Vie Photography

Photo by Jackie Alpers

© Susanrae/Dreamstime.com

Flavors, Fillings & Decorations

Wedding cakes should be delicious to eat and divine to behold, and there's no need to sacrifice one for the other. With plenty of gorgeous cake designs and scrumptious flavors and fillings to choose from, it's easy to bring a sweet finale to your wedding meal.

Find inspiration for your cake flavors in the season, theme, and overall style of your wedding. Chocolate is a perennially popular wedding cake flavor. Get creative with variations like red velvet, dark chocolate, or mocha. White cake is the most traditional cake flavor. It can be combined with almost any kind of filling and frosting. Carrot cake and spice cake have gained popularity at weddings, though their dense texture may make it difficult to stack the layers too high. Other common cake flavors are lemon poppy seed, almond, orange blossom, and banana.

If you're throwing an elegant evening affair, delicate classic flavors like Madagascar vanilla cake with white chocolate and raspberry filling will match the atmosphere. If you're having a tropical wedding, look to exotic flavors like banana, passion fruit, guava, or mango. Choose light and airy citrus cake complete with lemon curd and mousse filling for an outdoor spring wedding, or a decadent mocha cake filled with chocolate ganache and toasted hazelnuts for a romantic winter celebration. If you and your partner have special cake flavors you adore, let your personalities shine through by choosing different flavors for each layer and letting your guests choose their favorite.

© photo by Junebug Weddings

© photo by Junebug Weddings

Photos by Jackie Alpers (unless otherwise noted)

Buttercream frosting is rich and delicious, comes in many flavors, and is made with real butter, so it requires cool temperatures and careful handling. Fondant is made from powdered sugar and water and is rolled out to form a smooth cake covering. It can be colored, cut, or sculpted to amazingly decorative effect, and it stands up well in most environments. Other tasty ingredients like cream cheese, chocolate, citrus, and spices can be added to frosting recipes to create specialty flavors.

Wedding cakes can have multiple filling flavors between their layers. Classic fillings include chocolate ganache, buttercream, lemon curd, mousse, or vanilla cream. Liqueurs, like limoncello, amaretto, rum, Grand Marnier, and espresso, can be soaked into your cake. Bavarian cream and fresh fruit make wonderful seasonal cake fillings.

When it comes to cake decorations, let yourself be inspired by special wedding details like your flowers, your invitation design, your color palette, or the architecture of your wedding location. Practical considerations like the climate and length of your event should also be considered. Some types of frostings and decorative accents hold up to the heat and long hours better than others, and some may need refrigeration or special handling that your reception site manager should be made aware of well in advance.

Have a matching stand custom made or find one that coordinates with your wedding theme. Flowers made from sugar paste or marzipan can be made to look like real-life flowers or can be whimsical interpretations of nature. Real flowers should be free from pesticides and chemicals. Seasonal fruits make beautiful decorations. Use berries in the spring and summer and pears, apples, or figs in the fall and winter.

Experienced wedding cake designers know the limitations of a cake's ingredients and structure and can guide you in the right direction while at the same time creating nearly anything your imagination can dream up. Meet with several different professionals to find the one who can best bring your vision to life.

Photo by Kristen Jensen

Photo by Kristen Jensen

Chapter 8

THE CEREMONY

The ceremony is often considered the main attraction of your big day. When it comes to wedding planning, the ceremony is one of the most important things you'll plan. A highlight of the day—if not *the* highlight of the day—the ceremony is perhaps the most memorable and intimate moment, not just for you and your partner, but also for your many guests. Remember that celebrating is fabulous, but getting married is what your big day is all about.

You wedding day is often a blur, so try to take in the events of the ceremony in slow motion. The groom should make the first moment he sees his bride really count; he should take in how precious she is to him, and let her know it. While all eyes are on you the bride as she walks down the aisle, it's her eyes, locked with the groom's, that will make the moment oh so special.

When the ceremony begins, remember that even though there is an audience, there are only two VIPs in the crowd—you and your significant other. Look each other in the eyes as you say your vows, and keep your attention focused on each other. When your officiant pronounces that you're husband and wife—finally!—don't rush out too fast. Soak up the excitement of the moment and walk down the aisle hand in hand.

The moments leading up to the ceremony can be kind of rushed. Between getting ready, making last-minute adjustments, taking solo (and possibly group) shots with the

Photo by Kristen Jensen

photographer, and calming your own nerves, time can fly by before you even know it. To catch a breather, after the ceremony (and possibly before photos, if you're scheduled to have your pictures taken right after the ceremony), set aside some time together to connect—as husband and wife!—before your reception begins.

PICKING THE PERFECT LOCATION

While over 75 percent of today's couples choose to get married in a church, synagogue, or mosque, any space that feels sacred to you can be the perfect place for your ceremony.

If you're members of a particular faith, then getting married at your house of worship may be your most comfortable choice. Talk to the on-site coordinator to book your date early and be sure to get detailed information on any rules and regulations you'll have to follow, including required counseling appointments, guidelines for writing your vows, and restrictions on

video recordings or photography. Ask if you can choose your officiant or if one will be designated for you.

If a traditional venue is not your first choice, then look for a private place with ambiance that matches your style and plenty of room for all your guests. Most reception sites offer lovely on-site ceremony locations, with indoor and outdoor options, and beautiful beach, park, and garden ceremony sites abound.

To help secure your first choice, try to book your site and your officiant twelve to eighteen months before your wedding day.

Ceremony Basics: Types of Services

There are basically two types of ceremonies: religious and civil. Religious ceremonies incorporate rules of faith and require a religious

officiant. If the officiant is willing to travel off-site, a religious ceremony can be held at any venue that feels appropriate to you and your fiancé. The privacy of a ceremony inside a house of worship creates a sense of intimacy, ensures the safety of your guests from the elements, and limits unwanted distractions.

The traditional civil ceremony takes place in a city hall but may take place at any location you love. Civil ceremonies require a legal official to marry you: a justice of the peace, magistrate, county clerk, mayor, boat captain, or even a friend ordained online. If you're getting married for the second time, don't feel that you have to choose a civil ceremony. You're free to celebrate the way that feels best to you.

Check with your location in advance if you want to release birds, include your pets in the ceremony, or throw flower petals or birdseed. Be sure you have an easy place to park, a comfortable place to "hide" from guests, and a fun plan to make your grand exit.

Choosing Your Style

There are no set rules when it comes to planning out your ceremony's style. Whether you go with a classic or an alternative style, you must first and foremost plan with your personalities in mind. Are you and your groom religious, or have you always dreamed of an intimate ceremony with family and close friends? Are you blending your faiths, or are you eager to elope? Regardless, remember that this is your day, and you should have a ceremony that reflects you.

Classic Ceremonies

Following family customs and choosing to have a religious authority to officiate provide the foundation for a classic ceremony. Ministers, priests, rabbis, or other religious figures provide spiritual guidance to couples looking for a classic ceremony that's rich with time-honored rituals and blessings. No matter what your religious affiliation, choosing a classic ceremony will most likely mean including the following elements:

© photo by GH Kim Photography

A processional: Music will signal both mothers being seated and your bridal party proceeding to their set places near the altar. Your grand entrance and walk down the aisle will be the highlight, as all guests stand to see you in your dress. You may walk down the aisle with either your father, both your parents, or alone, according to your traditions.

Opening remarks: Your ceremony will start with a welcoming blessing from your officiant.

Affirmation of intentions: For this important part of your rite, you'll proclaim that you've come freely to be married without legal impediment.

Charge to the couple and betrothal: Your officiant will remind you and your guests of the serious and sacred nature of your commitment, and then will ask if you promise to love and honor each other as long as you both live. Here's your big chance to say those special words, "I do."

Vow exchange: To affirm your intentions, you'll exchange or repeat vows. Many classic ceremonies begin, "I _____, take you, _____, to be my lawfully wedded husband. . . ." Time your ceremony from your guests' point of view. Fifteen minutes is too short, and two hours is probably too long. If you would like to customize your vows, be sure to check with your officiant before writing them. You may need permission.

> While most traditional ceremonies take place in a house of worship, more and more classic ceremonies are taking place at alternative locations, as an increasing number of religious officiants allow it.

The ring exchange: As a symbol of your love and commitment, you will exchange wedding rings. Your best man or ring bearer will present the rings to be blessed before you exchange them. You'll then present your beloved the ring as a symbol of your endless love. To be extra prepared, practice slipping the rings on at your rehearsal.

A pronouncement, followed by your kiss: To seal the deal, your officiant will pronounce you legally married and you'll be given permission to kiss. Stop and savor this moment! Then head

Photo by Kristen Jensen

back down the aisle to sign your license and celebrate. Forming a second aisle of guests outside the church, synagogue, or mosque for you to rush down and make your getaway is a sweet, classic tradition.

Blended Ceremonies

Today's world is a much more diverse place than it was just a few decades ago, and many people are finding love with partners who come from very different backgrounds than their own. If the two of you are looking to bring together two family cultures and two faiths, look to an interfaith ceremony as a way to create a bridge based on honor and respect.

If you're getting married in your church, synagogue, or mosque, you may not be able to alter the ceremony to honor your partner's faith, so you may consider having a secondary ceremony to achieve that goal. If you're getting married at a location other than a house of worship, or at a nondenominational church, there are lots of ways to weave together the cultural traditions that are important to you. Without a doubt parents and grandparents will be touched by your efforts, and you'll be enriched by the experience.

If neither of you are directly related to a particular culture, but you still want to have fun bringing cultural elements from the people and places you love into your ceremony, by all means go for it. The world is rich with romantic customs and rituals to call your own.

A chuppah, which represents God's love and the couple's new home together, shelters the bride and groom during the Jewish ceremony pictured in the top photo on this page. Other forms of marriage canopies like the Buddhist *poruwa* and Hindu *mandap* are used on every continent.

Catholic ceremonies may include a full mass and communion, which requires you to be a practicing Catholic to participate. Keep in mind that almost every religion requires preparatory classes to be married in its house of worship.

Marriage is a universal tradition that has been part of every culture on Earth since the beginning of recorded time. The Korean tea ceremony shown on this page, bottom photo,

© photo by Positive Light Photography

© photo by GH Kim Photography

© photo by GH Kim Photography

many other cultures around the world. Middle Eastern brides are decorated with intricate and beautiful henna designs.

Ceremony Alternatives

Your wedding ceremony is all about making a lifetime commitment to the one you love in a way that is most authentic to the two of you. Fortunately there are lots of alternatives to choose from when it comes to creating a genuine ceremony that you'll both love and remember. Here are just a few.

demonstrates respect for parents and ancestors by asking for their marriage blessing. Many modern Chinese brides are still married on auspicious days according to astrology and wear red for good luck. Almost every culture has lucky colors, numbers, or dates associated with it. A groom breaks a glass at the end of a Jewish ceremony to signify the fragile nature of happiness compared to the enduring nature of love.

Each ceremony will have its own unique set of blessings. Here are just a few from the world over: The red paste known as *kum kum* is placed on the bride's and groom's foreheads in the Indian blessing. Sugar is used in many cultural wedding traditions to protect the couple from the bitter aspects of life. The custom of lighting one candle from two other candles is a symbol of combining couples and families and is prevalent the world over. Dishes are smashed to signify many good years ahead during Greek wedding ceremonies.

Presenting couples with money in envelopes or pinning it on them when they dance is customary in the Filipino culture and in

Military weddings: If either or both of you are in the military, you've earned the honor of getting married in full dress uniform by the chaplain of your branch and faith. Of course there will be rules to follow, so contact your chaplain to help you prepare as soon as you're engaged. You deserve exclusive treatment, and who doesn't love a man or woman in uniform?

The Arch of Sabers pictured at the top of the facing page is an honor reserved for those who have served or are serving in the armed forces. Commissioned officers and Marine NCOs are the only soldiers who can carry these special swords and sabers. The groom will also use the saber to cut the cake at the reception, and officers will be seated according to rank.

Civil ceremonies: Not just for couples looking for a quick nonreligious courthouse ceremony, civil ceremonies provide flexibility and an inexpensive way to tie the knot where and when you

© photo by Cheri Peerl Photography

want to. All you have to do is follow the most basic legal requirements, and the rest is up to you—plus you still have the option of throwing a lovely wedding reception following your ceremony or in the future.

Commitment ceremonies: If you're in love with someone of your same sex, you may be lucky enough to live someplace where you can get legally married. If not, you can still celebrate your relationship by planning a commitment ceremony. Other than some minor differences,

© photo by La Vie Photography

beautifully planned commitment ceremonies are planned just like weddings. A growing number of U.S. states and over twenty countries around the world recognize gay marriage as legal.

Elopements: Want to get away from it all, or just be completely spontaneous? Then eloping might be perfect for you. Every year tens of thousands of couples take off for fun and dreamy destinations to get hitched without the hassle. Over 150,000 couples get married in Las Vegas every year because it's quick, easy, and legal. Be sure to check the requirements for your destination. If you're eloping to avoid sensitive family issues, consider how the news may affect those closest to you. After you elope, throw a party on your first or tenth anniversary to renew your vows.

CEREMONY DETAILS

Just like with a reception, there are a fair amount of details—both big and small—that go into pulling off the perfect ceremony, one that is intimate, personalized, and reflects the values and traditions of the couple. But don't sweat—once you've decided the "style" of your ceremony, the rest falls into place quickly.

Choosing an Officiant

Choosing a person to officiate your wedding ceremony is a very personal decision. You want someone who can represent your values and spiritual beliefs and speak from a place that truly represents your relationship.

If you decide to get married in your church, synagogue, or mosque, your officiant will probably come with it or you may have more than one officiant to choose from. No matter where you're getting married, you'll need to reserve his or her time, make appointments for any necessary counseling, and pay a deposit to reserve the requested services (unless you're in the military, in which case your chaplain will perform the service for free).

Many couples choose to have a nondenominational minister officiate their wedding in order to blend religions or personalize their ceremony. If that's the best choice for you, find someone with lots of experience whom you like and trust and who will listen to what's important to you. Ask for a copy of his or her sample ceremony, read it carefully, then ask any of the following questions that are relevant to you: Can we personalize our ceremony? (Meaning, can you write or edit your own vows, include music and readings of your own choosing, or adjust

© photo by GH Kim Photography

the sequence of events to fit your style?) What restrictions are there on music, photography, or dress? Can we choose your own songs? Can our photographer use a flash? Will we or our guests be required to cover arms or shoulders, or wear something to cover the head? What is the fee, when do we have to pay it, and will we be signing a contract? Do you have backup in case of emergency? Can you attend our rehearsal and help with the processional and recessional as well as seating details? After asking these questions, ask yourself if this is the person you want to have with you on your wedding day.

Getting married in a church comes with several requirements; talk with your officiant early to be sure you clearly understand them. Before you schedule anything else, ask how long the ceremony will take and how much time you'll have afterward. Some ministers, priests, and rabbis will travel to other locations to perform ceremonies. Ask about this option, if it appeals to you. Be sure your consultant speaks to the church coordinator to ensure the other's plans do not conflict.

Many couples who believe in God or a higher power do not subscribe to all the rites and rituals of a particular religion. If this is true for you, choose a nondenominational officiant. Ask if there are videos available so you can see how he or she performs a ceremony. Conduct a local search on the Internet for wedding ministers and nondenominational celebrants. Look for websites with lots of client raves and a stated philosophy you agree with.

© photo by La Vie Photography

Getting married by someone you know and love can be a heartwarming experience. Your sister, brother, family member, or friend can be "ordained" online to perform your ceremony. Online ordinations from the Universal Life

Honoring Those You Love

One of the best ways to make your wedding special is to honor the people closest to you and ask them to show off their unique talents and personalities. For your ceremony choose inspirational people from your life as candle lighters, ushers, readers, and performers, or have someone you mutually admire act as your officiant. Enlist creative people to help decorate and design your ceremonial space. Have your uncle build you a floral arbor or have your aunt who's an artist create your program. To honor your parents, add the presentation of a single flower and heartfelt thanks to them at the opening of your ceremony.

Personalized Ceremonies

Whether your ceremony style is classic or casual, you may want to include some unique elements that make it feel more personal to the two of you. By adding a little or a lot of your own favorite music, poetry, rituals, and personal touches, you can create a one-of-a-kind ceremony that's totally you. Listed here are some suggestions:

Down the Aisle: Create a "sweet path" to the groom with your favorite fragrant flowers; they'll smell divine when they're crushed. (For more on flowers at the ceremony see page 309. Or line the aisle with candles, garlands, or a hand-painted runner with your initials on it. Make your entrance in a gown of antique gray, rich cranberry, or pink champagne and cause a stir. Choose your brothers, a close male friend, or your pup to take you down the aisle.

The couple pictured on the right literally "ties the knot" in a pagan handfasting ritual that inspired the saying. Look for ways to honor the coming together of your families. Have a sand ceremony, light a unity candle, or present your parents and grandparents with roses. When you write your own vows, you share a deeply personal side of yourself with your community and the one you love.

© photo by by John and Joseph Photography

© photo by Yours by John Photography

Involving Family and Friends: If either of you have children, welcome them into your marriage by including them in your ceremony. Get your guests involved; have them greet one another or silently remember their wedding vows while you say yours. Make your own ring pillow with a special pocket. Use it as a tooth fairy pillow for your children. For a cute touch have all the kids in your wedding come down the aisle together in a wagon pulled by your best man.

Unique Recessionals: Have your photographer line up guests on both sides of your exit. Give them flower petals to throw over you or pass out silver bells they can ring for good luck as you exit your house of worship. Bubbles provide a popular alternative to the ritual of throwing rice and they look great in pictures. Recessional music can be out of the box and perfectly tasteful. Make your exit to James Brown's "I Feel Good" or something similarly spirited.

Church are recognized in many states. There are celebrants who specialize in interfaith weddings, second weddings, pagan weddings, gay weddings, and marriages of every kind. There's definitely one that's right for you.

Be sure you know when and where you should sign the marriage license. It is the responsibility of your officiant to file this crucial document. If you are not familiar with the officiant you interview, ask for references and proof of their credentials before you give a deposit. Scams are very rare, but they do occur. Every state and country has different laws governing marriage. In Kansas and Colorado, for example, couples can get permission to perform their own ceremony!

Writing Your Own Vows

If you're looking forward to a classic, traditional ceremony, writing your own vows may feel out of the question. But if you're taking a more modern, casual approach to your ceremony, voicing your own feelings and interpreting your own commitment may be the only natural thing to do. If you're looking to personalize your ceremony by writing your own vows, ask yourself the following and write down the answers in detail.

Why and when did I know that my fiancé was "the one"? What memories do I hold most fondly of our time together? What qualities do I most revere in my partner? How does he or she complete me? What do I commit to do in order for the two of us to thrive and stay together for

© photo by GH Kim Photography

completing them. Once you have a good beginning, spend the rest of the night celebrating how fabulous it is to be in love.

When you write your first draft, write freely and from the heart without editing. Then go back and highlight what feels right for you. Consider your promises. Do you promise to love, honor, and cherish? How about being honest, forgiving, or willing to seek counsel when times are tough? Let yourself be inspired by the first time you met or by a special time you spent on vacation. Weave in phrases from cherished books or music that you love. Use phrases that mirror one another. For instance both of you say, "I, ___, promise to support you through all of life's triumphs and challenges." Have your officiant help you write your vows or look them over once you've written them. It can help to be sure you don't miss anything important.

Practice your vows several times before you get to the altar, and carry an extra copy with you "just in case." When you find yourself at the altar, remember there is only one person your words have been written for. Look into each other's eyes and forget about what anyone else is doing or thinking. This is a moment that belongs to the two of you.

Authentic words of love are guaranteed to bring tears to your eyes. Carry a tissue or hanky, or have your partner carry one for you. Use emotionally expressive words like "my beloved wife or husband" instead of "spouse." If you're facing one of life's challenges together, like an illness, military service, or raising children with special needs, consider making specific promises that address it in your vows. Marriages are about romance as well as real life. Holding hands during your ceremony helps keep you calm and present. Don't worry if you get choked up and have to pause. Your friends and family will be there to support you, and they'll feel touched by your emotion.

Make a calligraphy copy of your vows to frame or add to your wedding album. Read them again on your anniversaries and throughout the years when you need a little encouragement to keep them.

FLOWERS, FLOWERS & MORE FLOWERS!

The spot where you will take your vows and officially become husband and wife is a location to pay special attention to when it comes to floral decor. After all, the ceremony is the main attraction of the day! All eyes will be on you as you take your vows and exchange rings, and your ceremony photos will be an everlasting reminder of the big moment . . . that first kiss as husband and wife. The ceremony site decor you plan—which is the focus of this section—sets the stage and tone for your entire wedding. This is the first impression you make on your guests, as well, so think about what you want your altar flowers and ceremony florals to say to them.

Ceremony Style

Decorating your wedding ceremony location provides a wonderful opportunity to create floral decor to highlight your style. Whether you cover your

© photo by La Vie Photography

location in flowers from floor to ceiling or add tiny extra touches to an already spectacular venue, your floral decor can add romance, beauty, and theme to your ceremony.

If you're getting married in a church, the most common places for floral arrangements are at the altar and at the ends of the pews lining the aisle. Altar arrangements can be simple and subdued, gently dressing up your ceremony backdrop, or they can be over-the-top structures like trees, columns, or chuppahs, exploding with stunning floral arrangements. Be sure to discuss your plans with both your floral designer and your church wedding coordinator and put them in touch with each other so there is no miscommunication when your wedding day arrives.

In outdoor locations you may have more leeway to get creative with your floral ceremony style, but you may also need less decoration if it's already naturally lush. For a seamless look, choose flowers that complement the existing vegetation and landscape and tie in your wedding color palette by mixing in accents like ribbon, fabric, paper lanterns, or luminarias with your floral arrangements. Think of decorating areas like the altar, aisle, backs of chairs, trees surrounding the ceremony location, and entrance to the venue.

In an especially urban ceremony venue, you could choose to complement the clean look with strong modern shapes like tall, thin calla lilies in square vases, or you could go against the grain and soften things up with full blooming roses, peonies, and ranunculus in curving containers.

Whatever your style, be sure that your florist has enough time to set up before your ceremony begins and that he or she knows your venue's rules and regulations.

Classic: A single large floral arrangement at the altar looks classic and dramatic, while several smaller arrangements nicely fill up a larger area. Consider how many wedding party members

© photo by Yours by John Photography

will be standing to your sides when choosing the layout for your arrangements. Try not to crowd yourselves so you feel comfortable in the moment. Ask your floral designer to visit your ceremony location if he or she has never been there before, or provide your florist with photos and measurements of the available space.

Casual: Scatter flowers or flower petals on the ground as a beautiful way to create an aisle if one doesn't naturally exist in your outdoor location. In a casual garden ceremony, use tin pails or watering cans as creative holders for

allowed to have open flames on the premises. Use branches, reeds, or other delicate but large natural objects to create dramatic arrangements that will last and last.

Fun Extras: Hand out paper cones full of flower petals or lavender that your guests can shower you with as you walk back up the aisle as husband and wife. Give your officiant a boutonniere, corsage, or necklace of flowers to honor him or her as a special part of your day. Be sure

your floral arrangements. Work with the rustic details already present and accentuate their personality: fill an old wheelbarrow with blooms, wrap floral garland around fence posts, and hang floral wreaths from doors and gates.

Alternative: Candles create a glowing and romantic mood for your ceremony and are often less expensive than flowers. Be sure to check with your wedding venue to find out if you are

you have enough flower petals for your flower girl to scatter during the ceremony processional and to practice with in advance.

Altar Arrangements

Single altar arrangements are designed as a centerpiece on the table surface. Small arrangements are usually six to eight inches across and work best on small altar tops. Make sure to size your altar arrangements to look appropriate on the altar top, neither too large for a small surface

© RKS/Dreamstime.com

© photo by GH Kim Photography

nor too small for a big one. Single altar arrangements are best planned to be either a wide, low-set grouping or a tall, elevated centerpiece with lots of flowers and greenery.

On a wide altar, you may want to use a dual floral arrangement of matching pieces. Dual altar pieces can symbolize your two lives coming together as one or the joining of your two families. The flowers in your altar arrangements

do not have to precisely match the flowers in your bouquet. Design your altar arrangement with one or two pricey flowers, plus inexpensive filler.

If your wedding style is simple elegance, whether formal or informal, you want to choose smaller, low-set floral pieces with fewer types of flowers. If your wedding style is grand and dramatic, whether formal or informal, you want your altar flowers to be taller and more colorful and to contain anywhere from three to eight different types of flowers. If you're having an outdoor wedding, incorporate garden-type flowers such as peonies. Design an arrangement to match your bouquet. Include symbolic flowers, as well.

Chuppahs & Arches

When it comes to designing the floral decor for your ceremony, one of the most exciting tasks is designing your chuppah or a floral arch under

A Note on Altar Decor

When choosing altar decor, keep in mind that many houses of worship have strict rules about what they do and don't allow for on-site decor, so find out the house rules before you order a lavish altar arrangement. It would be a shame to design and create a floral masterpiece and then find out that you cannot place it on the altar.

which you'll take your vows. The deep symbolism of being sheltered and protected as you join your lives, as well as the pure freedom to design your choice of floral structure and the blooms on it, brings both couples and families together to design and often make this sentimental and spectacular decor piece together.

The floral design for an arch or chuppah must work with the formality of the wedding and usually contains the same types of flowers as found in the bride's bouquet and thus used in the rest of the site decor. Consider your location and create the same feel for your arch or chuppah.

Use the brightest mix of whites, pastels, and greenery to take a step beyond bridal white and incorporate the season. Besides roses, use spring tulips, peonies, ranunculus, and lilies of the valley. Create a natural design with

© Wico/Dreamstime.com

© Reminisce Photography & Design

flowers and greenery attached to the framework of the arch or chuppah, simulating the way flowers grow in nature. Set yourself apart from your backdrop or chuppah by carrying brighter-colored flowers than those used in its creation.

Formal arches and chuppahs are usually crafted with roses, gardenias, ranunculus, and other traditional summer blooms. Daisies and wildflowers are ideal for informal weddings. Use larger amounts of greenery on all surfaces of the

© istockphoto

chuppah or arch, and accent it with lilies of the valley, lisianthuses, or Stars of Bethlehem for a softer bridal effect. Informal weddings welcome large, bright flowers, including Gerber daisies and zinnias, especially in summer-friendly tones.

Autumn arches and chuppahs include rich, deep colors of fall, including persimmon, burgundy, gold, and hunter green. Jewel tones lead the fall and winter trends, so create your arch or chuppah with deep amethyst tones, navy blues, and cranberry. To save money in autumn, use seasonal items such as fall greenery, pinecones, and acorns. A new autumn decor idea is to drape bunches of dark purple grapes, which give a vineyard effect for an outdoor wedding.

Unique Arch and Chuppah Materials

Some unique materials for arches and chuppahs are wrought iron, cherrywood, bamboo, birch, and ash. Use a wooden trellis that you can find ready-made for painting at a home improvement store. Suspended chuppahs do not have wooden or metal legs, but are instead squares of rich fabric suspended from a tree and then decorated with florals, garlands and hanging flowers, and crystals on wire to catch the sunlight. The effect is a chuppah floating on air. Just the same, an arch shape can be created by suspending individual flowers and crystals from a tree using invisible wire at lengths to form the desired effect.

Pew or Row Flowers

Ceremony seating that consists of just rows of chairs with no floral or design accents at the ends of the rows says, "We cut this expense from our budget." It's a big, glaring symptom of cost cutting as well as not paying attention to the kinds of small details that can make a wedding special. These bare chairs attract the wrong kind of attention.

Don't overdecorate the ends of your rows or pews, either. Big, puffy tulle bows look like a bad homemade job that you took on to save money. The key is to choose a simple, classic design. The simple use of a single Gerber daisy on a bright green leaf costs under $5 and is deal for this decor.

You might decide to decorate only the rows or pews where your parents, grandparents, and other VIP guests will sit, rather than decorate forty to fifty rows of chairs. Another option is to make fabric bows for all the pews or chair rows, but just add floral and accents to the first three rows on each side where parents and grandparents will sit.

A single beautiful flower may make all the impression you need, so look for flawless roses or other blooms to use as pew decor. Give single blooms a good backdrop with a shiny leaf, a fern, or a satin ribbon bow. Pin the flower securely to its center. The flower should be at least one-half

© Dallaseven/Dreamstime.com

to two-thirds the size of the ribbon bow so that it doesn't get overwhelmed by too much fabric.

Hand tie a small bunch of coordinating flowers, such as a grouping of pink tulips for your spring wedding, and affix them to a satin bow. Bunches look best when their stems are fully wrapped, rather than tied with a bow in the middle of cut stems, for a finished look. The top trends in bunch flowers for pew decor are roses, daisies, Gerber daisies, and calla lilies for

DIY: Guest Flowers

Choose flawless single flowers for placement on guests' ceremony seats. Take each stem and strip it of thorns using floral scissors or a stem stripper. It's best to remove leaves from each stem. Place dry single flowers on each seat at a uniform angle. Do not use Stargazer Lilies or other flowers that have visible yellow or orange pollen on the blooms, since these pollen spores can stain the seats and your guests' clothing.

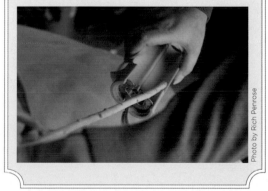

Photo by Rich Penrose

formal weddings and wildflowers for informal weddings.

Just like pew decor made from filler flowers, you can design greenery-only row accents. Hand tie a cascade of ivy for a "green" effect, with the added significance of ivy's fidelity symbol. Be generous with groupings of ferns, especially softer ferns with ultradelicate fronds, for a look guests will want to touch. Practice greenery origami by curling green or colored leaves such as pink-hued coleus into the shape of a calla lily. Affix these to satin or lace bows.

Petal Aisle Markers

Extend the floral bounty and the distinctive bridal look along both sides of your path down the aisle by sprinkling flower petals in lines along either side. This pretty and natural look has long been a favorite design choice of brides in all manner of formal, informal, indoor, and outdoor weddings, adding color and a tie-in to your entire floral scheme—all at a low price.

You might think this design style is a simple one, but there are so many options for a personalized aisle path. Choose petals in a single color, such as a line of bright pink flower petals, or mix the hues. You also have design options for the types of petals to use. While the traditional wedding features rose petals, the new trend is to use different types of flower petals for an unexpected and creative effect.

Your first concern might be the expense of such a design choice. Aren't rose petals expensive at certain times of the year? Yes, that's true,

which is why you might discover a different bloom or a different way to mark your pathway that can cut your budget in half. If you will self-decorate your cake table, guest tables, altar, and buffet table with petals sprinkled as decor, your purchase of big bags of flower petals from your wholesaler or floral designer means that you can stretch your purchase out into different purposes—including your aisle markers. Many brides save 40 to 60 percent by taking a petal supply meant for one task and using it for several.

The colors of the petals will set a tone and perhaps coordinate perfectly with the color mix of your bouquet. Create your aisle markers with all one shade or color family of petals, such as pale to deeper pinks. If you'll have a colored aisle runner, or if the flooring in your indoor site is a hardwood or colored carpet, use white petals. If you're carrying a bright bouquet, craft your aisle markers out of the same shade of bright petals.

Most couples choose to have two long, uninterrupted lines of petals along either side of the aisle. Create dashes of petals, such as a length of white petals, then a blank space with no petals, then a line of pink petals, and so on. Mark your aisles with dots of one-foot-wide circles of petals set every few feet. Make your aisle curvy or arched in petal placement. Set the petals wide enough apart for your escorted walk down the aisle.

While rose petals are the leading trend in site decor, you can bring in different petal effects by using the softer, rippled edges of peonies or

cooperate. Be sure to pick up a few of your aisle petals to preserve as a keepsake of your wedding day.

Flowers in the Ceremony

Flowers are not just for decor. They can also play an active and meaningful part in your ceremony. Maybe you want to hand flowers to your mothers in recognition and gratitude for a lifetime of love and support. Or you want to enact centuries-old cultural rituals as your ancestors did during their own weddings, exchanging blooms as a symbol of unity. The living beauty of a flower has long played a part in marriage rites, and today's modern wedding couples who look for ways to pay homage to loved ones often turn to the flower as the perfect offering.

It's not just the rings that are exchanged today; more couples love the beauty of a flower exchange during the readings, vows, or cultural rituals. Incorporate your birth-month flowers, as each of you gives the other the flower from your own birth month. Your groom can give you a flower to incorporate into your bouquet or set in front of a religious statue, as a blessing on your marriage.

Some religious ceremonies contain a ritual of shaking hands with guests seated near you, wishing them peace. You can turn this ritual in your wedding mass into an opportunity to give single-stem flowers to your mothers as you hug and kiss them.

Flowers may also be offered to religious icons or statues, requesting blessings on the

ranunculus. Calla lily petals provide larger, curled singles for you to line your path. Longer, straighter petals from bright Gerber daisies could give you the artistic look you desire. If you'd like to stick with roses, look into rose varieties with some colored edges at the tips of the petals.

Some sites will not allow you to decorate with flower petals because they may pose a slip risk to guests who may in turn sue the establishment, so get permission first. At an outdoor site, a breezy day could mean your aisle marker petals will get blown all over the place before your ceremony begins, so think about skipping the aisle markers and using your petal supply elsewhere if you discover the weather won't marriage, or handed to children as they participate in your wedding ceremony.

Research any religious lore or symbolism in which flowers play a part, such as lilies being a symbol of Easter and rebirth, as well as additional cultural rites, such as exchanging a certain variety of flower with the groom's family matriarch, or with your own grandmother, or the use of certain flower petals in a unity ritual. Flowers can play a part in religious ceremonies, multifaith ceremonies, and more spiritual marriage rites, all with the universal messages of gift, promise, beauty, and life. You have the freedom to attach your choice of symbolism to any floral element in your ceremony, so work together to write vows or readings that bring the message of flowers into your day. This is one area where the language of flowers comes in particularly handy (see page 163).

If you'll enact the tradition of the unity candle, choose pretty flowers to encircle the bases of all three candleholders. You can also create a floral chain that extends between the candleholders for effect and meaning. If your mothers will light the outside candles, they can set their single-stem flowers next to their candles as a blessing on the marriage. Design a lush floral arrangement in which your three unity candles stand.

Present single-stem white roses to your mothers to thank them for a lifetime of love. Presentation flowers can be incorporated into your bouquet as separately wrapped blooms that you appear to pluck out of your bouquet to present to the mothers. Brides are

© Karenr/Dreamstime.com

extending the list of presentation flower recipients. Grandmothers, godmothers, and stepmothers are popular choices. If you or your groom has a child or children, present flowers to each during a portion of your vows that unify your new family.

Start your ceremony early by having your greeters hand each guest a rose upon arrival at the ceremony site. Instead of sprinkling rose petals, the flower girls can hand single flowers to each guest seated at the ends of rows. Have the child attendants present guests with single-stem flowers upon their exit from the ceremony, along with whatever departure toss-it (birdseed, flower petals) you've chosen to shower you as you dash to the getaway car.

Chapter 9

THE RECEPTION

The wedding reception is where guests can really kick back, kick off their shoes if need be, and join you both in celebrating your special union. Like you, each reception is unique, and so, as you might have guessed, there are lots of decisions and choices to be made when it comes to this part of the wedding planning. The reception also reflects the style and feel of your overall day. If you're having a more casual affair, you might choose to have your reception in your parents' backyard, at a golf or country club, or even at a nontraditional venue, like an old barn or art gallery. A more formal gathering might find you at a hotel ballroom.

The reception is also where you'll spend the majority of your budget, on things like food and drinks, entertainment, decor, and catering staff. Some venues also charge a straight-up venue fee for use of the facility. You'll want to keep your budget in mind when shopping around for reception places—remember there's a place for every type of wedding and every budget.

© photo by GH Kim Photography

Find a place that's special to you, one where you can envision your wedding day actually taking place. We recommend you narrow your search to a handful of places. Start by weeding out places by their location (too far away, etc.), their seating capacity, and their estimated costs (get per-head quotes). Then go visit the places still left on your list. You might need to go back to the venues several times before making your decision, especially if you need to consult with the person paying for your wedding, if it isn't you.

RECEPTION DETAILS

As mentioned, there are a lot of details that go into planning the reception. Here are some questions you'll ask yourself (and others around you): What's the seating setup like? What kinds of linen color and chair options do I have? Can

I bring in outside items, like my own food and wine or decor items? What kinds of restrictions are there? And so on. This section tackles all those questions—and gives you a full list of questions you should be asking—and more.

Seating

Your guests will spend the majority of their time at your reception seated at a place of their choosing, or at one you've selected for them. Their view of the events, the amount of space they have around them, and the company of the other guests at their table will all be factors in how much they enjoy the experience.

To create the most comfortable atmosphere, first consider the size of your venue and the type of meal you'll be serving. If tables and chairs aren't included at your location, visit a

© photo by John and Joseph Photography

rental showroom to choose some and bring a floor plan of your venue with you. Meet your consultant there or ask a salesperson to assist you. Once you've found options that suit your style and budget, use the map of your dining space and be sure that the arrangements leave plenty of room for people to move about freely. Choose chairs with padded seats or use tie-on pads to make guests more comfortable. If you're planning a cocktail hour in addition to or instead of a seated reception, use tall cocktail tables that make it easy for your guests to mingle, or go all out and create a one-of-a-kind lounge space complete with couches and pillows to help your guests relax.

photo by GH Kim Photography

Seated Dinners: The long table arrangement shown on page 316 is considered ultraformal. Many couples today use long tables in their design but omit the chairs on one side so the couple and bridal party can face the dining room without obstruction. Formal seating arrangements frequently include individual seating cards that assign each guest to a particular chair. If you're renting tables and chairs without the help of a consultant, most rental companies will help you make a map that fits your needs.

Buffets: Round tables are most commonly used for events because they can comfortably seat the most guests per table. A sixty-inch round table fits eight people easily but not ten. Don't be tempted to squish folks together. Set out table assignments for your guests at the entrance to

your reception. Then have your DJ or best man call your guests to the buffet one table at a time. Square tables are also available to bring a more restaurant-like look to the room.

Cocktail Tables: Cocktail tables provide guests a place to put their plates and glasses while they move throughout the room. Generally used just during the cocktail hour, they can also be used for late-afternoon or after–dinner hour

photo by La Vie Photography

Creating a seating chart is a must and a social art that your consultant can't help you with. Before you assign your guests to seats, consider each person's personality and think of each table as a separate party. Combine people with similar interests who are likely to get along well.

receptions. Some guests will prefer to be seated at a table, so keep that in mind when creating your layout. Shared tables can get messy quickly; use dark colors to hide stains, or lay an oversize napkin, which can be replaced, across the table.

Lounge-Style Seating: Decorative lounge-style atmospheres are all the rage of late. The space shown below was inspired by the luxury of Indian Mughal tenting. If you choose to create a cocktail atmosphere throughout your reception, consider leaving children off the guest list and hosting an adults-only party. In addition to party rental companies with generic tables and chairs, most cities have specialty rental and prop companies that carry unique furniture, lighting, and decor.

Linens & Chair Covers

Whether your style is classic or casual, dressing up your tables and chairs with fabrics is one of the easiest ways to bring beauty and color

© photo by Raj Tents

to your reception venue. From rich velvets and brocades that shout "winter wedding," to sheer silks and organzas that show off a summer celebration, there is just about every weight, color, and texture available from specialty party rental companies.

Unless your tables are lovely to behold all by themselves, look for tablecloths that are floor length to hide any imperfections. Many venues offer shorter options that look too casual for formal affairs, so double-check before you go with their linen package.

Also, think creatively about your napkin choice; a specialty napkin and the right table accents can dress up a plain tablecloth and finish a look all on their own. Be sure the napkin fabric you choose is absorbent, and order plenty of extras to give to guests when needed and to dress up the cake and cocktail tables.

Once you've seen what your venue offers, visit a rental showroom that has table decor of all kinds. Take a photo of your venue with you, as well as any inspirational photos you've downloaded or torn out of magazines.

Classic Linens: Ivory linens and chair covers look harmonious in a classic ballroom setting and don't compete with the architecture; plus they are often included in the hotel's package. If you're looking to dress up a less-ornate room, look for linens with bright colors or patterns that complement your color palette. Set up a mock table with a table setting to see how your linens, chairs, and tableware will look all together and in your venue.

Casual Linens: The "placemat" made of white rock and the starfish accent on the linen napkin shown below make a beautiful combination for a beach wedding. Look for accents that show off your theme. No matter how casual your wedding, linens will always look better than vinyl or paper. Don't forget to decorate your cake table. Cover it with a special cloth or sheer overlay. Put a draped screen behind it, or make it a focal point of the room.

© photo by Junebug Weddings

Decorative Chairs: The chairs of the bride and groom are often decorated with special flowers, fabrics, or signs. Decorating your chairs can be a fun, inexpensive DIY project that helps put a finishing touch on your wedding style. Chair coverings range from simple tie-on seat pads that provide color and comfort to elaborately draped works of art. Simply tie a thick silk or velvet ribbon around your chair cover to add a splash of color from your palette.

© photo by La Vie Photography

Fun Extras: Bring a fancy touch to your table by using an overlay cloth and "pickups" (small embellishments that you pin to your tablecloth to create a ruffled effect). Save money by adding accents to the options your venue provides instead of upgrading. Dress up your napkins with fresh flowers, ribbons, napkin rings, or elaborate folds.

Party rental companies carry fabrics and carpets that can transform almost any space and create an intimate atmosphere even in the largest venues. Keep in mind that transformation comes with a price tag and requires professional installation. If you're on a budget, finding a venue that needs little alteration can save you big bucks.

Setting the Table

Once the look and layout of your tables have been decided, move on to making them beautiful, functional, and easy to use by adding just the right mix of dishes, glassware, and flatware.

Meet with your caterer to determine the items you'll need for each course of your meal. Your caterer may be able to supply all the necessary items you're looking for, or you may choose to rent them. Discuss your dishes and glasses first. Set up a mock table with dinner plates, bread plates (if you need them), and glasses. Factor in the size of your centerpieces and leave extra room for condiments and your table card. If you're having a formal seated dinner, consider your utensils carefully. You may need room for an array of forks, knives, and spoons at each place setting, or if you're having a buffet, you may not need standard utensils on your table at all.

Once you've determined what items you need, choose the options that best fit your style. White china with a gold or silver rim is the most popular and easy-to-find option for formal dinners, while plain white or glass china is most popular for more casual events. If you love the linens and centerpieces you've chosen, you may not want to add any more color or design detail to your table, and these options will work perfectly for your setting. However, if you're looking for something totally unique, try searching the Internet for specialty resources in your area to see what's available and ask your consultant or caterer for suggestions. When you're done setting your table, sit down and imagine you're a guest from start to finish. Putting yourself in their shoes will help you create a successful and unforgettable event.

Classic Table Settings: A gold-rimmed charger is at the center of the classic setting is featured below left. A charger is a decorative plate that is not meant to hold food but acts as a frame for other dishes. The charger can be removed before the first course or at any time up until the dessert course. A single orchid adds beauty to the setting and sets off the black napkin beneath it. If you need to create less clutter on the table, have servers bring new forks and wineglasses for each course.

Casual Table Settings: The table shown below on the right is elegantly set for a country brunch reception in the spring, perfectly mixing both

casual and classic elements. You don't need specialty china to set a lovely table. Use a colorful tablecloth, napkins, and flowers to dress up plain white or glass dishware. For a whimsical DIY approach, try setting every table in the room with a different china pattern. Borrow china sets from friends and family and create one-of-a-kind, low-cost table settings.

Alternative Table Settings: Square metal chargers can echo the shape of a square table and give a modern look to the setting. Square dinnerware is available at most party rental companies. If you're serving a family-style meal, be sure that your serving dishes and glassware are sturdy so nothing gets tipped over when plates are passed. Do you collect candy bowls, salt and pepper shakers, or porcelain figurines? Add some of your collection to your settings for a unique, personal touch.

© photo by GH Kim Photography

© photo by Junebug Weddings

Fun Extras: Table cards can be simply or elaborately designed with numbers or creative table names that match the theme of your wedding. Clusters of candles or cabaret lamps with pretty shades can help create an intimate nightclub atmosphere. Leave breadbaskets, candy dishes, bottles of wine, or specialty foods on the table for guests to share with one another. These additions will help break the ice and be appreciated between courses.

© photo by La Vie Photography

Fun Reception Extras

Goodie bags, favors, creative guest books, and specialty foods and services are just some of the treats that make receptions extra special. If you're looking to go the extra mile for your guests, consider adding these optional items to your celebration. Here are just a few ideas to fit every budget and style.

Favors: Crystal ornaments, silver bells, wine stoppers, CDs of your favorite music, and customized word magnets with your names,

photos, and romantic adjectives included all fit nicely in little gift boxes and bring a smile to guests' faces. The tradition of giving out wedding favors dates back hundreds of years to a time when European aristocrats gave out precious boxes of metal, porcelain, or crystal called *bonbonnieres.* The boxes held five almonds or candies that represented love, life, success, happiness, and longevity. Many couples choose favors to match the theme, season, or location of their wedding or to highlight their cultural backgrounds, like rice candy or sake for their Japanese celebration or fiery hot sauce for their Mexican affair.

Slip a pack of your favorite flower seeds on top of your guests' napkins, or create a centerpiece of potted topiary for your guests to take with them when they leave for an ecofriendly parting gift. Choose organic, locally made products and gifts.

Yum! Yum! Everyone loves homemade goodies like fudge and fruit jam. Make your own labels and give them out with your recipe for a personal touch. Who doesn't want cookies and milk for the ride home? Give your guests a peanut butter cookie and chocolate macaroon and you'll create a sweet memory. Family members can help make homemade favors, and it gives them a great way to contribute. Don't have time to cook? Then choose a delicious treat that shows off the local flavor of your wedding location, like coffee and mugs for your Seattle wedding or chocolate macadamia nuts for your Hawaiian celebration. Test ordered foods to be sure they're fresh and delicious before you choose them for your guests.

Guest Book Ideas: The tradition of signing a guest book was on its way out of style until savvy brides came up with new twists like turning it into a wish book or having guests sign the mat of a large engagement photo instead. Think of your own way to make your guest book special, and it will be worth carrying on the tradition. Rent a photo booth or leave out a Polaroid for guests to take their own pictures. Then have them paste them into your guest book along with a special message. Display your matted engagement photo on an easel at the entrance to your reception. Get your family or bridal party to sign it first so guests will follow suit. Buy a porcelain serving platter that comes with a permanent marker for guests to sign. It will make a fun family heirloom.

© photo by GH Kim Photography

THE BIG EVENTS

With so much going on during the wedding planning process, you might easily forget what events happen when and where on your big day. This section breaks down the highlights for you.

The Highlights

Wedding receptions are set apart from other celebrations by the romantic events and rituals that move them along from one touching moment to the next. To ensure that your event unfolds gracefully, arrive thirty minutes after the majority of your guests and have your best man or MC announce you. This presents a great opportunity to thank your guests for coming and welcome them to enjoy themselves.

Once you've made your grand entrance, give yourself another thirty to forty minutes to

---

Get Creative

European sports cars and classic American convertibles are perfect for entrances for the casual wedding reception. Antique motorcars and stretch limousines add an elegant touch to formal affairs. Horse-drawn carriages, motorcycles, bicycles, boats, and trolleys make fun alternative transportation. If you'll be using your own car, chances are someone will decorate it. Be sure your best man knows that shaving cream eats paint but window paint found at party-supply stores doesn't.

mingle with family and friends before the main course is served or the buffet line is opened. Traditionally you are served first, so take the time to get enough to eat right away and be prepared to move to the toasts and cake cutting as soon as the last guests finish their meals.

Toasts: Traditionally your best man, father, or friend will kick off the toasts and any presentations such as a video or slide show that you want to share with your guests. Be sure to organize this time well so there's enough time to include those who would like to speak and not

limitations when you initially ask them to speak. Leave the open microphone for other occasions. Knowing who is going to speak and what they are likely to say can help you stay calm and collected. If you're having a video presentation, show it immediately before or after your toasts.

Cake Cutting: When it comes time to cut the cake, put your hands on the knife together and slice off one piece from the bottom layer. Give each other one bite and then kiss. Do not smash the cake into each other's mouths; it's messy and not very romantic. It's customary to freeze the

Photo by Kristen Jensen

© photo by John and Joseph Photography

so much time that your guests lose interest. If you would like to include more than six speakers, try scheduling their toasts between each menu course.

Toasts should last one to five minutes and be focused on good wishes for both of you. Gracefully let speakers know your time

top layer to eat on your anniversary. If old cake isn't your favorite dessert, save the topper and put it on a fresh cake next year.

Your First Dance: When it comes time to hit the dance floor for your first dance, go for it without hesitation. Your guests will be delighted whether

© photo by J. Garner Photography

© photo by GH Kim Photography

you simply sway back and forth or put on a full-blown performance. Either way, you can't hope for a more supportive audience. Dancing with confidence is no sweat when you've practiced or taken lessons. It's always a good idea to brush up on your moves. Some couples have their first dance when they first arrive at their reception. Do what feels best for you. Just look into each other's eyes, smile, relax, and enjoy! Choose your father, his father, or your closest male friend or relative to dance with you next.

Garter and Bouquet Toss: To put the finishing touch on your reception, you may choose to throw the bouquet and/or toss the garter to your single guests. If your guest list is light on people yearning to get married, choose another event as an alternative to these traditions. The bouquet and garter toss originated back when a bride and groom had to give something away to avoid being mauled by their guests. Thank goodness today's guests are decidedly more

civilized! To ensure a picture-perfect toss, practice throwing a fake bouquet prior to your reception. For an alternative, design a break-away bouquet with two parts to present to your mother and mother-in-law as gifts of appreciation, and save your garter as an heirloom.

AND . . . MORE FLOWERS!

Included here in this section is information on flowers used for the reception, not including centerpieces, which can be found on page 249. Yes, it's true—you can go overboard on flower decor (although some might argue that point). But sometimes a lone cake and cake table are just begging for a few roses to dress it up. Or perhaps you're looking for a place to reuse the spray of flowers from the ceremony site. This section gives you inspiration and ideas for even

Hosting like a Pro

Creating a truly memorable wedding day isn't about how much money you spend or how many people you invite; it's about artful planning and accurately anticipating the needs of your guests.

Put yourself in your guests' shoes and consider the length of time you want them to attend, the distance you want them to travel, and what is likely to make them feel pampered while they're with you. When people arrive, will they know where to go? Consider having your parents or members of your bridal party ready to greet them at the entrance of your reception. Imagine you're a guest receiving your invitation. Will they know how to dress, know who they can bring, and be offered a reasonable amount of time to plan and reply? Have you taken

into account any special needs your guests may have? Will you need handicap ramps or child care for young children? It's easy to get overwhelmed by all the products and possibilities that exist for weddings, so taking a step back like this can help you make smart decisions.

Previsualize their experience all the way from receiving your invitation to watching you wave good-bye, and then plan how to keep them comfortably content from beginning to end. Carefully imagine your wedding day schedule unfolding to be sure that no one, including the two of you, is rushed from one thing to another, or left waiting around with nothing to do.

Consider what your guests will be seeing, and do your best to highlight the important things and make them forget about all the work behind the scenes. Plan your cake cutting against a complementary background, put spotlights on the dance floor for your first dance, and keep facilities, parking, and restrooms out of sight.

Don't forget that you're going to be the center of attention from morning until night, so plan your entrances and exits gracefully, with both you and your guests in mind. Have a place to relax quietly and gather your thoughts from when the guests begin to arrive until they see you come down the aisle. Arrive at your reception with finesse and allow guests to greet you. When it comes time to leave, make it a celebratory and special moment. Design your own exciting exit, like a fireworks send-off. To end your day on a high note, post the end time for your reception on your schedule and leave before the majority of your guests do. Consider having snack bags for your guests to take home. Guests will welcome them after a long day. Far too many exits are wrecked by the overconsumption of alcohol. Have fun, but don't go overboard.

more places to add flowers, which will certainly help your reception venue come alive with color.

Reception Style

Continue your wedding style throughout your celebration by choosing floral reception decor that builds on the theme set at your ceremony and liven up the tone for the rest of the event. The average wedding budget allots 8 to 10 percent of the total wedding cost for flowers, and this number can reach higher if you want more complex decor.

For larger events, consider choosing an event designer who can incorporate your floral design with your lighting, tabletops, and decor.

For smaller weddings a florist whose work you love can probably supply everything you need or can recommend additional rental companies to complete your event's look.

When meeting with your florist, explain your color palette, wedding party's attire, theme, and mood you want to create. Give the florist three adjectives to describe your ideal event, along with magazine and website images that inspire you.

Make the most of your floral decor by repurposing the flower arrangements from your ceremony. Vases on the head table, around the wedding cake, or on another surface needing attention will safely hold and showcase the

wedding party bouquets. Use large arrangements and candles from around the altar to decorate a stage, buffet table, or entryway. Arrange for your florist or coordinator to be in charge of transportation.

Classic: Classic centerpieces like the ones on the facing page made with lilies and gardenias, fill the room with sweet fragrance and add to the romantic effect. Most rental companies have numerous options for centerpiece holders. Choose the same one for every table for a streamlined look, or mix up the shapes and heights of the centerpieces to add depth and texture to the room. Use similar flower arrangements to decorate your guest book table, the restrooms, and other areas around your venue.

Casual: Rich, bright, colorful blooms add cheer and excitement to your wedding reception. Be sure the existing decor at your venue will coordinate and not clash with your bold color choices. Sometimes centerpieces make it difficult for guests to see the people across the table from them. Keep them low and wide or tall and slim for easy socializing. Add a few small votive candles to your arrangements for some warmth and sparkle when the lights go down.

Alternative: Nonfloral decor that incorporates candles, branches, foliage, and moss makes dramatic and creative arrangements. Fresh-flower alternatives like paper and fabric flowers are a low-maintenance option. Use potted plants as centerpieces and send them home with guests as gifts at the end of the night. Instead of a traditional floral wreath, create one in the shape of your initials or monogram and hang it at the entrance of your venue to welcome guests.

Fun Extras: Hang garlands or other flowers from the backs of the guest chairs or just from the backs of the reception chairs for the bride and groom. Use fresh flowers to decorate your

© photo by Positive Light Photography

© photo by Junebug Weddings

Flowers Postwedding

After your wedding is over, what will happen to your flowers? All that beauty shouldn't go to waste, so arrange for them to be delivered to a local retirement home or hospital, or offer them to guests or vendors to take home at the end of the night.

wedding cake, but be sure they are organically grown or free from harmful toxins. If you're concerned about this, use the fresh flowers on the cake table and sugar flowers on the cake itself. Edible crystallized flowers are beautiful additions to a wedding cake or any dessert.

Entryway Flowers

When guests arrive at the cocktail party, you'll welcome them with an immediate impression on the style of your wedding through the florals you set at the entrance. A formation of grand, oversize bridal blooms in crystal vases sets the stage for an elaborate, formal wedding, while bright scattered vases of wildflowers says, "Welcome to our relaxed garden party."

Here is your chance to "paint" the first moments of your guests' experience at your celebration, and you'll do so with the floral arrangements—large and small—awaiting them before they even reach the party setting.

It's the smallest details that can make the largest impact, and the good news is that you can choose smaller, more subtle floral arrangements for this section of your wedding floor plan, letting the food at the cocktail party take center stage. Perhaps you want to leave the wow factor for your reception ballroom or tent, so you see this setting as a chance to go a bit smaller with your floral designs and still impress. Then, when the doors open to your reception area, your more dramatic and detailed florals will make an even bigger statement in comparison.

Visit your site in person and take photos of the architectural elements that already exist there, such as a circular table just inside the foyer, a grand staircase to the left, a chandelier, antique tables and chairs, or a fireplace.

Then use these photos to guide your floral decor plans.

Set pedestals on either side of the doorway to your cocktail party and place floral arrangements on them. Place fully in-bloom potted flowers, for a less formal look than arrangements in vases, on pedestals on either side of the doorway. Set a large floral arrangement on a table just inside the door, surrounded by silver platters of champagne flutes and berries. For an understated look, simply hang a color-coordinated floral wreath on the outsides of both entryway doors.

You will attract attention to the guest book table with an oversize, color-coordinated floral arrangement placed behind the guest book. This floral piece does not have to match your bouquet design exactly; you could have an all-white entryway floral theme, while you carry pastel flowers. Instead of one large floral arrangement, consider three small, low-set or single flowers in bud vases, alternating with votive candles.

You don't need floral arrangements for both the men's and ladies' rooms; most weddings feature floral arrangements just in the ladies' room. A large arrangement is not needed; just a low-set bunch of six to eight flowers in a glass bowl makes a great impression. If you're on a budget, this might be the floral item you decide to cut from your plans.

Buffet Table Flowers

Flowers on your buffet table serve a dual purpose: They're there for beauty, and they can work as a budget-saving trick. Floral arrangements and flowers placed on a buffet table fill the space and add lushness and color that make it look like you have a much bigger, fuller buffet table than would appear if you had only a half a dozen chafing dishes and a few platters set on a big, long table.

Adding the elements of color and texture to a buffet table makes the food look more appetizing as well, because it's received a royal treatment of decor. This is not the same spread of dishes that everyone has seen at every family picnic and birthday party even if you have the exact same menu items. By virtue of dressing up your buffet table with florals, you turn even a budget buffet into a smashing smorgasbord.

Floral arrangements and vases between food platters create a more lush-looking buffet table. Greenery in the floral arrangements coordinates with the greenery of salads and platter garnishes. Place platters and chafing dishes at least two feet apart so that items are well spread out. With floral arrangements placed around a buffet table, you might need one-half

© Ginaellen/Dreamstime.com

to two-thirds the amount of food to make your buffet look plentiful.

Design one large centerpiece for each buffet table, aiming for a two- to three-foot width as an eye-catching design accent that still takes up lots of space and requires fewer dishes. Each centerpiece on each buffet table should match in color and style. If you're planning a "green" wedding or just like the look of all-natural greenery, design your table centerpieces to include just greenery and perhaps some rounded river stones for effect.

Add plenty of height to your buffet table arrangements to give the impression of a grander floral presence. Use flowering branches that stand up to three feet high, arising out of a larger floral arrangement. Use decorative branches and twigs such as white birch to use the bridal white color scheme in a more architectural way. Add height through the use of tall (twenty-four- to

---

Safely Using Florals with Food

Because guests will be very interactive with the food items on your buffet table, be sure that a reaching guest cannot knock florals or leaves into platters of food. Glass vases containing florals do a great job of keeping flowers and greenery out of reach and out of serving platters. Do not use any flowers, greenery, or flowering branches with berries on them, as most berries are extremely toxic. Talk to your floral designer about the safest types of greenery to use near food.

---

thirty-six-inch) glass vases, which you'll fill with water and submerged flowers.

Sweetheart Table

When you forgo the big, long table that has traditionally served as the seating for the bride, groom, and entire bridal party and instead have just one small table for you and your groom alone, this is called the "sweetheart table." This seating arrangement has become a trend for several reasons: A small, round table for two is easily set up right at the front of the dance floor, and room for a schematic-busting long table for sixteen people is no longer needed. What's more, a sweetheart table gives the bride and groom a few minutes alone to eat in peace and share some undisturbed conversation time. When the bride and groom are seated at their table, guests don't usually approach.

This means you have a spotlight table all to yourselves, and it invites your choice of special floral decor. After all, your table at the front of the dance floor is in full view of all of your guests. Often, the wedding cake is placed right next to or behind it, which means lots of pictures will capture the beauty of your table decor.

The sweetheart table is functional as well as fashionable. Your guests must be able to see you, and you must be able to see what's going on in the room. It's silly to hide behind a gigantic table centerpiece when you're the only ones at the table. So think low set and design floral accents for the front of your table, since that is in guests' eye line as well.

Design a smaller version of the guest table centerpieces, such as four low-set roses instead of twelve. Set out three to four small glass vases in a row across the front edge of the table and fill them with single flowers, such as gardenias, peonies, roses, ranunculus, or other wide blooms. Use small, round vases, fill them with water, and set a single floating flower in each. Add some sparkle to low-set centerpieces by adding crystal-studded wire stick-ins or theme adornments.

Save over $100 by simply placing your bridal bouquet front and center on the table as your centerpiece. Using your own bouquet on the sweetheart table can set your tabletop decor apart from guest tables' pastel or bright decor. Lay the centerpiece flat on the table for a natural look; with a ribbon-wrapped handle, you won't be able to stand it upright in a vase full of water.

Give your bridesmaids a place to put their bouquets by having them set them in a line on top of your sweetheart table. Six to eight bouquets usually form a complete, uninterrupted line across most sweetheart tables. Flower girls' and moms' nosegays can be placed at both ends of your bouquet lineup centerpiece for the perfect height and color blend. If you have a small table, set your bouquet on top and surround it with bridesmaids' bouquet on each side.

Cake Table

You would think a grand, elaborate wedding cake wouldn't need any extra accenting to make an impression, but even the most majestic cake masterpiece can be made all the more impressive with the right placement of florals on the table surrounding it.

Think about the cake design you plan to request or have already ordered. Depending on your personal style, and the formality and theme of your wedding, it might be a highly detailed cake of five tiers that costs more than your wedding gown, or it might be a simple, elegant cake of three tiers with the most subtle icing decoration. No sugar-paste hummingbirds or flowers for you.

Whatever your style and size of cake, well-placed flowers placed all around it can enhance the look of any decor your baker plans to create for your cake. So that elaborate cake with pink floral icing pops with the addition of fresh pink florals around the bottom layer of the cake. Or a small cake looks larger with a ring of matching white florals around the base.

The color scheme of your cake table florals is up to you. You can match the color of the frosting, such as white or off-white, but keep in mind that some buttercream frostings do appear off-white, so ask to see a sample before you order pure white flowers. Or, you can use your florals to bring out the hues of the colored icing details, such as piped-on roses, dots, swirls, or other embellishments.

There is a formula to figure out what size cake table flowers to use: They should be no taller than one-third the height of the bottom layer. Any more and it obscures the bottom layer from view, actually making your cake look smaller.

Instead of using your bouquet and bridesmaids' bouquets on your sweetheart table, place them around the base of the wedding cake. Use only the bridesmaids' bouquets to encircle the base of the wedding cake, as you may wish to take additional photos with your bouquet throughout the reception. Have your floral designer create nosegays to match the bridesmaids' bouquets, and use these expressly to encircle the cake base.

© Mrorange002/Dreamstime.com

Instead of bouquets, set single roses in low-set vases around the base of the cake. Vases can be set one foot apart in good, natural spacing to allow the cake base decor icing to show. Surround your cake base with roses that have been stem cut to three to four inches in length. Match roses to the cake's color scheme, such as white frosting and pink roses.

If daisies are included in your bouquet and wedding decor, it's a brilliant tie-in to bring daisies onto your cake table. Set out low vases and fill them with three to six white or yellow informal daisies or two to three larger Gerber daisies. For a more informal look, place wide, colorful Gerber daisy heads on the table around the base of the cake. Your baker can create sugar-paste Gerber daisies or ice colorful Gerber designs on the cake.

Flowers on the Cake

One of the lasting top trends in cake design is the cascade of fresh flowers starting at the top layer of the cake and extending down to the bottom layers. Your cascade design could be lush and full, with dozens and dozens of flowers, or you might choose to go more subtle with just a few flowers arranged on each cake layer.

∾

Chapter 10

PARTIES SURROUNDING THE BIG DAY

No wedding planning journey would be complete without the inclusion of a few big parties to celebrate, well, you! Generally speaking, the main parties include an engagement party (often thrown by the couples' families), a bridal shower, and a bachelorette and bachelor party. And, to conclude all the parties—minus, of course, your actual wedding day—there's sometimes a postwedding brunch. Phew, you tired yet?

This chapter may be more helpful for bridesmaids and groomsmen, and other family members, who are looking to help honor the bride and/or groom, and to help these people in planning out these mini events. You might consider subtly sticking this chapter under your wedding party's noses!

Just like with the rest of wedding planning, there are no hard-and-fast rules when it comes to throwing these parties. There are traditions, yes, of course, but many a modern bride and groom are bucking trend and having, for example, a Jack-and-Jill type shower, where the groom is also included. It's really just a matter of taste and personal preference. If you're included in the planning (some brides and grooms are left to be surprised), feel free to make your desires and wishes known to your wedding party. These are parties in honor of you, after all.

Parties Before

The days before your wedding are full of activity, and there are a few special events that will need planning. These parties will be hosted by various

© photo by Positive Light Photography

people, from your parents to your bridesmaids and groomsmen. Some people choose to keep these events a secret from the bride and groom, as they might be surprises. If that's the case, try not to pry too much. You might be able to drop hints here and there, but since you have so much to worry about for the wedding, why not leave the planning of the other parties to your family and friends?

Engagement Party

The engagement party is often thrown by one or both families of the bride and groom in honor of the recently betrothed. It's an opportunity for family and friends to celebrate together, and for the bride to show off her shiny new ring. Many families choose to throw engagement parties in the intimacy of their own home, while others may rent out party spaces in restaurants or at their local country club. Attire is generally less formal than that of the wedding, and guests can often expect just heavy appetizers and drinks with low-key music. Of course styles of engagement parties vary, and some events might be more casual while others are more decked-out affairs. It's really a matter of personal choice.

Guests will often bring gifts off the couple's registry, if they have one, but gifts won't be nearly as expensive as wedding gifts. Often a small token is perfectly acceptable.

One or both sets of parents (or sometimes just one parent) will provide a toast at the party in honor of the engaged couple. Toasts may include funny stories or warm wishes for

their joint future. The bride and groom are not expected to also give a toast, but it is fine if they wish to do so.

Bridal Shower

Wedding and bridal showers are fun-filled events that allow you to spend time with the people you love and to start celebrating! Traditional bridal showers take place with the women in your life and are full of gifts to prepare your new home. These days there are no hard-and-fast rules for these events, and you may very likely have a number of them thrown in your honor. The various groups could include both male and female family members, just girlfriends, coworkers, or other specific groups of people close to you.

Even though you aren't the one who is planning the party, do communicate your desires clearly and be gracious for all the effort people put forth for you. Tell whoever is planning the event (likely your maid of honor, your sister, or your mother) who is on your wedding guest list. You don't want to invite anyone to a shower if you're not also inviting them to the wedding.

Choosing a theme for the shower is a popular way to organize this kind of event. Since you may not need all the basics to start a home, a theme could be chosen that carries all the way through from the invitations, decorations, and food served to the games played and the kinds of gifts given.

You'll need to send out thank-you notes within two weeks of the shower, so purchase them ahead of time and get the address of each guest from the host of the party. As you open your gifts, be sure to have someone by your side to take careful notes on which gift came from which person. It will make writing thank-you notes infinitely easier, and you'll be reminded of the gift giver each time you use the item.

© photo by Junebug Weddings

Classic: Classic bridal showers include party games that involve the bride. Ask guests trivia questions about how the bride and groom met, their most romantic moments, and their favorite things. Ask the groom ahead of time and then see if the bride can guess his answers. Luncheons can easily be hosted at home or at a restaurant. For lighter fare, schedule the event for the afternoon and have a tea party with finger sandwiches and hors d'oeuvres.

Casual: Invite the ladies over for brunch. Serve mimosas, Bloody Marys, French toast, quiche, fruit, and pastries, and send guests home with locally roasted coffee beans or homemade gourmet granola. Enjoy the sunshine with a picnic

in the park. Bring lots of large picnic blankets, throw pillows, and some folding chairs for those who can't easily sit on the ground. Host a pajama party at home or at a hotel, complete with DIY beauty treatments and the bride's favorite snack foods.

Alternative: Throw an evening cocktail party at a swanky bar or restaurant. Find out if the venue has a private area you can reserve and have a specialty cocktail named after the bride. Get the groom in on the action and throw a coed wedding shower (often referred to as a Jack-and-Jill shower). For a beautiful East Indian–themed shower, serve yummy curries and flat breads and sweet mango lassis, decorate with jewel tones, and hire a henna artist to decorate each guest's hands or feet.

Thematic: A lingerie-themed shower will make opening gifts a lively event, and each item will be a welcome addition to her honeymoon wardrobe! Be sure the bride's sizes are included in the

© photo by GH Kim Photography

invitation. Let the bride's favorite hobbies lead the theme. If she loves cooking and baking, have a culinary-themed party with specialty foods and gifts for the kitchen. If she loves fashion, use fashion magazines as your decor inspiration and ask guests to bring fun accessories as gifts.

Bachelor Party

The bachelor party is a time-honored tradition that shouldn't be missed by any groom. It's the time for the groom to kick back, relax, and celebrate his friendships as well as the big and exciting event to come.

Traditionally it's the best man's responsibility to plan the event, but he can always ask for help from the other groomsmen if he lives out of town or doesn't know all the guys involved. The best way to begin the planning process is

for the best man to sit down with the groom and get a feel for the kind of party he's hoping for. Bachelor parties range in style from simple and subdued to wild and crazy, so a little direction from the man of honor is a safe bet.

Once his thoughts have been heard, talk about the guest list. Who are the most important people to invite? Will any family members be involved, like fathers, brothers, or cousins? What will be appropriate activities for them?

The event planning should begin well in advance, and some things should be kept under wraps as a surprise for the groom. If the event requires travel, give everyone lots of time to make arrangements and be sensitive about budget restraints that may exclude some people from participating.

Classic: The groom can make a special toast to his friends. This is his chance to recognize their efforts in supporting your celebration and to say thanks. The men should take taxis, rent a car service, or stay in a hotel so no one has to worry about driving home. If the best man is going for a classic bachelor party, he should be sure the groom's fiancée is comfortable with the plan. One night out is not worth fighting over during such a special and emotional time.

Casual: The men can play eighteen holes of golf and have a barbecue in the evening. Is the groom a video-game guy? A Wii video game competition could be fun, or an old-school Atari or arcade game battle. The guys could head to the

© photo by J. Garner Photography

© photo by Barbie Hull Photography

© photo by GH Kim Photography

hills for mountain biking in the summer or snowboarding in the winter. If the groom loves to hunt, but it's not the right season, the men could go to the firing range and learn to shoot a new gun, or play paintball.

Themed: For a Rat Pack or Swingers theme, the men could hit a local casino, organize a poker tournament, or arrange a Scotch or whiskey tasting or a classic cocktail–mixing lesson at the groom's favorite bar. Does the groom love the movie *The Big Lebowski?* A bowling tournament with his buddies would be a fitting party, and they can all drink White Russians. Or they could head to the racetrack and have everyone pitch in money for the groom to place his bets. Someone should call ahead to see if the party can get a private tour.

Weekend Destinations: Best buddies can spend a weekend away at a local destination for some serious male bonding before the big day. Or they can visit a city the groom has always wanted to see, like New York, Las Vegas, Chicago, or Austin, and meet up with friends from around the country. A camping, hiking, or fishing trip provides lots of activities to keep the guys busy, as well as downtime for catching up and spending quality time together.

Enjoy a Joint Party

If the bride and groom share one big group of friends, and the bachelor and bachelorette parties are taking place on the same night, meet up later for a joint celebration or at the end of the festivities for a late-night breakfast and recap of all the fun!

~

Bachelorette Party

During the busy time leading up to the wedding, time spent just with girlfriends is a must for every bride-to-be. The bachelorette party can be organized by anyone close to the bride, and whether it's classic, casual, simple, or spectacular, it should be all about fun!

If the party will take place locally, it should be scheduled at least two or three days before the wedding to allow for proper recovery time. Out-of-town guests should be made aware of the date so they can arrive in time to attend. If a destination weekend is more the bride's style, it should be planned way ahead and the host should be sensitive to different people's budgets.

The bride is the guest at this party, so the host should communicate with the rest of the group to organize payment in advance. Some of the events should be kept a surprise for added intrigue, and the host should choose events and locations she knows the bride will love.

Gag gifts and racy toys are welcome at most bachelorette parties, and it's the perfect time for

© photo by GH Kim Photography

girlfriends to give the bride sexy lingerie and other fun items she may not have been comfortable opening at the bridal shower. Gifts at the bachelorette party can be far more casual or forgone for simply the gift of everyone's presence at the party.

Classic: Now's the bride and her girlfriends' chance to get dressed up in their most fabulous fashions and hit the town! Girlfriends may treat the bride to a lovely dinner, and let her know how much she means to them. The host should be sure to reserve a table ahead of time. All the girls can let loose and go dancing. There's nothing but fun out on the dance floor with girlfriends. The hostess can call around to find out where the bride's favorite kind of music will be played that night.

Casual: Whether it's a full day at the spa, or mini mani-pedis, a bachelorette party that involves pampering beauty treatments is a surefire

Surprise the Bride

Create a surprise gift for the bride by asking guests to write a note about how they became friends, their first memory of hearing about the groom, or how special the bride is. Compile them into a custom book that shows how much you all honor her friendship.

winner. The bride can be taken to a karaoke bar where she can sing her heart out to her favorite tunes. The hostess should find out if the venue has private rooms if any of her girlfriends are on the shy side. Another idea is to rent a hotel suite and have a sleepover. Girlfriends can order room service, have a dance party, and spend quality time catching up.

Themed: The hostess can rent a boat and get the girls out on the water for an afternoon of lounging at sea. Or she can host a wine tasting and invite an expert speaker to teach the girls all about wines from a region the bride loves. Girlfriends can pitch in on a wine-of-the-month club gift for the newlyweds to enjoy. Or the girls can take a fun hip-hop or swing-dance class, or invite a belly-dance instructor to the bachelorette party to teach the girls some new moves.

Weekend Destinations: The girls can get out of town for an extended bachelorette party that includes both relaxation and excitement. The girls should remember to bring any gag gifts, props, decorations, or presents along so they can get there and be relaxed and ready for fun. The hostess should choose a known party city, like Las Vegas, Miami, or New York, or a low-key destination the bride will love. Camping, hiking, and playing sports aren't just for the guys. The girls can get together for a sporty weekend of outdoor fun.

Rehearsal Dinner

Each wedding ceremony is unique, so it's important to schedule a rehearsal time to familiarize everyone involved with the specifics of yours. It will give you a great chance to see your planning come to life and make any final adjustments to the timing, flow, and physical spacing of the ceremony. Check with the location coordinator so you know how much time you have there, and ask your maid of honor to keep an eye on the time so you're sure to cover everything.

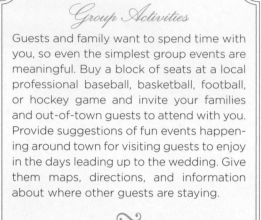

Group Activities

Guests and family want to spend time with you, so even the simplest group events are meaningful. Buy a block of seats at a local professional baseball, basketball, football, or hockey game and invite your families and out-of-town guests to attend with you. Provide suggestions of fun events happening around town for visiting guests to enjoy in the days leading up to the wedding. Give them maps, directions, and information about where other guests are staying.

Schedule time a day or two before the wedding to practice your ceremony in your actual wedding location, and run through the program at least twice. Everyone involved in the ceremony should attend, including family and ushers. Bring a bouquet made of ribbon from your bridal shower gifts to hold as you walk down the aisle. Be sure all the guests involved know how to get to your ceremony location, since you may not have much time available there.

After the rehearsal, the groom's parents traditionally host a dinner for the families, wedding party, and other important out-of-town guests. A rehearsal dinner can be as casual as a backyard barbecue or as fancy as the wedding itself; it's totally up to you and the host. Try to make it an early night so you can all be well rested for the big day ahead.

At the rehearsal dinner the two of you should make a toast to your families, wedding

© photo by GH Kim Photography

party, and anyone else who has helped you along the way. For a more formal dinner, use a private room at your favorite restaurant or rent an event location and have a catered party. For a casual dinner, host a barbecue, picnic, or softball game in the park. It's a great way for family and guests to get to know each other.

PARTIES AFTER

So the vows have been said, the dances have been danced, and the cake has been cut. Guests start filing out of the reception and say their good-byes . . . but wait! The celebration isn't over just yet. Many couples choose to do a casual post-wedding brunch the morning after the nuptials to give guests one last chance to say good-bye. It's particularly helpful for out-of-town guests staying in local hotels to have somewhere to eat with family and friends and reminisce about the memories of the night before.

But that's not the only "party" to look forward to postwedding. Then there's the honeymoon, which many couples choose to embark on immediately following their wedding. It's a time for couples to unwind from the busy months of planning leading up to the big day, and to savor getting to know each other as husband and wife.

Day-After Brunch

A postwedding brunch is a great way to catch up with friends and family, reminisce about the fun memories at the wedding, and to say good-bye to out-of-town visitors. The postwedding brunch is typically held the morning immediately following the wedding at a nearby restaurant, family member's house, or catering facility.

Schedule enough time so you can easily visit with your guests and say good-bye to out-of-town visitors, as well as eat a delicious breakfast. Reserve a private dining room at a location near where guests are staying, or ask a family member to host it at his or her home. Help organize the event, but don't host brunch at your own house; you deserve to relax and rest the day after your wedding.

Some Notes on the Honeymoon

Ah, the honeymoon—a perfect chance to get away and to catch up on R&R after a few busy months of wedding planning. Some couples prefer to go on their honeymoon directly following the wedding day. Others choose to put off their honeymoon for a short bit, which is completely fine. Typically, the groom plans the honeymoon—or, at least, he's in charge of organizing a good majority of it.

The groom should be sure to check all your reservations in advance, including transportation to and from your accommodations, twice. He should not be fooled by ads and photos. He needs to ask lots of questions, get referrals, and find out if any events or construction may affect your visit. If you're traveling out of the country, he should arrange for all travel requirements for passports, blood tests, and immunizations. And, finally, he should have dinner reservations ready for the night you arrive.

The Wedding Timeline Checklist

12–8 Months before Wedding

- ❐ Determine Your Wedding Style _____
- ❐ Set Your Date _____
- ❐ Consider Hiring a Consultant _____
- ❐ Book Your Ceremony Venue _____
- ❐ Book Your Reception Venue_____
- ❐ Book Your Officiant_____
- ❐ Consider Transportation, If Necessary _____
- ❐ Book Your Photographer _____
- ❐ Book Your Videographer _____
- ❐ Start Your Registry _____

8–4 Months before Wedding

- ❐ Find Your Dress & Arrange Alterations _____
- ❐ Choose Your Bridal Party_____
- ❐ Start Looking for Bridal Party Attire_____
- ❐ Start Looking for Your Accessories _____
- ❐ Hire a Caterer, If Necessary _____
- ❐ Decide on a Menu _____
- ❐ Order Any Necessary Rental Items_____
- ❐ Book All Musicians (DJ/Band/Other) _____
- ❐ Book Your Cake Maker _____
- ❐ Order All Stationery: Invitations, Etc._____
- ❐ Hire a Florist _____
- ❐ Book Hotel Rooms _____

4–2 Months before Wedding

- ❐ Set Up Cake Tastings _____
- ❐ Shop for Wedding Bands & Gifts _____
- ❐ Update Your Gift Registry _____
- ❐ Research Marriage License Paperwork _____
- ❐ Update Passports & Travel Documents_____
- ❐ Book Your Honeymoon _____
- ❐ Confirm Playlists with Musicians _____
- ❐ Confirm Photography Lists _____
- ❐ Meet with Your Cater for Tastings _____
- ❐ Meet with Your Florist_____
- ❐ Start Final Fittings for Attire _____
- ❐ Send Out Invitations 8 Weeks Early _____
- ❐ Book Rehearsal Dinner Venue _____

2 Months to 1 Day before Wedding

- ❐ Finalize Ceremony Details _____
- ❐ Write Vows, If Necessary_____
- ❐ Confirm Musicians & Readers _____
- ❐ Confirm All Reception Details _____
- ❐ Book Hair & Makeup Trials _____
- ❐ Have a Bachelorette & Bachelor Party_____
- ❐ Have a Bridal Shower _____
- ❐ Get Mani-Pedis_____
- ❐ Send Out All Final Vendor Payments _____

Beauty Appointments Schedule & Planner

Keep track of your consultations, trial runs, beauty regimen, and other appointments.

Hair:

Initial Consultation with Hairstylist

Date: ______________________________

Time: ______________________________

Place: ______________________________

Stylist name: ________________________

Stylist contact information: ___________

____

Notes:______________________________

____

____

Trial Run with Hairstylist

Date: ______________________________

Time: ______________________________

Place: ______________________________

Stylist name: ________________________

Stylist contact information: ___________

____

Notes: _____________________________

____

____

Hair Color or Highlighting Appointments

#1: Date: ________________________

Time: ________________________

#2: Date: ________________________

Time ________________________

#3: Date: ________________________

Time: ________________________

#4: Date: ________________________

Time: ________________________

Photo by Kristen Jensen

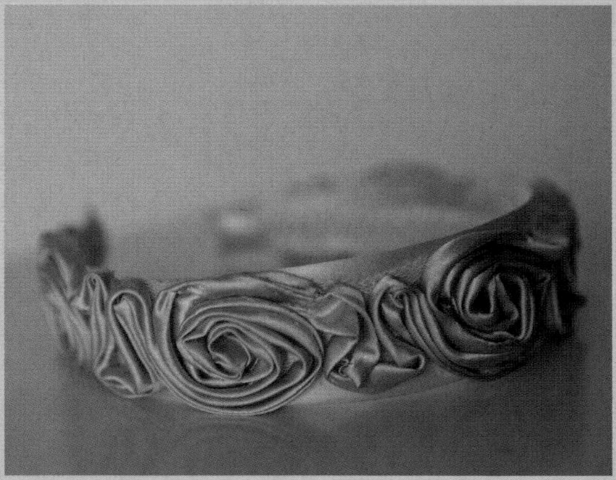

Makeup:

Initial Consultation with Makeup Stylist

Date: _____

Time: _____

Place: _____

Stylist name: _____

Stylist contact information: _____

_____

Notes: _____

_____

_____

Trial Run with Makeup Stylist

Date: _____

Time: _____

Place: _____

Stylist name: _____

Stylist contact information: _____

_____

Notes: _____

_____

_____

Skin:

Initial Consultation with Skin Aesthetician

Date: _____

Time: _____

Place: _____

Aesthetician name: _____

Aesthetician contact information: _____

_____

Notes: _____

_____

_____

Appointment Schedule with Skin Aesthetician

Date: _____

Time: _____

Place: _____

Aesthetician name: _____

Aesthetician contact information: _____

_____

Notes: _____

_____

_____

Facials and Skin Care Appointments

#1:   Date: _____

          Time: _____

#2:   Date: _____

          Time _____

#3:   Date: _____

          Time: _____

#4:   Date: _____

          Time: _____

Massage Appointments

#1:   Date: _____

          Time: _____

#2:   Date: _____

          Time: _____

#3:   Date: _____

          Time: _____

#4:   Date: _____

          Time: _____

Additional Beauty Appointments

#1:   Date: _____

          Time: _____

          Location: _____

#2:   Date: _____

          Time: _____

          Location: _____

#3:   Date: _____

          Time: _____

          Location: _____

#4:   Date: _____

          Time: _____

          Location: _____

Wedding Day Morning Hairstyling:

Time: _____

Location:_____

Stylist name: _____

Who else will accompany: _____

_____

Styling details for bridesmaids,
moms, and others: _____

_____

Wedding Day Morning Makeup Styling

Time: _____

Location:_____

Stylist name: _____

Who else will accompany: _____

_____

Styling details for bridesmaids,
moms, and others: _____

_____

Wedding Day Morning Mani-Pedi

Time: _____

Location:_____

Stylist name: _____

Who else will accompany: _____

_____

Styling details for bridesmaids,
moms, and others: _____

_____

Additional Notes: _____

_____

_____

Photo by Kristen Jensen

Wedding Day Beauty Countdown

Use this chart to create your wedding day beauty schedule so that you stay on track and on time, avoid rushing, and have time to enjoy taking prewedding photos before it's time to depart.

Pre-Salon Visit:

Time: _____

Task: _____

Who: _____

Time: _____

Task: _____

Who: _____

Time: _____

Task: _____

Who: _____

Salon Visit:

Time: _____

Task: _____

Who: _____

Time: _____

Task: _____

Who: _____

Time: _____

Task: _____

Who: _____

Time: _____

Task: _____

Who: _____

Photo by Kristen Jensen

DIY Hair & Beauty:

Time: _____

Task: _____

Who: _____

Time: _____

Task: _____

Who: _____

Time: _____

Task: _____

Who: _____

At-Home Touch-Ups:

Time: _____

Task: _____

Who: _____

Time: _____

Task: _____

Who: _____

Time: _____

Task: _____

Who: _____

Photo by Kristen Jersen

Photo by Krister Jensen

Flowers by Season

Spring Wedding Flowers
Anemone
Bells of Ireland
Casa Blanca lily
Crocus
Daffodil
Delphinium
Hyacinth
Lilac
Narcissus
Peony
Ranunculus
Stargazer Lily
Sweet pea
Tulip

Summer Wedding Flowers
Alstroemeria
Bells of Ireland
Chrysanthemum
English lavender
Forget-me-not
Freesia
Gerber daisy
Hydrangea
Iris
Larkspur
Lily
Lisianthus
Queen Anne's lace
Snapdragon
Stephanotis
Stock
Sunflower
Tuberose
Yarrow
Zinnia

Photo by Kristen Jensen

Fall Wedding Flowers

Allium
Aster
Alstroemeria
Amaranthus
Anemone
Chrysanthemum
Cosmos
Dahlia
Freesia
Gerber daisy
Gladiolus
Hypericum berry
Iris
Juniper
Kalanchoe
Lily
Marigold
Orchid
Rose
Salvia
Star of Bethlehem
Sunflower
Yarrow
Zinnia

Winter Wedding Flowers

Acacia
Amaryllis
Anemone
Asiatic lilies
Bells of Ireland
Camellia
Carnation
Casa Blanca lily
Chrysanthemum
Cosmos
Cyclamen
Daffodil
Evergreen
Forget-me-not
Gerber daisy
Helleborus
Holly
Jasmine
Narcissus
Orchid
Pansy
Phlox
Poinsettia
Ranunculus
Stargazer Lily
Star of Bethlehem
Sweet pea
Tulip

Photo by Kristen Jensen

Birth-Month Flowers

Spring Birthdays

March: daffodil or jonquil

April: daisy or sweet pea

May: lily of the valley or hawthorn

Mix these with non–birth-month spring flowers such as peonies and hydrangeas for extra floral effect and texture.

Summer Birthdays

June: rose or honeysuckle

July: larkspur or water lily

August: gladiolas or poppy

Fall Birthdays

September: aster or morning glory

October: calendula or cosmos

November: chrysanthemum

The key is in the autumn color base; use plenty of reds, oranges, golds, and browns.

Winter Birthdays

December: narcissus or holly

January: carnation or snowdrop

February: violet or primrose violet

Wedding Flowers Available Year-Round

Baby's breath	Gladiolus
Bachelor's button	Heather
Calla lily	Lily of the valley
Carnations	Orchid
Delphinium	Rose
Eucalyptus	Scabiosa
Gardenia	

Photo by Kristen Jensen

Flower Delivery

Use this chart to organize your floral deliveries by location and time, with special instructions noted.

Site #1:

Address: _____

Items to Be Delivered: _____

Delivery Time:_____

Delivery Details: _____

Contact Phone #:_____

Site #2:

Address: _____

Items to Be Delivered: _____

Delivery Time:_____

Delivery Details: _____

Contact Phone #:_____

Site #3:

Address: _____

Items to Be Delivered: _____

Delivery Time:_____

Delivery Details: _____

Contact Phone #:_____

Site #4:

Address: _____

Items to Be Delivered: _____

Delivery Time:_____

Delivery Details: _____

Contact Phone #:_____

Notes

Flowers We Want to Use:_____

_____

_____

_____

Flowers We Don't Want to Use: _____

_____

_____

_____

Others' Favorite Flowers:

[ ] Bride's Mother: _____

[ ] Groom's Mother: _____

[ ] Bride's Stepmother: _____

[ ] Groom's Stepmother:_____

[ ] Bride's Grandmother:_____

[ ] Bride's Grandmother:_____

[ ] Groom's Grandmother: _____

[ ] Groom's Grandmother: _____

[ ] Bride's Godmother: _____

[ ] Groom's Godmother:_____

[ ] Child:_____

[ ] Child:_____

[ ] Other: _____

[ ] Other: _____

[ ] Other: _____

[ ] Other: _____

INDEX

buttercups, 174–75
calla lilies, 202, 204, 222, 229
carnations, 171
cattails, 175
centerpieces, 249–60
for the ceremony, 309–18
choosing a florist, 27
chrysanthemums, 171
and the color yellow, 171
corsages, 243–44, 248
daisies, 169–71, 202, 204, 222, 240–41
ecofriendly choices, 178
fall flowers, 177, 179, 357
ferns, 197
floral clubs and organizations, 212
flower baskets, 235–37
flower bunches, 203–4
flower delivery, 359
flowering cabbages, 175
flowers for grandmothers, stepmothers. and
    other special women, 247–49
flowers for the mothers, 243–47
flowers symbolizing abundance, 173–75
gardenias, 172, 244
hyacinths, 170, 171, 172
in-season flowers timeline, 178–79, 356
ivy, 175, 196–97
the language of flowers, 163–75
lilies, 166–67
lilies of the valley, 172–73, 197
orchids, 173, 229, 244, 245–46
for the reception, 329–38
roses, 164–66, 202, 203–4, 221, 229, 240,
    244, 245
seasonal flowers, 176–79, 231

spring flowers, 176, 179, 356
stem treatments, 206–7
summer flowers, 176–77, 179, 356
traditional bridal flowers, 171–73
tulips, 167–69
wildflowers, 204–8
winter flowers, 177–78, 179, 357
wristlets, 244–46, 248

G

groom
    attire, 76–81
    boutonnieres, 228–31
    honeymoon planning, 23
    jewelry, 69–71, 80–81
    responsibilities, 22–23
    support team, 23
groomsmen
    attire, 83–85
    boutonnieres, 228–31, 234–35

H

honeymoon, 24, 28, 347

I

invitations and invitation packages
    addressing your guests, 263
    designs, 263–71
    for destination-themed weddings, 271
    ecofriendly options, 263
    including information for guests, 271–74
    ordering and designing, 26–27, 29
    photograph of, 29
    postage and postage stamps, 271
    RSVP cards, 262–63

SPECIAL CONTRIBUTORS

The creation of this book was the ultimate collaborative process, and it would not have been possible without the generous support of the professional wedding community. Below are the names of the people who contributed to this book and supported our vision. We thank them for sharing their talents, artistry, and energy with us!

With many thanks to the team at The Adam Broderick Salon and Spa (www.adambroderick.com) who dedicated so much of their time and talents to help us style and capture some of these lovely photos for your inspiration. Our beauty professionals from the Adam Broderick Salon, including Adam Broderick himself and:

Marcia Jaquez, our coordinator and stylist
Zekira Kobas, model and makeup artist
Susana Gannon, model and make up artist
Laura Lewis, model and makeup artist
Kaylyn Touhey, makeup artist
Jennifer (Mykayla) Kovacs, makeup artist
Amanda Raymond, stylist
Courtney Cinque, stylist
Rachel Raposo, stylist
Joseph (Dino) Santos, stylist
Marisel Snyder, stylist
Amanda (Grace) Raymond, stylist
Joanne (Faith) Frulla, stylist
Sooki Vitarelli, hair stylist and model
Doreen Chan, hair stylist and model
Suzanne Headley Harriott, model
Grace Heiser, model
Leigh Ann Parisi, colorist and model
Felicia Leighman, stylist and model
Dawn Williams, model
Beth Santoli, model and stylist
Krysti Johannesen, nail tech
Robin Jones, nail tech

Photo courtesy of Kristen Jensen

Photo by Kristen Jensen

Reba Gaines, esthetician
Damien Bourbeau, massage therapist
Dina Lopes, model

Thank you also to these models whose faces grace these pages:
Vivian Hsu
Amanda Wall
Alyssa Cave
Leah Ferrel

Thank you to the bridal salon owners and dress designers for sharing their style:
The Bridal Garden: www.thebridalgarden.com
Lea-Ann Belter: www.lea-annbelter.com
Birnbaum & Bullock: www.birnbaumandbullock.com
Judd Waddell: www.juddwaddell.com
La Belle Reve: www.labellereve.com
Manuel Mota for Pronovias: www.pronovias.com
Erica Koesler: www.ericakoesler.com
Heidi Hull Designs: www.heidihulldesigns.com
Ann Marie Lingerie
Simone Perel
Jonquil: www.jonquillingerie.com
Sherry et Cie: www.sherryetcie.com
Huit: www.huit.fr
Isadora's: www.isadoras.com
Madina Vadache: www.madinavadache.com
Luly Yang Couture: www.lulyyang.com

In addition, we thank Occasions Bridal and Eveningwear Boutique (www.efashioncentral.com/occasions) for providing some of the lovely accessories and bridalwear shown in this book.

Thank you to the cake designers who make our mouths water:
New Renaissance Cakes: www.newrenaissancecakes.com
Jen's Desserts: www.jensdesserts.com

Lisa Dupar Catering: www.lisaduparcatering.com
Crème de la Crème: www.cakesbycremedelacreme.com
Mike's Amazing Cakes: www.mikesamazingcakes.com
Trophy Cupcakes: www.trophycupcakes.com
Tallant House: www.tallanthouse.com
B&O Espresso

In addition we would like to thank Marc Jayson from The Goodie Shoppe in New Fairfield, Connecticut.

Thank you to the florists whose passion for beauty enriches us all:
Juniper Flowers: www.juniperflowers.com
Bella Rugosa: www.bellarugosa.com
Acanthus Floral: www.acanthusfloral.com
Christopher Flowers: www.christopherflowers.biz
Woodland Flowers: www.woodlandflowers.com
Fiore Blossoms: www.fioreblossoms.com
Aria Style: www.ariastyle.com
Garden Party Floral: www.gardenpartyflowers.com
Loves Me Flowers: www.lovesmeflowers.com
Athena Flora: www.athenaflora.com
Laurie Cinotto: www.lauriecinotto.com

Photo by Kristen Jensen

Thank you to the invitation designers who know how to tell it:
Brown Sugar Design: www.bsdstudio.com
All About Weddings: www.allaboutweddingsnw.com
Bella Figura: www.bellafigura.com
Ephemera Custom Letterpress: www.ephemera-press.com
Izzy Girl: www.izzygirl.com
Paper Moxie: www.papermoxie.com
Mmm Paper: www.mmmpaper.com
A and O Design: www.aandodesign.com

Thank you to the jewelers who bring the sparkle and shine:
E.E. Robbins, the Engagement Ring Store: www.eerobbins.com
Ritani: www.ritani.com

Gelin & Abaci: www.gelinabaci.com
Jeff Cooper: www.jeffcooperdesigns.com
Coast: www.coastdiamond.com
Lieberfarb: www.lieberfarb.com
Frederick Goldman: www.fgoldman.com
Trent West: www.trewtungsten.com
Twist: www.twistonline.com
Jamie Joseph: www.jamiejoseph.com
Me & Ro: www.meandrojewelry.com
Reinstein/Ross: www.reinsteinross.com
L. Frank: www.lfrankjewelry.com
Marie-Helene de Taillac: www.mariehelenedetaillac.com
Taru
Fancy: www.fancyjewels.com
Greenlake Jewelry Works: www.greenlakejewelryworks.com
Isadora's: www.isadoras.com

Photo by Kristen Jensen

A special thank you to Michelle Webb for allowing us to showcase her beautiful collection of vintage hair accents.

Thank you to the event professionals who provide products and expertise that exceed expectations:
Good Taste Events: www.goodtasteevents.com
PHEW Kits: www.phewkits.com
Totally Tabletops: www.totallytabletops.com
Clara French Ceramics: www.clarafrench.com
Tolo Events: www.toloevents.com
Pedersen's Event Rentals: www.pedersens.com
Rented Elegance: www.rentedelegance.com
Grand Event Rentals: www.grandeventrentals.com
Mosaic Linens: www.partymosaic.com

Thank you to Erin Skipley of Bellatrix Studio, whose way with hair and makeup makes getting gorgeous easy: www.bellatrixstudio.com.

Thank you to Pravda Studios for providing a fun, hip place to take commercial photos in Seattle: www.pravdastudios.com.

PUBLISHER'S ACKNOWLEDGMENTS

A special thank you to all the photographers who contributed their work, especially:

Barbie Hull Photography (www.bariehull.com)

Cheri Pearl Photography (www.cheripearl.com)

GH Kim Photography (www.ghkim.com)

Jackie Alpers (www.jackiealpers.com)

Jenny Jimenez (www.photojj.com)

John and Joseph Photography (www.jkhphoto.com)

Junebug Weddings (www.junebugweddings.com)

J. Garner Photography (www.jgarnerphoto.com)

Kristen Jensen (www.kristenjensen.com)

La Vie Photography (www.laviephoto.com)

One Thousand Words Photography (www.onethousandwordsphotography.com)

Positive Light Photography (www.positivelightphotography.com)

Rich Penrose

Susan Bourgoin (www.visualcuisines.com)

Yours by John Photography (www.yoursbyjohn.com)

Photo by Kristen Jensen